THE HISTORY OF THE JAPANESE WRITTEN LANGUAGE

THE HISTORY OF THE JAPANESE WRITTEN LANGUAGE

YAEKO SATO HABEIN

UNIVERSITY OF TOKYO PRESS

Publication assisted by a grant from The Japan Foundation.

ISBN 4–13–087047–5 (UTP 87470)
ISBN 0–86008–347–0
Printed in Japan

CONTENTS

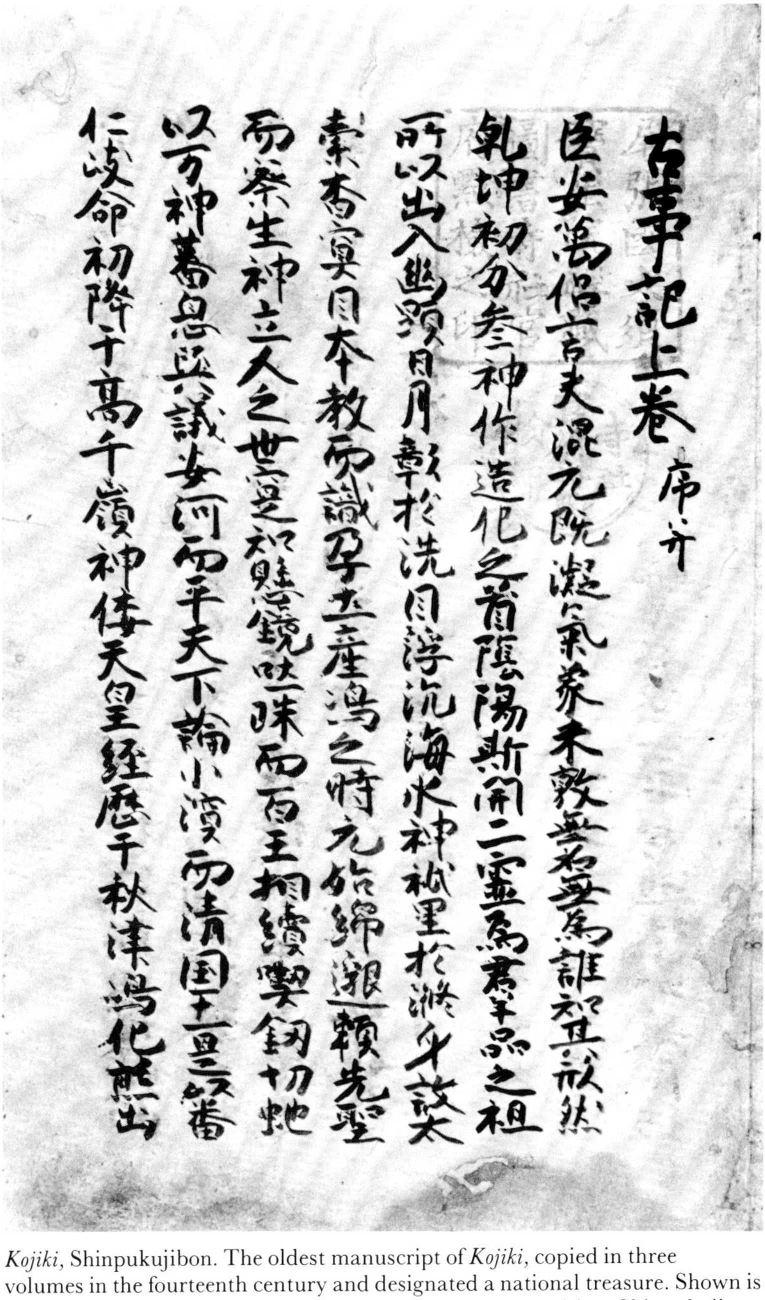

Kojiki, Shinpukujibon. The oldest manuscript of *Kojiki*, copied in three volumes in the fourteenth century and designated a national treasure. Shown is the opening page of the preface in *kanbun*, Chinese-style writing. Shinpukuji Hōseiin Collection, Aiichi prefecture. Photograph courtesy of Shōgakukan Publishing Company.

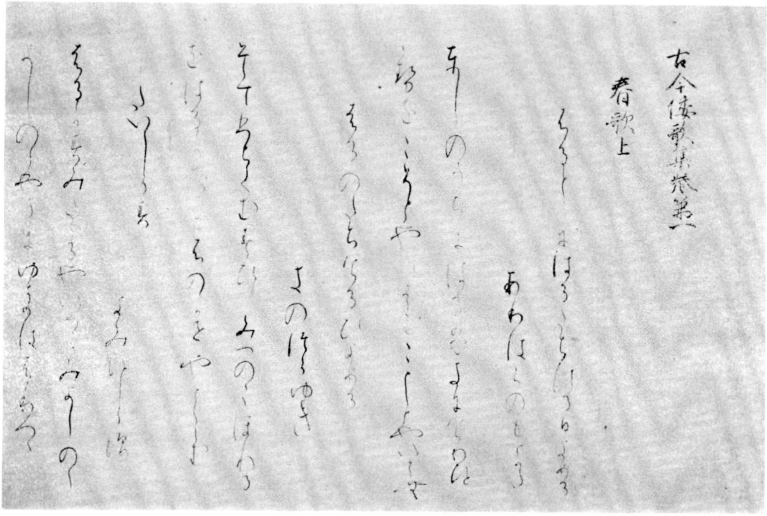

Kokinshū. Opening page from the oldest manuscript of *Kokinshū*. Although traditionally attributed to Ki no Tsurayuki, one of the compilers, the manuscript is dated, on the basis of its calligraphy, about 150 years after Ki no Tsurayuki's time. The page shown here is from the first of twenty volumes, written almost entirely in *hiragana*. Gotō Museum Collection, Tokyo. Photograph courtesy of Shōgakukan Publishing Company.

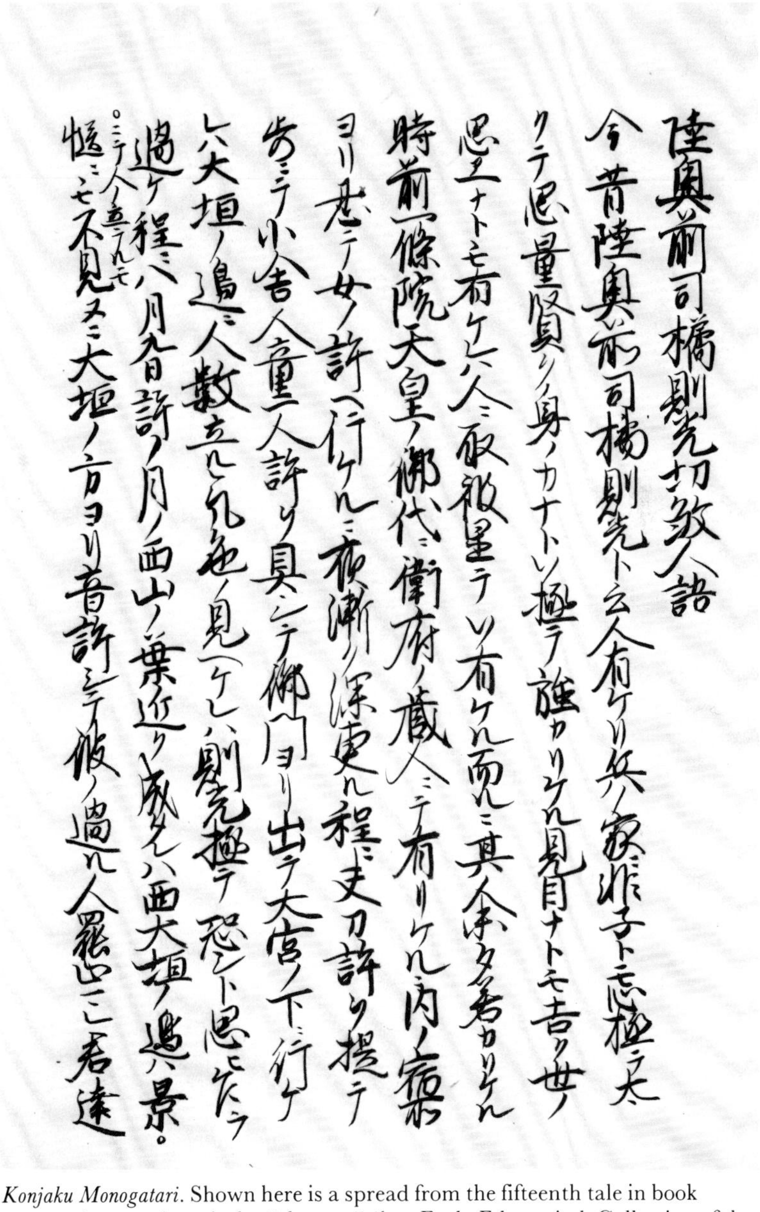

陸奥前司橘則光切殺人語
今昔陸奥ノ前司橘則光ト云人有ケリ兵ノ家ニ非子トモ心極テ太
クテ思量賢ク身ノ力ナトソ極テ強カリケル見目ナトモ吉ク世ノ
思エナトモ有ケレハ人ニ所被置テソ有ケル而ルニ其人若カリケル
時前ノ一條院天皇ノ御代ニ衛府ノ蔵人ニテ有ケル内ノ宿所
ヨリ忍テ女ノ許ヘ行ケルニ夜漸ク深更ル程ニ大刀許ヲ提テ
歩ニテ小舎人童一人許ヲ具シテ御門ヨリ出テ大宮ノ下ニ行ケ
ハ大垣ノ邊ニ人数立ル気色ノ見ヘケレハ則光極テ恐シト思ヒケルニ
過ケ程ニ八月九日許ノ月ノ西山ノ葉近ク成タレハ西大垣ノ邊ハ景。
○ニテ人ノ立ルモ
慥ニモ不見エヌニ大垣ノ方ヨリ音許シテ彼ノ過ル人罷止マレ君達

Konjaku Monogatari. Shown here is a spread from the fifteenth tale in book twenty-three, written in *kanji-kanamajiribun*. Early Edo period. Collection of the Department of Japanese Literature, Faculty of Letters, University of Tokyo.

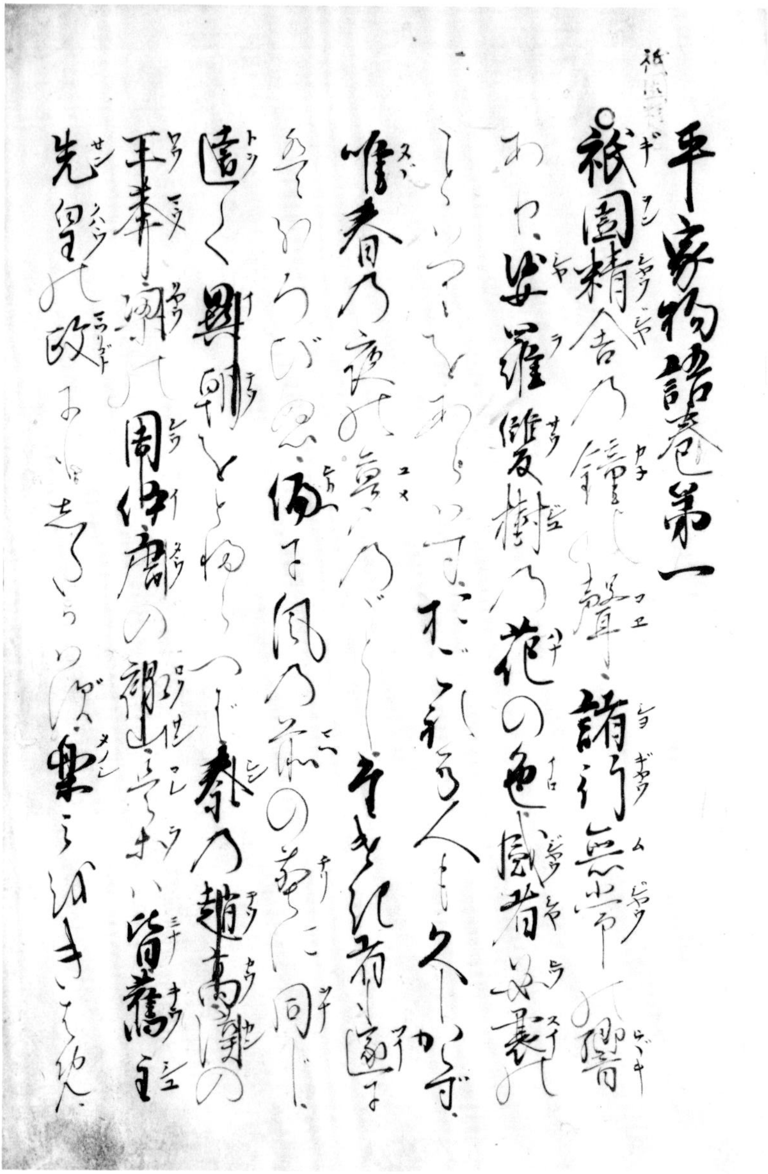

Heike Monogatari, Kakuichibon. This manuscript was supposedly dictated by Kakuichi, a noted blind *biwa* player and reciter of *Heike Monogatari* in the fourteenth century. The opening page of book one, written in *hiragana kanamajiribun* with *furigana* in *katakana*, is shown. Collection of the Department of Japanese Literature, Faculty of Letters, University of Tokyo.

PREFACE

The object of this book is to introduce the history of the Japanese written language to the student who needs to read classical Japanese of any period. The book is divided into two parts: a survey of the history in English and reading selections in Japanese as samples of the written styles and languages discussed in the survey section. The reading selections may serve as a reader for classical Japanese.

I am neither a linguist nor a specialist in language history. However, my experience in teaching Japanese, both modern and classical, to non-Japanese speakers made me realize that an introduction to the history of written Japanese would be extremely helpful for students, especially the student who reads classical Japanese.

Since this book is written as an introduction to the history of written Japanese, detailed discussions of different views and theories on any topic have been purposely avoided. However, I have tried, as much as possible, to discuss the history in accordance with the general consensus of Japanese specialists on the classical writings of the various periods. Numerous books and articles have been written in Japanese on various aspects of the written language, and this introduction will, I hope, prepare the student for further reading in this field in Japanese.

The manuscript for this book was prepared under a grant from the University of Hawaii Japan Studies Endowment, funded by a grant from the Japanese government, and publication was aided by a subsidy from The Japan Foundation. I wish to express my sincere appreciation here for the above assistance.

I am also deeply indebted to many colleagues of the Department of East Asian Languages and Literatures, University of Hawaii at Manoa, especially Professor David Ashworth for advice in the early stage of writing and Professor Gerald B. Mathias for his patient editing of the final manuscript in English, without whose assistance this book could not have been written. My deepest appreciation goes to the staff of the University of Tokyo Press for much encouragement and assistance in the publication of this book.

THE HISTORY OF
THE JAPANESE WRITTEN LANGUAGE

INTRODUCTION

For any language the history of written language does not necessarily parallel the history of spoken language, since a written language normally evolves far more slowly than a spoken language. Also, the history of a written language is usually complicated by the nature of the writing system used for the language. The history of the Japanese written language is influenced very much by the fact that the Japanese people started to write or attempted to write in Chinese in the early period of Japanese history. China had an advanced and sophisticated culture when the Japanese first imported Chinese script in Chinese writings, and since the Japanese people did not have a writing system of their own, it was natural for them to study Chinese and to write in Chinese script.

Since the Chinese language is totally different in its phonology, syntax, and vocabulary from the Japanese language, writing in Chinese does not represent the Japanese language at all. However, Japanese intellectuals were serious students in the study of Chinese until the end of the nineteenth century, and they mastered the ability to read Chinese, or classical Chinese, and some of them acquired the skill of writing in Chinese. The fact that Japanese intellectuals had a reading knowledge of classical Chinese very much influenced both spoken and written Japanese. The influence was especially strong in the area of vocabulary; a large amount of Chinese vocabulary, with Japanized pronunciation, was assimilated into Japanese over time, and today vocabulary originally from classical Chinese is inseparable from the Japanese language.

The native style of writing, which was completely free of Chinese influence at its outset, was begun some time in the ninth century as writing in Japanese syntax and vocabulary using *hiragana*, a native syllabary, and was established and perfected by the beginning of the eleventh century. This style of writing, which reflected the spoken language of the period, remained a model for many centuries, during which the spoken language underwent various changes at various periods. Although the influence of the spoken language, as well as of the Chinese vocabulary, caused the emergence of various modified versions of the native-style writing, the basic grammar of the written language remained similar to that of the eleventh century until the end of the nineteenth century. Naturally, some attempts were made at writing in the spoken language of various periods, but writing in the spoken language was not really accepted as a written style until the beginning of the twentieth century.

The history of the Japanese written language does not coincide neatly with the divisions of Japanese political history, nor with the divisions of the history of the spoken language. Although the usual historical divisions are used for the discussion of the historical changes of the written language in this book, the major dividing line is at the end of the decline of the aristocratic society of the Heian period which separates it clearly from the following period when reading and writing began to spread among non-aristocratic society.

The earlier part of the history, up to the end of the Heian period, is the history of the introduction of reading and writing to aristocratic society, which eventually became extremely accomplished in literary skills, establishing sophisticated writing styles. It is the history of the study of Chinese script, the invention of the Japanese syllabaries, and the discovery and perfection of the native-style writing, through a period when Chinese was also written and writing in Chinese was highly esteemed.

The latter part of the history, after the Heian period, is the history of the dissemination of reading and writing among the broader public, causing diversification and complication of writing styles. Changes in the spoken language and the evolution of society accompanied this diversification and complication for the period of about seven centuries. At the end of the Edo period in the latter half of the nineteenth century, Japanese intellectuals began to study Western culture and languages. They were faced with the problem of finding the answer to "how to write," while they inherited the various written styles, many of which used simple Heian grammar.

Over the entire history of the Japanese written language, Japanese intellectuals, whether they were aristocrats or not, were confronted with the problem of "how to write Japanese" twice: the first time, in the early history when the problem was "how to write Japanese" when they had only Chinese script, and the second time, in the early Meiji period when the problem was "what style of Japanese to write in" to make it compatible with contemporary spoken Japanese.

The discussion of the history of the Japanese written language will provide the reader with some insight on how the Japanese solved or attempted to solve this problem, while giving an overall picture of the written materials produced during a period of about fourteen centuries.

I

THE INTRODUCTION OF WRITING

Early Japan and the Nara Period (710–93)

1. The Introduction of Chinese Script

One of the major difficulties in discussing writing systems in the early history of any civilization is the fact that surviving evidence is scarce, and, therefore, it is difficult to have a consensus among historians. We have the same problem with the early history of Japan. Although it is generally agreed that the Japanese people did not have their own writing system before the introduction of Chinese script, it is difficult to determine exactly when Chinese script was introduced.

The ancient Japanese chronicle *Kojiki* (Record of Ancient Matters), written in 712, records that the ten volumes of *Rongo* (Lunyü; The Analects of Confucius) and one volume of *Senjimon* (Ch'ientzu wen; The Thousand-Character Classic) were brought to Japan by a Korean scholar named Wani in the sixteenth year of Emperor Ōjin's reign. Another chronicle, *Nihon Shoki* (Chronicles of Japan), written in 720, also mentions the arrival of Wani to teach one of Emperor Ōjin's sons. However, these chronicles begin with mythology and blend legend with the history of early Japan, and the historians' general agreement is that they first become accurate around the seventh century. Since there is disagreement over the dates of Emperor Ōjin's reign, ranging from the late third to the early fifth century, we are simply left with the Wani legend.

It is assumed that the first introduction of Chinese script must have been in the form of inscriptions on such items as mirrors or swords, brought from China or Korea before the fourth century, the exact time being difficult to determine. It is not known to what extent these inscriptions were studied by the Japanese of the time, but we have extant inscriptions on swords and a mirror which are considered to have been made in Japan and date from the fifth and sixth centuries. These may have been inscribed by a Korean or Chinese who came to Japan and taught Japanese how to read, or by a Japanese who studied under such teachers.

Judging from later evidence, we know that Chinese books on philosophy and Chinese translations of Sanskrit works on Buddhism must have been brought into Japan and studied by Japanese in the fifth and sixth centuries. The earliest known Buddhist temple, Hōkōji, was erected at the end of the sixth century in the area of Yamato, where the emperors took their residence before 710. The Japanese court must have been involved in studying various aspects of Buddhism, including reading Buddhist literature in Chinese, for a long time before they built the temple, which was the embodiment of their faith in Buddhism.

Written evidence from which we can begin our discussion of the history of the Japanese written language is available to us from the seventh century. These written materials can be classified into two categories: documents recorded in chronicles written in the eighth century and inscriptions in stone or metal, *kinsekibun* in Japanese. The earliest writing of the seventh century, recorded in its entirety in *Nihon Shoki,* is *Kenpō Jūshichijō* (The Constitution of Seventeen Articles), attributed to Prince Shōtoku (574–622), and composed in 604. (See Reading Selection 1.)

Kenpō Jūshichijō was written in *kanbun* (Chinese style of writing), modeled on classical Chinese. The strong influence of Confucian and Buddhist writings can be observed in its writing style, as well as in the underlying philosophy. The tradition of writing *kanbun,* a language quite unlike Japanese and which few of the writers could actually speak, thus began by around the seventh century and continued for many centuries to come.

While *Kenpō Jūshichijō* and other official documents of the seventh century were written in an authentic Chinese style of writing, or were so recorded in the eighth-century chronicles, the written style of inscriptions shows more variety. Some of them contain irregular uses of vocabulary or characters and contain some syntactical anomalies in comparison with genuine Chinese writing.

One special usage of characters found commonly in the inscriptions is the writing of proper names, both place names and personal names, in *man'yōgana,* a phonetic usage of Chinese characters. Precedent for this is found in some Sanskrit terms in Chinese Buddhist writings which were untranslatable and were therefore transcribed phonetically. Similarly, as many Japanese proper names were not translatable into Chinese, phonetic usage was the inevitable outcome. Although not all the characters are decipherable, there are examples of this predating the seventh century.

As long as the syntax of writing is Chinese, even though it may contain Japanese proper names in *man'yōgana,* it is considered to be genuine Chinese writing, or *jun-kanbun,* since a Chinese person can read it. However, if the writing includes some syntactical irregularities, such as the presence of Japanese honorific terms, which are different from those in Chinese, or the misplacement of a verb, the writing is considered modified Chinese writing, *hentai kanbun.*

Some inscriptions contain Japanese honorific terms expressed through a special application of a Chinese character. Whoever the writers of these inscriptions may have been, their intention is clear to us: even when writing a Chinese sentence, they wished to communicate respect by using honorific terms, which were established in the Japanese language by this time. The misplacement of a verb in a sentence may have been an error, or it may have been done intentionally. Since the position of the verb in a sentence is a crucial difference between Chinese and Japanese, its misplacement may have been intentional in order to make the sentence closer to the Japanese language.

A few inscriptions of the seventh century were written in a style of Chinese verse, using rhymes. In order to rhyme, the writers had to be well versed in the Chinese pronunciation of the characters. On the other hand, there is one extreme example on a late-seventh-century monument which was written completely in Japanese word order. (See Reading Selection 2.) The writer's desire to write in Japanese seems obvious, although it was written entirely in Chinese characters as a Japanese syllabary had not yet been developed. Also, the usage of *many'ōgana* in this period was limited to proper names, so that inflections and particles of the Japanese language were not written at all.

There can be two reasons for the emergence of these modifications found in the seventh-century inscriptions. First, not all the Japanese who wanted to write could master the technique of writing in authentic Chinese, which was not only a foreign language to them but was also already highly refined and sophisticated. Another reason was the strong desire of the Japanese to express themselves in a manner closer to their own language but which could not be achieved by using Chinese syntax and vocabulary. These modifications continued to be practiced in the next century and further developed into more varieties of written style, of which we have records dating from the eighth century.

2. The Emergence of New Usages of Chinese Characters

The cultural advancement of ancient Japan reached one of its peaks in the Nara period (710–93), when the imperial palace was located in Heijō-kyō, the present city of Nara. We have ample materials believed to have been written or compiled in this period and they are extremely important works for the study of language, literature, and history.

The following works are representative of the different written styles of the eighth century and will be discussed in the next chapters:

(1) *Kojiki*, 712, written in a modified Chinese-style writing, *hentai kanbun*, with poems and proper names in *man'yōgana*;
(2) *Nihon Shoki*, 720, written in a genuine Chinese-style writing, *jun-kanbun*, with poems and proper names in *man'yōgana*;
(3) *Kaifūsō* (Fond Recollections of Poetry), 751, a collection of Chinese-style poems;
(4) *Man'yōshū* (Collection of a Myriad Leaves), compiled in or

after 759, a collection of Japanese poems, written in *man'yōgana.*

However, we cannot readily assume that these monumental writings in various styles emerged all at once in the eighth century. Both *Kojiki* and *Nihon Shoki* cite older documents on which their writing was based. *Kaifūsō* and *Man'yōshū,* being anthologies of poems, also record old poems that existed at the time of compilation. The poems in *Kaifūsō* were composed from the middle of the seventh century up to the time of compilation. The earliest poems in *Man'yōshū* were supposedly composed in the fourth century and transmitted orally until they were written down in some documents. Even though these documents may have been written in the seventh century, since they are no longer extant, we are compelled to confine our discussion to the eighth century.

a. *Man'yōgana* in Poetry Writing

As we can find the earliest poems written in *man'yōgana* in *Kojiki* and *Nihon Shoki,* it appears that the Japanese people attempted to write their poems in Japanese syntax from the very beginning. The native poems had a long history of oral transmission, which also preserved myths and legends in a society where there was no writing system. Research on the relationship between the early poems and folksongs, which were transcribed later, indicate that most of these poems were once sung as folksongs. Although they may be attributed to certain gods or legendary persons in these chronicles, they are in fact anonymous.

The eighth-century Japanese had two methods available to them to transcribe the poems in their recited form. The first was to use Chinese characters for their meaning to express the Japanese words. This is called *kun,* the semantic usage of the characters. The other was to employ the Japanese approximation of the Chinese reading of the characters to write Japanese syllables, with no regard for the meaning of the characters. This is called *man'yōgana,* the phonetic usage of the characters.

In *Kojiki* and *Nihon Shoki* more than one hundred ancient poems were written in *man'yōgana,* although some proper names in the text of the chronicles were written with characters used for their meaning. In *Man'yōshū*, in its 20 volumes, more than 4500 poems were recorded combining the two methods. Since the most extensive employment of characters is found in *Man'yōshū*, we will first discuss how they were used there. (See Reading Selection 5.)

The first method, the use of Chinese characters for their meanings only, e.g., using 山, 秋, 朝, 神 for the Japanese words, *yama* (mountain), *aki* (autumn), *asa* (morning), *kami* (god), seems quite established by the time *Man'yōshū* was compiled in or after 759, the year in which the last datable poem was composed. This method corresponds with the usage of the *kun* reading of the characters in modern Japanese, but in the eighth century a wider variety of characters was applied in writing a given Japanese word than in the modern Japanese usage. For instance, in *Man'yōshū* poem no. 27, the five different characters, 淑, 良, 吉, 好, 芳, all meaning 'good,' with nuances, were used to write one word, *yoshi* (good), and its inflected forms, *yoki* and *yoku*. The native Japanese vocabulary was small, and each word was semantically broader than the Chinese vocabulary which the characters represented. Therefore, the Japanese could choose several characters which have similar but slightly different meanings in Chinese to write one Japanese word. This usage of characters is called *shōkun* (regular *kun*), to differentiate it from another usage of *kun*, which is discussed below.

The term *man'yōgana* derives from the combination of *man'yō*, from the title *Man'yōshū*, and *kana*, the syllabary. In *man'yōgana*, two kinds of reading of characters were applicable. One is the Japanese reading of Chinese characters in approximation of the Chinese pronunciation, with a complete disregard for their meaning, e.g., using 久 (long time), *ku*, and 母 (mother), *mo*, to write *kumo* (cloud). This usage is called *shakuon* (sound-borrowing). The other is the borrowing of *kun* readings to write Japanese syllables, again in complete disregard for their meaning, e.g., using the *kun* reading of 庭, *niwa* (garden), to write particles *ni* and *wa* in sequence. This usage is called *shakukun* (*kun*-borrowing).

The *shakuon* found in *Man'yōshū* can be further divided into the following groups:

(1) One character was used to represent one syllable, e.g., 阿 for *a*, 志 for *shi*, 多 for *ta*, 奈 for *na*, and 母 for *mo*.

(2) A part of the reading of the characters was used to represent the syllable, e.g., 君 (*kun*) for *ku*, 丹 (*tan*) for *ta*, 南 (*nan*) for *na*, 民 (*min*) for *mi*, and 欲 (*yoku*) for *yo*.

(3) One character was used to represent two syllables, e.g., 兼 (*ken*) for *ke mu*, 三 (*san*) for *sa mu*, 漢 (*kan*) for *ka ni*, 難 (*nan*) for *na ni*, and 楽 (*raku*) for *ra ku*.

Many different Chinese characters which had similar sounds were used to write one Japanese syllable, e.g., for the syllable *ka*, 加, 迦, 可, 箇, 架, 嘉, 何, 珂, 甘, 敢, 甲, and 香 were used. Approximately 480 characters in *Man'yōshū* use *shakuon*, although some scholars may arrive at slightly different figures.

The *shakukun* found in the *Man'yōshū* can also be grouped as follows:

(1) One character was used to represent one syllable, e.g., 見 for *mi*, 来 for *ku*, 田 for *ta*, 十 for *so*, and 津 for *tsu*.

(2) A part of the *kun* reading was used to represent one syllable, e.g., 苑 (*sono*) for *so*, 面 (*omo*) for *mo*, 鳥 (*tori*) for *to*, 跡(*ato*) for *to*, and 沼 (*numa*) for *nu*.

(3) One character was used to represent two syllables, e.g., 鶴 (*tsuru*) for *tsu ru*, 鴨 (*kamo*) for *ka mo*, 借 (*kari*) for *ka ri*, 霜 (*shimo*) for *shi mo*, and 夏 (*natsu*) for *na tsu*.

The number of characters used for *shakukun* to write the Japanese syllables is much smaller than the characters used for *shakuon*. However, since the total number of characters used for *man'yōgana* is so large, we do not have the impression that these characters were chosen only out of necessity. In addition to the usages discussed, there is some *gikun*, the playful usage of *kun*, such as 十六 for *shi shi*, since the multiplication of *shi* (four) by *shi* (four) is 十六 (sixteen). This kind of writing gives us the impression that the writers of these poems were certainly enjoying their freedom in selecting characters for *man'yōgana*. Some influence from Chinese syntax, such as placing the character for negation before a verb—the sign of negation comes after the verb root in Japanese—is also found. All the commentaries for the poems were written in the Chinese style of writing.

It has not been determined who compiled *Man'yōshū*, and there is little uniformity in the compilation of its 20 volumes. In some volumes the poems are grouped under categorical divisions, and under each category, arranged chronologically with the names of the poets provided. In some volumes they are simply grouped in the various categories, without the names of the poets. The selection of the categories is not consistent, either, and in some volumes there are no categorical divisions. Therefore, we assume that there was more than one compiler of *Man'yōshū*, and we believe that it was not edited at the time of compilation. Some poems may have been written or rewritten at the time of compilation, while others had already been written in private collections and were simply assembled into the anthology.

The choice of characters also reflects the lack of uniformity. In some volumes, most of the characters are used for *shakuon*, using one character for one syllable, and in some volumes, the larger number of characters are used for meaning, *shōkun*. In volumes 17 through 20, which appear to be the private collection of Ōtomo no Yakamochi (718?–85), presumably one of the compilers, most of the characters use *shakuon*, except in volume 19 where there are a slightly larger number of *shōkun* characters. The poems in these volumes, as well as volumes 5, 14, and 15, are written as in the following example:

宇	奈	波	良	介	霞	多	奈	妣	伎	多	頭	我
u	na	ha	ra	ni	kasumi	ta	na	bi	ki	ta	zu	ga
祢	乃	可	奈	之	伎	与	比	波	久	介	弊	之
ne	no	ka	na	shi	ki	yo	(h)i	wa	ku	ni	he	shi
於	毛	保	由									
o	mo	ho	yu									

(When the spring mist is over the sea and the voice of cranes is sad, I long for my home, far away. Poem no. 4399, vol. 20)

In this poem all but one character, 霞 *kasumi*, use *shakuon*. In the following example, on the other hand, all the characters use *shōkun*, and no particles or inflections are written:

遠	妹		振	仰	見	偲		
tōki	imo	ga	furi	sake	mitsutsu	shinobu	ramu	
是	月		面		雲	勿	棚	引
kono	tsuki	no	omo	ni	kumo	na	tana	biki

(My love, far away, is probably looking at the moon and thinking of me. O, cloud, do not cover the face of the moon! Poem no. 2460, vol. 11)

In the following example, some particles and inflections are written in *shakuon* and the rest is written with *shōkun* characters.

暮 去 者 小倉 乃 山 尓 鳴 鹿 者
yū sare ba ogura no yama ni naku shika wa
今 夜 波 不鳴 寐 宿 家 良 思 母
ko yoi wa nakazu ine ni ke ra shi mo
(The deer in Ogura Mountain cry, when the evening comes, but they are not crying tonight, so they have probably gone to sleep. Poem no. 1511, vol. 8)

The Japanese poems do not rhyme but have a rhythm based on repeating phrases with five and seven syllables. Although some early poems in *Man'yōshū*, as well as the poems in *Kojiki* and *Nihon Shoki*, have phrases with irregular numbers of syllables, in the eighth century the basic rhythm using five- and seven-syllable lines was fully developed. The most popular form of the poems in *Man'yōshū* was the five-seven-five-seven-seven form, although a number of longer poems with a similar alternation are included. Therefore, in order to read the poems with unindicated grammatical elements, such as poem no. 2460, meter is also taken into consideration, along with the various alternatives for reading the characters and the meaning of the poems themselves.

Studies of *Man'yōshū* reveal that the poems were composed with native Japanese vocabulary, except for a very small number of Chinese and Sanskrit words mainly of Buddhist reference. When we consider the fact that there are some poets whose names appear both in *Man'yōshū* and *Kaifūsō*, it is interesting to note that the influence of Chinese vocabulary was minimal in *Man'yōshū* poems. The study of Chinese and writing in Chinese were done by only a small number of people, namely the court nobles and priests, but *Man'yōshū* contains poems from a broader segment of society, as we can see in the poems by anonymous authors. It appears that *Man'yōshū* poems established a precedent for composing Japanese poems with native vocabulary for many centuries to come, since this type of poem was composed only with native vocabulary, *yamato kotoba,* even after Chinese vocabulary was incorporated into Japanese in greater quantities.

However, composing a poem places certain restrictions on the selection of vocabulary, and the Japanese vocabulary used in *Man'yōshū* probably is not an exact reflection of the spoken language. It is known that certain words were avoided, due to considerations of meter or to their unpoetic qualities. Since poems have a unique impersonal dimension, as compared with prose, the use of honorific terms was limited to the extreme cases of praising a god or emperor. Nevertheless, *Man'yōshū* is an extremely important work for the observation of the native vocabulary, in the oldest form possible, since a large number of poems were recorded in *man'yōgana.*

Studies of *man'yōgana,* mostly done in the twentieth century, have led to the discovery of many important aspects of the phonology of eighth-century Japanese. There were eight vowels in this period, unlike modern Japanese which has only five vowels, and when the vowels were different, e.g., *ko* and *kö*, the syllables were written with different characters. The sounds of some consonants were different from those of modern Japanese; e.g., the *h* is believed to have been a labial, resembling a *p* sound. The characters used to write the syllables with the consonants *k*, *s*, *t*, and *h*, which are called *seion* (voiceless sounds), were usually different from the characters for writing the syllables with *g*, *z*, *d*, and *b*, which are called *dakuon* (voiced counterparts of *seion*). This distinction in the writing of *seion* and *dakuon* syllables was abandoned for unknown reasons when the Japanese syllabaries were developed in the ninth and tenth centuries.

When we think of the fact that the usage of *man'yōgana* was limited to proper names in the seventh century, it is a wonder to have this imaginative and creative use of *man'yōgana* in *Man'yōshū*. It is true that the liberation of *man'yōgana* in the eighth century was achieved by poets who wanted to write their poems in Japanese.

b. *Senmyōgaki* in Prose Writing

Although Japanese poems were written in *man'yōgana* in the eighth century, the official style of writing of the Japanese court from the beginning of the seventh century was Chinese-style writing. In fact, the study of Chinese advanced more and more in the eighth and ninth centuries, along with the official communication between the Japanese court and the court of the T'ang dynasty (618–907) in China. This resulted not only in the writing of documents but also in the production of Chinese poems, which were compiled into the anthology *Kaifūsō* in 751. (See Reading Selection 4.)

Kaifūsō is the first anthology of Chinese poetry composed by Japanese. It contains about 120 poems which were composed from the middle of the seventh century to the time of compilation, and its compiler is unknown. It is not considered to be a literary masterpiece, since many of its poems lack originality and some of them are simple imitations of Chinese models. However, the mere attempt to write verses in Chinese with rhymes, which Japanese poems do not have, is clear evidence of the enthusiasm for composing Chinese poetry and of the extent to which the study of Chinese flourished at that time. Mastering Chinese pronunciation in order to obtain correct rhyme could not have been easy for the Japanese poets; nevertheless, the practice of composing poems in Chinese became a tradition among the Japanese literati, who continued to produce many anthologies until the beginning of this century.

Nihon Shoki was also written in an authentic Chinese style of writing. It was written on the basis of documents which existed at the time of its writing and legends and myths transmitted by oral tradition. Both *Kojiki* and *Nihon Shoki* were written around the same time, and their sources appear to be similar, since they contain similar myths, legends, and records of ancient emperors. However, the writing styles of *Kojiki* and *Nihon Shoki* are quite different.

Since *Nihon Shoki* is an account of the history of ancient Japan, it inevitably contains, in *man'yōgana*, proper names and early poems which could not be translated into Chinese. The *man'yōgana* used in *Nihon Shoki* encompasses a large variety of characters, and it is believed that the *kan'on* reading of the characters was used. The *kan'on* reading of characters, which is the approximation of the Chinese pronunciation brought from the T'ang capital by envoys and scholars, was adopted as the official reading of Chinese characters by the Japanese court in the eighth century. The *go'on* reading, which is based on the Chinese pronunciation brought into Japan earlier, probably by way of Korea, was already widespread, e.g., the *shakuon* in *Man'yōshū* is according to the *go'on* reading of the characters, so the adoption of the *kan'on* reading naturally met some resistance. However, the compilers of *Nihon Shoki* obviously made it their policy to write it in the most up-to-date style of the time.

As the Chinese pronunciation of characters was brought into Japan at different times over the course of history and from different areas of China, there are several alternative readings for the characters, each reflecting their historical and geographic origins. In *Kojiki* and inscriptions of the seventh century, there are readings of characters even older than *go'on* used as *man'yōgana*. The *go'on* reading for many characters survived the official court promotion on the adoption of the *kan'on* reading. It survived especially for Buddhist terms, since these terms were established and widespread among the literate people of the eighth century.

Kojiki was written in a modified Chinese style. (See Reading Selection 3.) However, the preface was written in *jun-kanbun*, genuine Chinese style, evidence that its author, Ō no Yasumaro (?–723), could write in that style. There is a passage in the preface where he expresses the difficulty of choosing an appropriate style of writing for *Kojiki*, a prose narrative of considerable length. The writer said that if he used only *kun* characters, the words would not express the Japanese ideas fully. What he meant by "using only *kun* characters" was Chinese-style writing, excluding the phonetic usage of characters. That is, he would have had to translate Japanese ideas into Chinese with the inevitable loss of something in the translation. On the other hand if he were to use *man'yōgana* to write Japanese sentences syllable by syllable, the sentences would become inordinately long and their meanings would not be immediately clear. Poetry was successfully written in *man'yōgana* because each line in a poem was no longer than five or seven syllables, no matter how long a poem was.

Ō no Yasumaro finally compromised on a mixture of the two, in modified sentences with basically Chinese syntax. Proper names and poems were written in *man'yōgana*, and some expressions which the writer did not think translatable are also in *man'yōgana*. Honorific terms were used, and explanations that some characters should be read as *man'yōgana* were added. The writer also stated, in the preface, that since some proper names were already written with certain characters, he did not change them. This statement is interpreted today to mean that usage of characters for certain proper names was already established, but eighth-century writers no longer knew how those characters had come to be used.

As a result of Ō no Yasumaro's efforts, the written style of *Kojiki* is closer to the language used in the oral transmission of the myths and legends than the style of *Nihon Shoki* is. This may be the major reason why *Kojiki* is treated as literature, while the *Nihon Shoki* is generally treated as a historical document. The decision of *Kojiki*'s author may not have been totally novel at the time of writing, since there were similar attempts in earlier inscriptions. However, his awareness of the inappropriateness of any existing style for writing narrative prose was quite significant in the history of the Japanese written language.

One step closer to the Japanese language from the style of *Kojiki* is the style called *senmyōgaki* (the style of *senmyō*), which was used to write *senmyō* (imperial rescripts) and *norito* (prayers in Shinto rituals). It is difficult to determine the exact date of writings in *senmyōgaki*, since they are found only in books compiled later. The earliest *norito* is found in the collection of *norito* in the *Engishiki* (Institutes of the Engi Period), compiled in 927, and early *senmyō* are found in the *Shoku-Nihongi* (Continuation of Chronicles of Japan), written in 797. It has been determined that the oldest *senmyō* was composed at the end of the seventh century, and we have enough evidence to believe that *senmyō* and *norito* were composed and written in the eighth century.

In *senmyōgaki* two sizes of characters were used. (See Reading Selection 6.) The large characters used *shōkun* readings and the small characters were used to write the inflections and particles, etc., in *man'yōgana*. The important aspect of *senmyōgaki* is that it was mostly written in Japanese syntax and the particles and inflections were included.

The reason for not using *kanbun* to write *senmyō* and *norito* is obvious: *norito* had to be recited orally in certain rituals without changes in wording from its historic tradition. *Senmyō* also had to be expressed orally, usually by a minister acting on behalf of the emperor, according to the emperor's exact statements, which were made in Japanese. Both *senmyō* and *norito* had a fixed format, as well as fixed phrasing, and were probably recited with a certain rhythm, so they were not a free type of prose. However, the appearance of *senmyōgaki* is significant in the sense that it was the first attempt to write Japanese prose in Japanese syntax and including all the grammatical elements. The fact that a different size of character was used for the Japanese inflections and particles suggests that the writers were aware of the need for a set of phonetic symbols to write the Japanese language, in addition to the Chinese characters.

The poems in *man'yōgana*, the chronicles in both genuine and modified Chinese styles, and *senmyō* and *norito* in *senmyōgaki* are the representative styles of writing in the Nara period. There are a few other materials written in this period, which are not discussed, but they are similar to the styles discussed here. Although the number of literate people in this period may have been small, the variety of written styles they employed tells us that their attempts at writing Japanese using Chinese characters was extremely energetic and productive.

From what we have seen of the written works in the Nara period, we can conclude that only the materials written in *man'yōgana* and *senmyōgaki* and some Japanese vocabulary found in the modified Chinese style of writing can tell us about the nature of the spoken language of the period. Writings in prose are insufficient to provide much linguistic evidence, but there are sufficient materials in poetry for the study of the sound system and vocabulary of the period. Chinese vocabulary used in Chinese syntax is naturally not considered as a part of the Japanese language. However, a small number of Chinese and Sanskrit words used in *Man'yōshū* and *senmyōgaki* writings were in the process of becoming part of the Japanese vocabulary.

II

THE ESTABLISHMENT OF JAPANESE-STYLE WRITING

The Heian Period (794–1192)

1. The Development of Japanese Syllabaries

The approximately four hundred years of the Heian period offer us far richer written materials than the previous period, especially in the area of prose writing. What contributed to the richness of the written materials in this period is the fact that this relatively peaceful era within an aristocratic socioeconomic setting offered the people involved with the imperial court—the court members, priests, and scholars—a greater opportunity to read and write.

In fact, this aristocratic society placed a great value on reading and writing. Men studied Chinese and wrote in the Chinese style of writing, and women practiced writing Japanese poems in *hiragana*, the Japanese syllabary developed in this period. Although women were generally excluded from the study of Chinese and did not write anything in Chinese, their education included composing and writing poems in graceful handwriting in *hiragana*. In the mid-Heian period, newly emerged women writers, most of whom served in the court, produced masterpieces of Japanese prose literature when ancient Japan reached its highest cultural peak.

However, the first part of the Heian period, the ninth century, is the so-called dark ages for Japanese-style writing, including poetry, and the study of Chinese and writing in Chinese prevailed due to the strong cultural influence of the T'ang dynasty. The evidence can be observed in the compilation of imperial anthologies of Chinese poetry, composed by the Japanese, which demonstrate a higher quality than *Kaifūsō* of the Nara period. Official documents and official diaries, modeled on Chinese works, were all written in the genuine Chinese style of writing.

However, two new writing systems, *katakana* and *hiragana*, developed in the ninth century and were to play extremely important roles in the history of the Japanese written language.

a. *Katakana* with the Japanese Reading of Chinese

It appears that around the beginning of the ninth century priests who were studying Buddhist texts in Chinese began to use diacritical marks as an aid in reading Chinese. The marks were, in the beginning, created individually for personal use. The oldest copy of a Buddhist text which has these marks is dated 828. These marks are called *okototen* (marks for *o*, the object marker, and *koto*, the nominalization marker) and were used to indicate with which Japanese inflections and particles the characters in Chinese sentences should be read.

The appearance of these marks, *okototen*, is a clear indication that the priests were reading Chinese text in Japanese, that is to say, translating Chinese into Japanese. Since there are no marks to indicate the word order, they probably were translating only partially. We have no proof as to how the people in the Nara period read Chinese, so we do not know if they read it with genuine Chinese pronunciation or in *on* reading, which is a totally Japanese approximation of the Chinese pronunciation. Neither do we know whether they read with Chinese syntax or in a partial translation style. However, we have the evidence that the priests in the Heian period used *kun* readings, translation reading, since the *okototen* were created as a device for doing so. They probably used *on* readings also, using the *go'on* reading of characters, as Buddhist priests still do today when reciting Buddhist sutras.

Although the *okototen* usage started on an individual basis in the beginning, eventually they became a regular feature in teaching Chinese and were developed secretly and independently in different denominations of Buddhism. In the middle of the Heian period, scholars who held official positions in the court for the study of Chinese learned the use of *okototen* and developed it in their own way. Thus, by the end of the Heian period eight different schools of *okototen* existed.

The various kinds of marks were written, in different schools and at different times, with white or red ink on or beside the characters, which were written in black ink. The following is a partial example from a set of *okototen* used by one of the eight schools in the Heian period. In the following illustrations, each square represents a character and the black dots represent *okototen,* which indicate the given character is read together with the particles and inflections in Japanese.

 The particle *o* is to be appended to the reading of this character.

 The word *koto* is to follow the reading of this character.

 The particle *no* is to be appended to the reading of this character.

 The particle *wa* is to be appended to the reading of this character.

 The particle *ni* is to be appended to the reading of this character.

 The inflection *te* is to be appended to the reading of this character.

 This character is read as a verb by adding *su.*

 This character is read in the future tense by adding *mu.*

Katakana, which was called *katakanna* (imperfect *kanna*) in the Heian period, was developed together with *okototen* in the same environment. The priests used *man'yōgana,* which was called *magana* (genuine *kana*) in the Heian period, along with *okototen* to write some particles, inflections, or *kun* readings of characters in the early Heian period. However, it was not convenient to write *man'yōgana,* some of which are very complex, in the small spaces between the characters. Also, this took place when the priests were studying Chinese under a lecturer, so they had to write quickly. Thus, they began to develop their own personal simplified letters.

Writing a part of a character in place of the entire character was practiced earlier in Japan, e.g., writing 寸 for 村 (village), as well as in China, e.g., writing 女 for 汝 (you). However, this kind of abbreviation was done only as a temporary expedient and was never standardized or widely used. The priests in the early Heian period might have taken some hints from these abbreviated characters for their own simplifications.

This is the beginning of *katakana* in the ninth century, and the earliest text containing *okototen* also has some *katakana*. All of these simplified letters were abbreviated forms of *man'yōgana*, except the letter for the syllabic *n*, and were used phonetically to write Japanese syllables. Although there is not always a consensus among scholars as to which *man'yōgana* the original character for a particular *katakana* was, we can say that the *katakana* was created by taking a part of the original character, e.g., カ from the character 加 and ア from the cursive writing of 阿.

Since *katakana* was originally developed for personal use with less uniformity, more than one character was abbreviated for one syllable, e.g., 三 and 見 for the syllable *mi*, and also the way of abbreviation was not uniform, e.g., both イ and 尹 from the character 伊 were used to write the syllable *i*. However, it appears that *katakana* began to have more uniformity in the middle of the Heian period, and it was used in writing as well as in reading aids for Chinese. We have some scanty evidence of the fact that *katakana* mixed with Chinese characters was used for writing sentences or poems on a personal basis. Also, in one tale of this period, *Utsubo Monogatari* (The Tale of the Hollow Tree), *katakana* was mentioned as being practiced by young people for calligraphy.

By the end of the Heian period, *katakana* was freely used to write Japanese sentences, along with Chinese characters. By then, *katakana* replaced the small characters in *senmyōgaki* of the Nara period to write the particles and inflections of the Japanese words in Japanese syntax. However, this did not take place until the other syllabary, *hiragana*, was fully developed and practiced widely for writing poems and prose in Japanese.

The emergence of *katakana* to write Japanese syllables is extremely important in the history of writing in Japanese, since it made the writing of Japanese grammatical elements possible and easier than the use of *man'yōgana*. We will study the use of *katakana* in the late Heian period after we discuss how *hiragana* was developed.

b. *Hiragana* in Poetry Writing

Unfortunately, we have less information concerning the early stages of the development of *hiragana*, than we do of *katakana*, mainly because materials written in *hiragana* or in its developing stage were lost. We can assume that they may be Japanese poems, private letters, and notes, materials which are easily lost.

Judging from a few pieces of information from the early Heian period, *man'yōgana* apparently was first written in the cursive hand, *sōgana*, which still had a close resemblance to the original Chinese characters. Also, in *sōgana* each character was still written separately, unlike later *hiragana*, in which the letters were frequently connected to each other. Some pieces of writing in *sōgana* still exist, attributed to well-known calligraphers who were all men.

Hiragana developed from *sōgana* and is a simplified and more cursive form of *sōgana*, so that there is little resemblance between the original *man'yōgana* and *hiragana* that was developed from it. *Hiragana* was called *onnade* (woman's handwriting) or *onnamoji* (woman's letters) in the Heian period, since women, who were excluded from the study of Chinese and did not write *man'yōgana*, wrote their poems and letters in *hiragana*. In contrast with the terms *onnade* and *onnamoji*, *man'yōgana* written squarely was called *otokode* (man's handwriting) or *otoko no te* (man's letters) in this period. But men were not excluded from writing in *hiragana*, since written communication between men and women was done in *hiragana*.

Although there is a legend telling us that *hiragana* was created by Kōbō Daishi (Saint Kōbō, 774–835), we do not believe that it was created by a single person. Like *katakana*, several different *man'yōgana* were simplified for writing one syllable and different forms of *hiragana* simplified from the same *man'yōgana* existed in this period. Besides, we are not sure how much *hiragana* was developed during Kōbō Daishi's time.

Legend attributes *Iroha Uta*, which was used for *hiragana* writing practice, to Kōbō Daishi, but this poem has 47 syllables altogether, using all the syllables once in the form of poem. *Ame-tsuchi* (Heaven-earth), a similar exercise, which is merely a list of words using all the syllables once, has one more syllable than *Iroha Uta*, *e* and *ye* being distinguished with different letters. Therefore, we assume that *Ame-tsuchi* was created in the beginning of the Heian period and was in fact used for writing practice in the ninth and tenth centuries as mentioned in certain tenth-century tales, but *Iroha Uta* was created by someone after the *e* and *ye* sounds had coalesced into one, probably in the late tenth or early eleventh century.

The development of *sōgana* and *hiragana* had strong ties with the history of Japanese calligraphy. *Katakana* was never written for aesthetic purposes, but *sōgana* and *hiragana* were written to appeal to the aesthetic sense of the readers. While *katakana* was a convenient reading aid and was developed in the austere society of priests, *hiragana* was created in a more leisurely aristocratic environment, for writing poems and letters in beautiful handwriting. There are some letters resembling *sōgana*, as well as *hiragana* in its developing stage, mixed with *katakana* and *okototen* for reading aids in the ninth century, but their use was limited and soon discontinued.

From the beginning of the tenth century on, a number of literary works begin to appear, and, although the handwritten original texts no longer exist, we believe that these works were written in *hiragana*. Judging from the appearance of these works and from the fact that there are records of *uta-awase* (poetry contests) held at the court quite often from the end of the ninth century to the beginning of the tenth century, we can assume that *hiragana* was used widely and with a certain uniformity by that time and that the poems must have been recorded in *hiragana* at the time of the contests.

The following is a list of major works believed to have been written in *hiragana*:

(1) *Taketori Monogatari* (The Bamboo Cutter's Tale), written around the beginning of the tenth century;

(2) *Ise Monogatari* (The Tales of Ise), written around the beginning of the tenth century (See Reading Selection 8.);

(3) *Kokinshū* (Collection of Ancient and Modern Japanese Poetry), compiled in 905 by Ki no Tsurayuki and others (See Reading Selection 7.);

(4) *Shinsen Wakashū* (New Selection of Poetry), compiled in 918? by Ki no Tsurayuki and others;

(5) *Tosa Nikki* (The Tosa Diary), written in 935? by Ki no Tsurayuki (See Reading Selection 9.);

(6) *Yamato Monogatari* (The Tales of Yamato), written in 951?

Among these works, *Taketori Monogatari* may have been the earliest, but the date of writing is disputed; various dates are given by different scholars—from the early ninth to the early tenth century. *Taketori Monogatari* does contain the oldest vocabulary but there are no earlier copies, the oldest fragments belonging to the middle of the sixteenth century, and we are left with the question of how much of the original has been retained.

There is another aspect of *Taketori Monogatari* which is unique in comparison with the others. The influence of Chinese writing is more manifest than in other *hiragana* writings. It is likely that the author of *Taketori Monogatari* was well versed in Chinese, and, in fact, the tale is a mixture of two elements: (1) the basic frame of the tale, that of a Japanese folktale, and (2) various episodes strongly influenced by Chinese lore. Therefore, some scholars assume that the original *Taketori Monogatari* may have been written in the Chinese style of writing, in the same manner as some of the Buddhist tale collections, e.g., *Nihon Ryōiki* (Miraculous Tales of Japan), compiled between 810 and 823, and then rewritten in *hiragana* before the original was lost.

The remaining five works are believed to have been written originally in *hiragana*, and they are all strongly associated with Japanese poems, *waka* (Japanese-style poems). *Kokinshū* is the first imperial anthology of poetry, and *Shinsen Wakashū* is also a poetry collection. *Tosa Nikki* is a diary of a journey and contains poems. *Ise Monogatari* and *Yamato Monogatari* are collections of tales, and even the shortest tale in them contains a poem or two. Some of the tales in *Ise Monogatari* and *Yamato Monogatari* are extremely short and almost identical to the commentaries on poems found in *Kokinshū*. There is little doubt that the tales in *Ise Monogatari* and *Yamato Monogatari* have developed around the poems, since the poems play a crucial role in the tales. *Ise Monogatari* and *Yamato Monogatari* are classified in the literary genre of *uta monogatari* (tales developed around poems), which is believed to have its origins in the practice of providing commentaries on poems. *Uta monogatari* is differentiated from *tsukuri monogatari* (fictitious tales), such as *Taketori Monogatari*, although the latter may also contain some poems.

Kokinshū has two prefaces: one written in the Chinese style of writing and the other in *hiragana*. The preface in *hiragana*, written by Ki no Tsurayuki (868?–945?), a well-known poet and *hiragana* writer of the period, may be the first prose written in *hiragana*. Even though we cannot be sure of this, since the dates of some of the tales are difficult to determine, the preface is regarded as early *hiragana* writing, which, by discussing the value of Japanese poems, elevated *hiragana* writing to the level of the Chinese preface.

The development of native prose writing, called *wabun*, to which these tales belong, began together with the development of *uta monogatari*. Therefore, most of the Heian period *wabun* style writings contain poems, although the weight of poetry varies among them. *Wabun* was written almost entirely in *hiragana* with Japanese vocabulary in Japanese syntax. It is believed to be very close to the spoken language of this period.

However, there is one respect in which *hiragana* writing failed to record the spoken language accurately. That is, there was no distinction in *hiragana* for writing *seion* (the consonants *k*, *t*, *h*, and *s*) and *dakuon* (the consonants *g*, *d*, *b*, and *z*) syllables. The disappearance of this distinction is also observed in the *man'yōgana* written in this period, for unknown reasons. Neither did *katakana* have a separate set of symbols for *dakuon*. Strangely enough, more vocabulary with voiced sounds presumably entered the language in the Heian period, due to the combination of morphemes and to the influence of Chinese vocabulary. Yet, all *dakuon* syllables were recorded as *seion* both in *hiragana* and in *katakana* in this period.

The emergence of *hiragana* was perhaps a more significant phenomenon than that of *katakana* in the history of the Japanese written language, since *hiragana* came to be used for establishing the *wabun* style of writing. By the beginning of the tenth century, after many centuries of studying Chinese characters and Chinese writings, the Japanese people found a way of writing that was completely free of Chinese influence.

In addition, *hiragana* writing made writing more accessible to women. Although the compilers of *Kokinshū* and *Shinsen Wakashū*, as well as the writer of *Tosa Nikki*, were men, and we suspect that the unknown authors of *Taketori Monogatari*, *Ise Monogatari*, and *Yamato Monogatari* may be all men, there are a number of famous women poets in *Kokinshū*, *Shinsen Wakashū*, and in other private anthologies, which we have not discussed here. We know of some whose beautiful poems are preserved in *Man'yōshū*, but we do not really know if these women themselves wrote their poems in *man'yōgana* or not. However, for the women whose names appear in the anthologies of the tenth century, we are certain that they wrote their poems in *hiragana*. They not only wrote poems and letters, but also wrote diaries in *hiragana* in this period, while men wrote their diaries in the Chinese style of writing. *Tosa Nikki* was written by a man, Ki no Tsurayuki, who had to pretend that he was a woman to write the diary in *hiragana*.

2. The Perfection of Prose Writing in *Hiragana*

Wabun-style writing flourished from the latter half of the tenth century, reaching its peak at the turn of the eleventh century. The court nobles, many of whom were women, produced masterpieces of *wabun*-style writings. This was due to various aspects of the aristocratic society centered around the court in Kyoto. The influence of China had been diminishing ever since the court ceased sending its official embassies to the Chinese capital and the glory of the T'ang dynasty came to an end in 907. As the influence of Chinese culture declined, the native culture gathered strength. For instance, in painting, *yamatoe* (Japanese-style painting) began to appear in the beginning of the tenth century, and calligraphy began to shed its Chinese influence. In the eleventh century *yamatoe* established itself as the mainstream of painting in Japan. Writing Japanese poems and poetry contests became important and common activities in court life.

Heian women of aristocratic lineage were expected to master three skills: in literary skills they had to excel in poetry composition as well as memorize all the poems in *Kokinshū*. Fine calligraphy was required; the ability to write their poems in a graceful hand was a must, since the poems exchanged in courtship were very often equivalent to love letters. And in music, they were expected to master a musical instrument. Needless to say, they had to have proper manners, and excellent taste in colors in choosing their attire and the like was expected.

Hiragana was called *onnade* or *onnamoji* during this period not because women created *hiragana* but because women used *hiragana* more than men did—for women it was their only means of expressing themselves in writing. Educated and talented women were sought after and invited to the court to educate and entertain the wives and daughters of the emperors. It was usually the fathers of the emperor's wives who sought these talented women for their daughters and granddaughters. Since the emperors in this period had many wives who were kept in the court with their children, their fathers competed with each other to find the best ladies-in-waiting. These women, who usually came from the middle class of the aristocracy, could even read and recite Chinese poems, especially the poems of the T'ang-dynasty poets. They wrote *waka*, diaries, and tales in *hiragana*, and some of their works marked the height of *wabun*-style writing.

A large number of tales, diaries, etc., were written from the middle of the tenth century to the end of the Heian period. However, many of them were lost, and we cannot tell if they were tales or diaries from the titles surviving in other tales. The following is a list of major works of which copies survive today:

(1) *Utsubo Monogatari* (The Tale of the Hollow Tree), written some time in the latter half of the tenth century;

(2) *Ochikubo Monogatari* (The Tale of Lady Ochikubo), written at the end of the tenth century;

(3) *Kagerō Nikki* (Gossamer Diary), written in 974? by Fujiwara no Michitsuna's mother (936?–95);

(4) *Makura no Sōshi* (The Pillow Book), written in 1001? by Sei Shōnagon;

(5) *Genji Monogatari* (The Tale of Genji), written in the beginning of the eleventh century by Murasaki Shikibu (973?–1014);

(6) *Izumi Shikibu Nikki* (The Diary of Izumi Shikibu), written in 1007? by Izumi Shikibu;

(7) *Murasaki Shikibu Nikki* (The Diary of Lady Murasaki), written in 1010? by Murasaki Shikibu.

The authors of *Utsubo Monogatari* and *Ochikubo Monogatari* have not been determined. We can only say that the authors of these tales are likely to be men, judging from the style of writing and the use of vocabulary, both of which often indicate a knowledge of Chinese on the part of authors. The rest of the listed works, the *Kagerō Nikki*, *Makura no Sōshi*, *Genji Monogatari*, *Izumi Shikibu Nikki*, and *Murasaki Shikibu Nikki* are all written by women, and we have some knowledge of their authors.

Although no originals in the authors' hand are extant, it appears that various handwritten copies of these works existed already in the Heian period, since the comparison of some of the copies began in the thirteenth century. In order for these works to be read, someone had to hand-copy them, since printing techniques were not available except for very limited Buddhist documents in the Heian period. The copies usually contain some errors, especially when the copies were made centuries later. Some of the errors could be due to the changes in both the written and the spoken languages between the time of the original and the time when the copies were made. For instance, the poets in the middle of the Heian period were no longer able to read *Man'yōshū* written in *man'yōgana* without annotations and *kana*, so *Man'yōshū* had already become the object of scholarly study by the middle of the tenth century.

Fortunately, some of the works, such as *Genji Monogatari* and *Makura no Sōshi*, have been studied by many Japanese literary scholars since the Edo period. Studies have been done not only of plot formation and esthetic values, but also of the genealogy of surviving texts, with attempts at textual recensions. Also, the usage of vocabulary and the style of language used in the works have been quite thoroughly studied.

Genji Monogatari is the most widely studied and best-known tale of the Heian period, or perhaps, of the entire history of Japanese literature. (See Reading Selection 12.) It is the longest tale of this period, and numerous fictitious characters appear in it. A large number of poems are exchanged by the characters in the tale, according to the practice in Heian aristocratic society. However, the intention of the author, whose real name is unknown, does not appear to have been to write another *uta monogatari*, in which poems are the central focus of the tale. She was much more talented and ambitious than the poets of a century earlier. It appears that what she was essaying, using *hiragana* in the *wabun* style of writing, was a "history" book or a chronicle of the sort written by men in the Chinese style of writing. In other words, the *wabun* style of writing had been developed to maturity by this time, so that, provided with a talented writer, it could challenge the Chinese style of writing.

Genji Monogatari's contribution to the history of the Japanese written language is of great importance. It marked the pinnacle of *wabun*-style writing in its use of *yamato kotoba* to its full capacity. No other writer of the same period, nor the writers of the late eleventh century and thereafter, approached Murasaki Shikibu's ability to write a rich *wabun*-style of writing. Their usage of *yamato kotoba* is quite limited when we compare it with the fullness of its usage in *Genji Monogatari*, and from the standpoint of language, this is why it is considered to be the monumental work of *wabun*-style writing. There are, needless to say, many other reasons why *Genji Monogatari* is considered a literary masterpiece.

In *Genji Monogatari* a limited number of Chinese characters and Chinese vocabulary are used, limited to the common knowledge of its contemporary readers, mostly aristocratic women. *Sarashina Nikki* (Sarashina Diary), written in the middle of the eleventh century by the daughter of Sugawara Takasue, tells us that its author was eager to read all 54 chapters of the famous *Genji Monogatari* around 1028. This would indicate that *Genji Monogatari* was easily and widely read by contemporary aristocratic readers. It is obvious that its language was based on the spoken language of the period, as is true with all the *wabun* style up to that time, although slight differences are observed between the language of the dialogue and the narrative part of the tale.

Makura no Sōshi is not fiction, but classified as *zuihitsu* (miscellaneous writings), a category which is established as a literary genre on the basis of this work. (See Reading Selection 11.) As for the fullness of its *yamato kotoba* usage, it cannot bear comparison with *Genji Monogatari*, but its author, Sei Shōnagon, created beautiful and vivid expressions. A part of *Makura no Sōshi* is almost identical in form with the diaries of Heian women. Men wrote their diaries in Chinese-style writing to record daily activities, but these women's diaries in the Heian period are not records of daily activities. They are recollections of events, written afterward. Thus, they are more like the *monogatari* (tale), which could be either fiction or nonfiction, than like men's diaries of this period.

The establishment of the *wabun* style of writing in the Heian period has provided us with ample materials to observe the contemporary written and spoken languages. It should be noted that the language used in a large number of poems of this period had already become conservative, and the phonetic changes in the spoken language are little reflected in the poems. However, one change observed in poetry is that the usage of *makura kotoba* (pillow words), conventional epithets preceding certain words, was declining in this period, since the *makura kotoba* was a vestige of the time when poems were chanted and orally transmitted. The poems in the Heian period were written in *hiragana* by the poets who composed them; thus there was no need for oral transmission and the poems were more personalized. The techniques which came to be used more were the plays on words, namely, *engo* (associative word) and *kakekotoba* (pivot word or pun); the latter in particular was easier to use when *man'yōgana* was replaced by *hiragana*, which did not have separate symbols for *dakuon*, and one written word could mean two or more different spoken words.

Like *dakuon*, *yōon* (contracted sounds), which obviously existed in Chinese vocabulary, were not indicated in either *hiragana* or *katakana*. Recorded in *hiragana*, presumably as reflections of changes in the spoken language in this period, are these three kinds of *onbin* (euphonic change): (1) *i-onbin* (sporadic loss of *k, g, s,* etc., before *i*), such as *kisaki* (empress) changing into *kisai*, (2) *u-onbin* (the change of *ku, gu, hi, mi, bi,* etc., into *u*), such as *marabito* (guest) changing into *maraudo*, (3) *hatsuonbin* (the change of *mi, bi, ni, ri, ru,* etc., into *n*), such as *narinu* (became) changing into *nannu*. *Sokuonbin* (the assimilation of *chi, hi, ri,* etc., to the following consonant), must have occurred in the spoken language judging from the writing, such as *mote* appearing where *mochite* (gerund form of "to hold") would be expected, but presumably pronounced *motte*. At the end of the Heian period, *tsu* began to be written to indicate these assimilated sounds in *katakana* writings.

It appears that a number of Chinese vocabulary items were

totally assimilated into the spoken language in the middle of the Heian period, as we can observe such words in *wabun*-style writings. These words were often used with the Japanese inflectional endings: for example, *shifuneshi* (tenacious), which is the combination of *shifunen* (Chinese, tenacity) and *shi*, a Japanese adjective inflection; and *sauzoku* (to dress up) which is the combination of *sauzoku* (Chinese, attire) with *ku* written in *hiragana* for the Japanese inflection of a verb, making the word into a verb.

Honorific terms, used alone or together with verbs or other honorific terms, were extensively used in the tales and diaries of this period. It appears that the honorific terms in the spoken language developed along with the increasing complexity of the Heian society. Tales were often read aloud to groups of people during this period, and we can assume that the narrative parts in the tales and the honorific terms they used were also close to the spoken language, unlike the twentieth-century novels, which do not use honorific terms in their narrative parts.

The *kakarimusubi* (special system of sentence endings corresponding to particular particles which emphasize the preceding noun or phrase), which appears to have been a regular feature of the premodern Japanese language, is considered to be perfected and stabilized in the poems composed in the early tenth century, around the time when *Kokinshū* was compiled. However, some special sentence endings, not preceded by any of the special particles, began to appear in the dialogues in the tales in the middle of the Heian period. This is considered as a sign of the weakening of *kakarimusubi*, and its eventual loss affected the spoken language from the end of the Heian period through the subsequent period.

The works in the early eleventh century established a perfected *wabun* style of writing and were esteemed as models of this type of writing for a long time. Their influence can be seen in the themes, plots, and styles of many tales written later in the century, and even in the twelfth century when the *wabun* style of writing and the spoken language began to diverge. The tendency to follow the models actually lasted until the end of the nineteenth century, long after the spoken and written languages had evolved and become distinct.

At the end of the Heian period, the aristocratic hierarchy,

which had enjoyed the richness of its civilization for four centuries, began to deteriorate. This inevitably involved social upheavals, changes in life style and philosophy, together with the language involved in them. The written language of the aristocratic culture was the language used in the areas centered around the emperors' residence. But the social upheavals of subsequent periods were to bring in the language of different classes and different areas, as seen in the emergence of warriors and the introduction of a language from areas other than Kyoto, considered vulgar by aristocratic standards.

3. The Development of *Kanamajiribun*

In spite of the fact that the *wabun* style of writing flourished from the mid-Heian period on, the Chinese style of writing remained the official language. *Kanbun* was highly esteemed, and educated men wrote in this formal style throughout this period. The early Heian period is considered one of the peaks in the study of Chinese in Japan, and a time in which *kanbun* writing flourished. Official documents were all written in genuine Chinese writing, *jun-kanbun*, in the Heian period, as was the practice in the Nara court. In addition to daily communication in the court, all records, diaries, and chronicles written for official purposes were recorded in this style. And although the *wabun* style is more renowned than the *kanbun* writing of this period, the number of *kanbun* materials that survive far surpass extant *wabun*-style writings.

Aside from official documents written in *kanbun*, evidence for the peak of *kanbun* writing in the early Heian period can be observed in the compilation of three imperial anthologies of Chinese poetry: namely, *Ryōun Shinshū* (New Collection Surpassing the Clouds), compiled in 814?, *Bunka Shūreishū* (Collection of Literary Masterpieces), compiled in 818?, and *Keikokushū* (Collection for the Ordering of the State), compiled in 827. These collections are recognized for the excellent quality of their poems and firmly established Chinese poetry, *kanshi*, in the literary history of Japan.

The gradual influence of the poetry of the T'ang dynasty is

observed in these collections, the strongest influence being noted in *Keikokushū*. T'ang-dynasty poetry not only influenced Chinese poems composed by Japanese, but also made its mark on the Heian literature in general. Among T'ang poets, Po Chü-i (772–846), particularly his *Hakushi Monjū* (Poshih wenji) was very popular during the mid-Heian period and exerted the most influence on the literati, including the famous poet and statesman Sugawara no Michizane (845–903).

The poems loved by the Heian literati were not only widely read but also had a decorative effect as calligraphy accompanying screen paintings; they were also recited with a certain rhythm. Since reciting Japanese poems, *waka*, was a popular tradition, Fujiwara no Kintō (966–1041) compiled a collection of the most popular Chinese poems and *waka* for reciting. His *Wakan Rōeishū* (Collection of Chinese and Japanese Verse), compiled in 1018?, contains 234 *kanshi*, or parts of *kanshi*, composed by Chinese poets, 354 *kanshi*, or parts of *kanshi*, composed by Japanese poets, and 216 *waka*. More poems in the collection were compiled by Po Chü-i than any other poet, with second placc going to Michizane.

It is interesting to note that *waka* and Chinese poems, *kanshi*, were both collected for the same purpose of reading and recitation in *Wakan Rōeishū*. In the Nara period, *waka* were popular in a broader segment of society than Chinese poems were. In fact, in the Nara period reading Chinese poems and composing *kanshi* must have been somewhat foreign even for those who read and composed them. However, the fact that educated aristocrats enjoyed *waka* and *kanshi* both in the same way, writing them on screen paintings or reciting them on various occasions, convinces us that *kanshi* became a part of their normal life in the Heian period.

Diaries, men's letters, and family records for personal purposes were written in modified Chinese style, *hentai kanbun*. Since men were expected to write in *kanbun* and became familiar with it by studying Chinese books, choosing *hentai kanbun* for their unofficial writing was a natural outcome. In writing *hentai kanbun* they did not have to follow the Chinese syntax strictly, thus, they could write more at ease. In addition, they could use some Japanese vocabulary, including proper names and honorific terms. However, for descriptions of their life in the court system, which was modeled after the Chinese system, and for which there was no native vocabulary, they had to use Chinese vocabulary.

Diaries and unofficial letters exchanged between men were written in quite a free style of *hentai kanbun*, containing a number of honorific terms. The most well known diary of this period, *Midō Kanpakuki* (The Diary of Midō Kanpaku: Fujiwara no Michinaga) (966–1027), contains the following honorific terms: 参 (come), 奉 (an auxiliary verb), 給 (an auxiliary verb), 賜 (receive), 召 (summon), 奏 (say), 仰 (say), 侍 (attend). Also, some other native words, which are not found in Chinese vocabulary, were expressed in Chinese characters, such as *monoimi* (abstinence) written as 物忌. These terms were a reflection of the spoken language and are similarly found in *wabun* writings. The honorific terms were especially unavoidable elements in writing letters. For example, in *hentai kanbun* letters in the latter half of the Heian period, the term *haberi* (侍) meaning "to attend" or "to serve," used by itself or together with other verbs as an auxiliary verb, gave way to another honorific term, *sōrō* (候), with the same meaning as *haberi*. This type of letter writing with *sōrō* is called *sōrōbun* and became an established style of letter writing, which survived into the twentieth century.

The nature of their profession made Buddhist priests natural experts in *kanbun* writing. They hand-copied Buddhist sutras and wrote annotations in *kanbun*, or in *katakana* if necessary. However, *Nihon Ryōiki* (Miraculous Tales of Japan) was written in *hentai kanbun* by a priest named Keikai between 810 and 823. (See Reading Selection 10.) Judging from the fact that no records about Keikai exist today and from the information found in *Nihon Ryōiki*, which appears to be related to his own experiences, we assume that he was neither an aristocrat nor an official priest.

Until this period, Buddhism was patronized by the court and was available only to aristocrats. However, it appears that local non-aristocratic but powerful clans began to aspire to Buddhism and to build their own temples in the beginning of the Heian period. Some of them sought to join the order and became unofficial priests, resulting in more contact with lower-class people than a designated priest would have, and Keikai seems to have been one of them.

Nihon Ryōiki is a collection of Buddhist tales and each tale was written for a didactic purpose. It is also a collection of legends which had been transmitted orally, except for some tales which appear to be based on written materials. Keikai stated in his preface that he had read Chinese and Indian tales written in Chinese, and he wished to write a similar collection of Japanese tales. Although it is not clear whether the author anticipated that these tales would be used for preaching or not, he certainly expected them to be read by priests.

It is not the use of honorific terms that determines *Nihon Ryōiki*'s style as *hentai kanbun*. Rather, it is such grammatical characteristics as misplacement of verbs and terms for negation. Since the misplacement is inconsistent, the author was presumably able to write in genuine Chinese style. He may have been influenced by the fact that the tales were orally transmitted to expect that they would be read by *kun*, the partial translation reading, as was the practice among the priests in the ninth century.

Nihon Ryōiki is considered to be the first collection of *bukkyō setsuwa* (Buddhist legends) and is the only book of this kind written in the early Heian period. Another collection of Buddhist tales with illustrations, *Sanbō Ekotoba* (Illustrated Stories of the Three Treasures), was written in 984 under very different circumstances. This collection, in which many of the tales are copies of those in *Nihon Ryōiki*, was written for the second daughter of retired Emperor Reizei (950–1011).

The original of *Sanbō Ekotoba* is not extant, but its three existing copies, with no illustrations, pose an interesting question in the history of the Japanese written language. One copy is written in *hentai kanbun*; one in *hiragana*; and one in two volumes in a mixture of *katakana* and Chinese characters and one volume of *man'yōgana* and Chinese characters in the style of *senmyōgaki*. Some scholars argue that it was originally written in *hentai kanbun*. However, since *Sanbō Ekotoba* was written for a woman, it was probably written in *hiragana* first. Also, the edition in *hiragana* writing is dated 1120, the earliest of the three.

From studies on Buddhist writings, it is known that *katakana* began to have a certain uniformity in the middle of the Heian period. Graffiti found in the temple Daigoji indicate that *katakana* was used by itself, separate from Chinese characters and from the usage as marks for reading Chinese, in the middle of the tenth century. The graffiti appear to be three Japanese poems in *katakana*, and, together with the fact that Japanese poems written in *katakana* were mentioned in *Utsubo Monogatari*, suggest that poems were written in *katakana* in the tenth century more widely than we have direct evidence of.

It is not known exactly when and how *katakana* began to be used with Chinese characters in Japanese syntax. Some known factors that may have contributed to the emergence of this style, *kanamajiribun* (writing in a mixture of *katakana* and Chinese characters in Japanese syntax), are as follows:

(1) In addition to the fact that *katakana* was used for marks to aid in the partial translation reading of Chinese writings, some short sentences written in Chinese characters and *katakana* in a mixture of Chinese and Japanese syntax appear occasionally in Buddhist writings. Also, *Tōdaiji Fuju Monkō* (The Draft for the Recitation of the Sutra for Tōdaiji Temple) was entirely written in this style in the middle of the ninth century.

(2) Although we cannot tell how widely Japanese poems were written in *katakana*, from the little evidence we have we can assume that things ordinarily written in *hiragana* may have at times been written in *katakana*.

(3) In the middle of the Heian period *hiragana* began to replace *man'yōgana* in *senmyōgaki*, in which large-size Chinese characters and small-size *man'yōgana* had been used since the Nara period. This is a rather unexpected factor, just recently discovered. But since *hiragana* writing had already been established, it may be natural for *hiragana* to be used in place of *man'yōgana*, since *senmyōgaki* are in Japanese syntax.

The application of *kanamajiribun* began mainly in two fields, the field of *setsuwa* (legends) and the field of *gunki monogatari* (war tales). *Konjaku Monogatari* (Tales of Times Now Past) in the field of *bukkyō setsuwa* is probably the first book written in *kanamajiribun*. (See Reading Selection 13.) Since the *katakana* was written in a smaller size than the *kanji* in *Konjaku Monogatari*, some scholars call this style *senmyōgaki* or *katakana senmyōgaki*, due to its similarity to *senmyōgaki* of the earlier period.

Konjaku Monogatari contains more than 1200 short tales in 31 volumes, of which the first 10 volumes contain tales of Indian or Chinese origin. A large number of tales were based on tales found in writings in Chinese, including *Nihon Ryōiki*. Also, a number of tales of Japanese origin in the last 21 volumes appear to have been previously transmitted orally. Regardless of the sources of the tales, they all have the same format as orally transmitted tales ending with Buddhist morals.

The author or authors of *Konjaku Monogatari*, written probably around 1106, is not determined. Although it is written in Japanese syntax, the influence of Chinese writing is strong. A large amount of Chinese vocabulary, which was obviously not a part of the spoken language, was used, especially in the tales of Indian and Chinese origins; also the terms of negation frequently appear before their verbs, indicating the influence of Chinese writing.

The tradition of *kanbun kun* reading maintained a certain amount of old vocabulary, and it survived in *kanamajiribun*; for example, *gotoshi* (seem) and *iwaku* (say), which in *wabun* writing are *yō nari* (seem) and *iu yō* (say). They may have been a part of men's vocabulary, since they do appear in *wabun* writing by men, even if infrequently. Also observed is the usage of *zokugo* (slang or vulgarism), which was purposely avoided in the elegant style of *wabun* writing, especially *giseigo* (onomatopoeia) or similar terms. Since these *zokugo* are found more in the tales of Japanese origin, it is assumed that they are the reflection of the spoken language of non-aristocrats.

Many similar collections were written, probably by priests, in the twelfth century and thereafter in the same style as *Konjaku Monogatari*. For instance, *Uchigikishū* (Word for Word Collection) in 1133?, *Kohon Setsuwashū* (Old Book of Tales) in 1131?, and *Hōbutsushū* (Collection of Treasures) in 1178?, were all written in *kanamajiribun*. These tales had the practical purpose of being recited at religious gatherings. Some of the tales in *Konjaku Monogatari* for instance may not be obviously religious, but they were probably used to attract and entertain the audience.

The writers and readers of these tales were educated people, if not aristocrats, but the audience at a religious gathering was not necessarily educated nor aristocratic. Much Chinese vocabulary, *kango*, was absorbed by educated people into the Japanese language, through the process of reading Chinese writings, until the middle of the Heian period, but this process only changed the spoken or written language of a very limited circle of people. However, from the end of the Heian period, *kango* began to spread by word of mouth; *bukkyō setsuwa* contributed to this phenomenon first, and then *gunki monogatari* (war tales).

The first *gunki monogatari* is *Masakadoki* (or *Shōmonki*; The Revolt of Masakado), written in *hentai kanbun* in 940. This is the story of a warrior named Taira no Masakado who lived in the Kantō area, the eastern provinces, and of the battles in which he was involved, starting from clan disputes over territory and ending with his revolt against the administration of the court in Kyoto. Although *Masakadoki* was written in *hentai kanbun*, it is considered to have exerted some influence on the later *gunki monogatari* in *kanamajiribun*.

At the end of the Heian period, probably around 1186, *Hōgen Monogatari* (Tales of the Hōgen Period) and *Heiji Monogatari* (Tales of the Heiji Period) were written depicting the battles of the Hōgen era, in 1156, and the Heiji era, in 1159. (See Reading Selection 14.) Although there are many copies of these two books, which were written in a mixture of *hiragana* and *kanji*, there are some earlier copies written in *katakana* and *kanji*. We assume that both *Hōgen* and *Heiji Monogatari* were originally written in *katakana* and *kanji*, probably by the same author.

The style of these war tales, although in *kanamajiribun*, differs from the style of *bukkyō setsuwa*. While Buddhist tales were all written in a simple and concise style, *Hōgen* and *Heiji Monogatari* have a more elaborate style, which reminds us of the ornateness of *Masakadoki*'s style. The latter is a mixture of *wabun* and *setsuwa*-type *kanamajiribun* and is called *wakan konkōbun* (the mixed style of Japanese syntax and Chinese vocabulary), which became the foundation of the present Japanese written style.

Since *Hōgen* and *Heiji Monogatari* were used as *katarimono*, tales narrated to the accompaniment of the *biwa* (lute) in the Kamakura period (1192–1333), and since all the extant copies were made in the Kamakura period or later, the style of these tales is obviously influenced by the fact that they were narrated with melody. Also, the *biwa* players in this period were known to be lower-class blind men, who transmitted the tales orally. The repetition of seven- and five-syllable lines, which was the basic rhythm of *waka*, was applied to the musical accompaniment of the tales.

Observed in *Hōgen* and *Heiji Monogatari* is the abundant use of *kango*: these included Buddhist terms, which began to penetrate into the broader society at the end of the Heian period, and terminology related to armor, weapons, and warfare, for which there were no Japanese equivalents. As *kango* began to spread to a larger segment of society, to people who could not read Chinese, the Japanization of *kango* became more evident. Also, as *kango* became readily available, the production of *yamato kotoba* vocabulary ceased.

At the end of the Heian period the spoken language began to undergo various changes. One crucial factor for this was the destruction of the unity of aristocratic society by the newly arisen warrior class that came into power. This class spoke a dialect that invaded the elegant language of aristocrats as is best reflected in *gunki monogatari*. The *zokugo* and the language of the warrior class make the language in the dialogue parts of *Hōgen* and *Heiji Monogatari* surprisingly close to modern Japanese. Most of the warriors originated in the Kantō area, where the presently spoken standard Japanese has its basis. However, the changes that took place in the twelfth century may be better observed a little later, since any changes in spoken language take time to be reflected in written language.

Although the polity of the aristocrats collapsed and their civilization came to end, what they had achieved in relation to their writing is of a great importance in the history of the Japanese written language. *Hiragana* and *katakana* were completely developed, and prose writing was established both in *hiragana* and in *katakana* and *kanji*. While Chinese writing, both in *jun-kanbun* and *hentai kanbun*, continued to be used, *wabun* and *wakan konkōbun* developed further influencing each other in the next period.

III

THE ESTABLISHMENT OF *WAKAN KONKŌBUN*

The Kamakura, Muromachi, and Azuchi–Momoyama Periods (1192–1602)

1. *Wabun* and Its Survival

Compared to the peace and unity of the aristocratic society in the Heian period, the medieval period, starting in 1192 and ending in 1602, was politically extremely unstable. During the Kamakura period (1192–1333) the sovereign power was divided between the imperial court in Kyoto and the warrior shogunate in Kamakura, in the Kantō area. The shogunate resided in Kyoto during the Muromachi period (1336–1573), but the court retained only minimal political power. Powerful daimyo reigned over various parts of Japan and fought constantly among themselves in the Azuchi–Momoyama period (1573–1602) until Tokugawa Ieyasu (1542–1616) united the country under his own leadership in 1603.

Decentralization of culture took place during this period. Although the aristocrats still maintained their authoritative position in some areas of culture, non-aristocrats began to take part in various cultural activities. Warriors in ruling positions often tried to imitate and compete with the aristocrats, resulting in the birth of a different culture. Buddhism spread among common people, and priests and recluses played an increasingly important role in the field of writing.

The area in which the aristocrats excelled the most and for the longest period of time was the field of *waka*. In fact, composing *waka* was their major literary concern in the Kamakura and Muromachi periods, during which they compiled 15 imperial anthologies, the last one being compiled in 1439. In the Heian period, beginning with *Kokinshū*, 6 imperial anthologies were commissioned; thus, a total of 21 anthologies were compiled by imperial order over a five-century period, from 905 to 1439.

The most representative work of the 15 anthologies is *Shin-Kokinshū* (New Collection of Ancient and Modern Poetry), compiled in 1205. (See Reading Selection 15.) The most noted poets, Fujiwara no Shunzei (1114–1204) and his son Teika (1162–1241, one of the compilers) were active in this period, and the *waka* tradition attained perfection in *Shin-Kokinshū*, which displayed the highest artistic stage of Japanese poetry. Relying completely on the themes, images, and vocabulary of the traditional *waka*, it produced highly sophisticated and picturesque poems, a final blossom in a declining aristocratic culture.

Saigyō (1118–90), a warrior who denounced the world and became a recluse while still in his twenties, was represented by the largest number of poems in *Shin-Kokinshū*, though his *waka* do not represent the style of the anthology. However, his poems best reflect the sense of transiency of life, a sense that was shared by many writers of the medieval period.

In spite of the fact that the spoken language was undergoing various changes in the Kamakura and Muromachi periods, the language of *waka* remained unchanged. The use of *kango* and *zokugo* was totally avoided so that there is no reflection of the spoken language in the *waka* of this period. In fact, the tradition of strictly following the Heian vocabulary and grammar was firmly established in this period and maintained until the end of the nineteenth century.

Literary works in the Kamakura period include many romantic tales in *wabun* style and women's diaries. These tales, which depicted the aristocratic life, were mostly lost; those that are extant, and the diaries, follow the models of the Heian period for their themes and style of writing, and they do not have much significance in the history of the written language. They all are reminiscent of the previous period and reflect little of the spoken language.

There are two works, written in *wabun* style in the Kamakura period, which warrant discussion in reference to the written style of this period. One of them is *Ujishūi Monogatari* (Tales from the Uji Collection), an anonymous work written around 1218. (See

Reading Selection 16.) It is a collection of *setsuwa* and repeats a large number of the tales in *Konjaku Monogatari* and other *bukkyō setsuwa* collections, only 30 percent of the tales being original. However, the underlying Buddhist philosophy is rather weak in this collection, and it does not give the impression that it was written for Buddhist teaching.

Judging from the fact that *Ujishūi Monogatari* was written in the refined *wabun* style, its author was probably an aristocrat who had a wide interest in the common people's life. A larger number of folk tales and humorous tales are included than in earlier *bukkyō setsuwa*. Particularly because of its portrayal of the life of ordinary people, the collection could not avoid the use of the contemporary language. In fact, various irregular uses of Heian grammar, as well as a different vocabulary, are recorded.

Tsurezuregusa (Essays in Idleness) written by the priest Kenkō in 1330? was similarly influenced. (See Reading Selection 17.) It is classified as *zuihitsu*, and, in fact, Kenkō may have had *Makura no Sōshi* of the Heian period in mind when he wrote it. However, *Tsurezuregusa* is perhaps more successful as *zuihitsu* than *Makura no Sōshi*, since the greater complexity of the author is manifest through his observations of life. It discusses miscellaneous topics of the time and lifestyles of the different classes.

Although it is apparent from his writing that Kenkō was an avid admirer of the Heian period, the language in his writing was influenced by the spoken language, which was already quite different from the Heian model. Kenkō himself was aware that the language of the past was not the same as the spoken language of his time. He stated that people said that *waka* alone remained unchanged, but that he doubted it. The language of *waka* certainly did not change, but he noticed changes in the style of *waka*, which he also composed.

The style of *Tsurezuregusa* is considered the representative *wabun* style of the medieval period. Although it was written based on the *wabun* style of the Heian period, a larger number of *kango*, especially Buddhist terms, were used; auxiliary verbs were simplified; and verb conjugations were different from those of the Heian model. As for honorific terms, the use of the verb inflections *ru* and *raru* increased, and *haberi* and *sōrō* were both used in both dialogue and narrative. These changes in *wabun* writing and some rhetorical influence from Chinese writing brought the *wabun* style of this period closer to *wakan konkōbun*.

Composing *waka* had a by-product in this period. *Renga* (linked verse) started as a game, in which two or more poets composed parts of *waka* by taking turns. That is to say, the first verse consisting of three phrases of a *waka* (five-seven-five syllables) was composed by one poet and a second verse, corresponding to the last two phrases (seven-seven syllables) by another poet, and then, another verse of three phrases (five-seven-five syllables) would be added by another poet to harmonize with the preceding verse, usually continuing for 100 verses. *Renga* started in the beginning of the Kamakura period and most of the poets who composed *waka* also enjoyed composing *renga*.

Waka composition lost intensity and creativity after *Shin-Kokinshū*, and *renga* became more popular and serious as poetry. As a form of poetry, *renga* was established when *Tsukubashū* (Tsukuba Collection) was compiled in 1356. Since composing *renga* was a group activity, it attracted people in various social standings. The well-known *renga* master Sōgi (1421–1502), who produced *Shinsen Tsukubashū* (New Tsukuba Collection) in 1495, was of lowly birth and even his family name is not known.

The serious *renga*, as a new form of poetry, followed the tradition of *waka* and used only the elegant language of *waka*. However, *renga* as a game also continued to be enjoyed and was very popular among common people in the Muromachi period. This type of *renga* is called *haikai no renga* (humorous linked verse) and a collection of it, *Inu Tsukubashū* (Dog Tsukuba Collection), was compiled between 1520 and 1530. The composers of *Inu Tsukubashū* were common people and some priests, and they used the vocabulary of their daily lives. The use of the common everyday language was maintained in *haikai*, a seventeen-syllable poem which originated from the initial verse of *renga* in the Edo period.

In the Muromachi period the writing of courtly tales seems to have ceased, and in their place a number of *otogizōshi* (tales for companionship) were written by unknown authors. Some of them followed the tradition of the Heian tales in describing romantic affairs of aristocrats. However, most of them had new themes: priests' lives and Buddhism, warriors' lives, etc., and also folk tales. These *otogizōshi* were printed later in the Edo period with illustrations, since they provided popular entertainment. They are generally longer than Buddhist tales, but they often end with a moral lesson, such as filial duty or a Buddhist teaching.

The written style of *otogizōshi* is the *wabun* style of the late Muromachi period, influenced by the spoken language with a number of *kango* assimilated into it. *Otogizōshi* were obviously written for less educated people, and their appearance is the evidence of the broadened scope of readers in this period. The tales were read aloud to those who were unable to read.

Due to changes that took place in the spoken language, certain irregularities began to appear in *katakana* writing first and then in *hiragana* writing from the beginning of the eleventh century. Confused use of *kana* is found for *i, wi,* and *hi*, excluding *hi* when it occurs at the beginning of a word; *e*, *ye*, and *he*, excluding *he* when it occurs at the beginning of a word; *o*, *wo*, and *ho*, excluding *ho* when it occurs at the beginning of a word; *wa* and *ha* and *u* and *fu* also began to be confused, except in the beginning of a word. The poets and writers of the Kamakura and Muromachi periods attempted to follow the *kanazukai* (*kana* spelling) of the Heian period with little success, since these *kana* no longer represented current pronunciation.

The noted poet Fujiwara no Teika was the first person to exhibit scholarly concern about *kanazukai*, in *Gekanshū* (Essays of a Humble Official) in the early thirteenth century. Teika also copied and annotated a number of works of the Heian period, including *Kokinshū*, *Makura no Sōshi*, *Genji Monogatari*, and *Sarashina Nikki*. In *Gekanshū* he listed words in which certain *hiragana* should be used, based on the Heian usage. His usage of *o* and *wo*, however, was not based on the Heian spelling, and recent scholars have found that his distinction of them corresponds with word accentuation.

In the fourteenth century, Gyōa, a scholar of *Genji Monogatari*, wrote *Kana-Mojizukai* (How to Use Kana). Gyōa claimed that because his grandfather learned *kanazukai* from Teika, the book contained Teika's spelling system. Due to Teika's authoritative position in the history of *waka*, his spelling system dominated and influenced the writers of this period, especially the poets who attempted to follow the Heian models.

2. The Establishment of *Wakan Konkōbun*

In the Kamakura period various works were written in *kanamajiribun*, as well as in *kanbun*, by Buddhist priests, some of whom were of the aristocracy or of the upper ranks of the priesthood and some of whom were simply recluses. These priests and their works played important roles in a society that had through generations suffered wars, plagues, and natural disasters. People had become acutely aware of the uncertainty of life, and many noted priests left their aristocratic and academic worlds to minister to the suffering people, and in doing so they created new sects of Buddhism. The sense of the transience of life is manifest in every work written in this period, and, indeed, it was the period when Buddhism spread through the populace of Japan.

As the *wabun* style of writing in the medieval period approached *wakan konkōbun* under the influence of *kango* and *zokugo*, the *kanamajiribun* of this period was written in both *katakana* and *hiragana*. The collection of Buddhist tales, *Shasekishū* (Sand and Stone Collection), written by the priest Mujū (1226–1312) in 1283, has a style similar to *Konjaku Monogatari*. (See Reading Selection 18.) *Shasekishū*, which has more humorous tales, folk tales, and legends originating in the temples than other similar collections, was written in a mixture of *katakana* and *kanji*. Copies of some *setsuwa* collections are written in both *hiragana* and *katakana*; *Hosshinshū*, for example, which was written between 1207 and 1219, probably by Kamo no Chōmei (1153?–1216?). The copy of *Hosshinshū* in *hiragana* has a style similar to *wabun* writing, while the copy in *katakana* has a style similar to other *setsuwa* collections in *kanamajiribun*.

Chronicles and historical accounts were still written in *kanbun* as a rule in this period. However, *Gukanshō* (My Foolish Ramblings), written by the priest Jien (1155–1225) in 1220, is the first historical account written in a mixture of *katakana* and *kanji*. It records history from the legendary reign of Jinmu to the time of writing, the reign of Emperor Juntoku (1210–21), but with a Buddhist philosophy underlying the description of historical events. Although Jien, who is also known as a poet, was of a distinguished noble family and maintained a high position in the Tendai sect of Buddhism, his writing in *Gukanshō* used the plain language with many *zokugo*. He wrote that there were so few true intellectuals among the contemporary priests and laymen; and of the nobles and commoners who could read *kanbun*, few could understand its meaning; he therefore decided to write in the plain language using *kanamajiribun*. His statement indicates that the quality of the study of Chinese deteriorated in this period, as well as tells us his concern that his book be read and understood.

Other noted priests of this period, such as Hōnen (1133–1212), who founded the Jōdo sect (Pure Land Buddhism), Shinran (1173–1262), who founded the Jōdo-shin sect (True Pure Land Buddhism), and Nichiren (1222–82), who founded the Nichiren sect, wrote their major works in *kanbun* but wrote doctrines for lay society, as well as letters to less-educated people, in *kanamajiribun*. For instance, *Tannishō* (Deploring the Heresies), Shinran's words written no more than 30 years after his death by his disciple Yuien, is a well-known work of this kind. It was written in *kanamajiribun* using *hiragana*. Also, Nichiren's letters include many *kango* and *zokugo* in *kanamajiribun*. One famous letter to a disciple from the Kantō area, who had a job in Kyoto, advises the disciple not to be influenced by the Kyoto language, but to use his own dialect in preaching.

Dōgen (1200–53), who was of a distinguished noble family and who established the Sōtō sect of Zen in Japan, even wrote his major work, *Shōbō Genzō* (Treasury of Knowledge of the True Law), in 1253 in *kanamajiribun* using *hiragana*. Since it does not have a preface—it may have been lost—we cannot tell the reason for this highly educated priest's choice of written style. However, we can say that the choice of written style was freer in this period than in the Heian period, and that the priests were quite aware of the existence of a broader segment of society that could read non-*kanbun* texts, and that sought Buddhist teaching.

Hōjōki (An Account of My Hut), written by Kamo no Chōmei

in 1212, is an essay reflecting upon the social changes during his life. When he wrote it, Chōmei was a recluse who had renounced the world. *Hōjōki* was written in *kanamajiribun*; the earliest copy is in *katakana*, and some *hiragana* copies exist too. In contrast with *kanamajiribun* written by the priests for Buddhist teaching, the style of *Hōjōki* is more flowery, much influenced by Chinese rhetoric, and therefore, is closer to *wakan konkōbun* of *gunki monogatari*. Chōmei also composed *waka* and although *Hōjōki* does not contain any, its prose indicates that he was a talented writer.

The term *wakan konkōbun* is used broadly for any style that combines *wabun* and *kanamajiribun*. However, the *wakan konkōbun* established in the Kamakura period has specific features because of its development for *katarimono* (narrated tale) and for writing *gunki monogatari*. *Heike Monogatari* (The Tale of the Heike) in 1219? was the most successful and popular *gunki monogatari* for recitation accompanied by *biwa* playing and is the most representative *gunki monogatari* of this period. (See Reading Selection 19.)

Heike Monogatari is an epic depicting the rise and fall of the Heike clan, involving a number of battles, which actually occurred from 1181 to 1185, between the Heike and Minamoto clans. It is a tale of heroic warriors, as well as of the tragedy of the victims of war and the grief of the people involved. A sense of the transience of existence is present and the Buddhist philosophy of "all is vanity" is manifest throughout the tale. Because of the frequent occurrence of battles at the end of the Heian and the beginning of the Kamakura periods, the tales of warfare recited by *biwa* players became a popular entertainment during the Kamakura period. *Hōgen* and *Heiji Monogatari* were also recited in this period, but the sorrowful tone of *Heike Monogatari* appealed most to society, including the warriors who turned farmers when they were not in battle.

It is impossible to determine who authored *Heike Monogatari*. It exists in highly varied and diversified copies today, and these copies can be classified into two categories: copies for personal reading and copies for narration. There are two kinds of *Heike Monogatari* copies for reading. There are relatively accurate copies of *Enkeibon Heike Monogatari*, originally copied in 1309 (the second year of the Enkei era), about 90 years after the assumed date of the original *Heike Monogatari*. *Genpei Seisuiki* (The Rise and Fall of the

Minamoto and Heike Clans), first copied between 1247 and 1256, and consisting of 48 volumes was written for reading and is an expanded version of *Heike Monogatari*, with many additional tales and information.

The other copies are believed to have been made for narration and were kept in the various schools of reciters, the *biwa* players. Recitation of the *Heike Monogatari* with *biwa* accompaniment, called *heikyoku*, continued through the Muromachi and Edo periods, and a small number of *heikyoku* players still exist today. We cannot tell which copy is closest to the original, but the most commonly read *Heike Monogatari* today is the version that Kakuichi, a blind *heikyoku* player, had someone transcribe in 1371.

Tsurezuregusa has a famous chapter telling how *Heike Monogatari* was created. It says that the priest Jien, head priest at the temple Enryakuji, kept and protected one Yukinaga, who had denounced the world after an unhappy incident at the court. This priest Yukinaga created *Heike Monogatari* and told the blind man Shōbutsu to narrate the tale. Naturally this is but one legend concerning the origin of *Heike Monogatari*, and we cannot determine who Yukinaga was. However, *Heike Monogatari* must have originated from an environment where priests and temples were involved. *Heike Monogatari* may have developed from simple *setsuwa*, or a collection of *setsuwa*, which originated in temples, and as the *biwa* accompaniment was originally Buddhist music, the *biwa* players were affiliated with the temples.

While it may have started as a simple *setsuwa*, *Heike Monogatari* has, over the generations, been developed and refined into the magnificent tale that we know today. The style of *Heike Monogatari* is extremely ornate, much influenced by Chinese rhetoric and the elegance of *wabun* writing. Many of its narrative parts maintain a rhythm of seven-and five-syllable phrases. It also employs the parallelism of Chinese literary style, producing another sort of rhythm with pairs of phrases of equal length. In spite of the fact that the style of *Heike Monogatari* was obviously tailored for narration and *biwa* music, the style of writing impresses us as far more logical and powerful than the *wabun* writing of the Heian period.

Its vocabulary is far richer than that of the Heian *wabun* writings, due to the use of many *kango*. It is rich in Buddhist terms in *kango*, as well as special terms for armor or other similar military words. The use of *kango* brought more clear-cut and specific terms into the writing, as compared to the vagueness and broad meaning of *yamato kotoba* in *wabun*. However, a relatively large number of *kango* were written in *kana* in some copies of *Heike Monogatari*. Those copies were written down as the tale was related by blind players, with or without accurate pronunciation. The *heikyoku* players contributed greatly to spreading of the use of *kango* orally in the populace.

For the study of the spoken language of the Kamakura period, *Enkeibon Heike Monogatari* is regarded as the most reliable of the numerous copies. However, most of the other copies also contain many *zokugo*, particularly in the dialogue parts, including onomatopoeia, vogue words, and dialecticisms, all of which made the tale extremely colorful. Although its syntax is still basically the same as that of *wabun*, the phonological and sporadic syntactical changes reflect the spoken language of this period, which was a transient stage between old Japanese and modern Japanese.

Some copies contain sporadic use of marks for *dakuon* and *sokuonbin*, certain sound assimilations. Compared to the earlier writings, *Heike Monogatari* has more words with *sokuonbin*, probably due to the influence of the warriors' language. Some copies use more *kanji* than others, and misuses of *kanji* and Japanized use of *kango* are observed, as well as the irregular usages of *kana* which are found in most writing of this period.

In the dialogue parts the use of the honorific *sōrō* is extensive, with men using *sōrō* and women using *saburō*. The use of the causative form became extended to include the sense of failure to prevent, e.g., *kodomo o shinasu* (to let the child die), instead of saying "the child died, since I could not prevent it from happening," and very often sentences end with the particles for emphasis, *koso* and *zo*. Also, the sentences ending with nouns increased, as well as those ending with *rentaikei* (the inflected form of an adjective, verb, and auxiliary verb used before a noun), which was used in place of *shūshikei* (the inflected form of an adjective, verb, and auxiliary verb normally used at the end of a sentence). While these changes reflected the spoken language, they add a masculine quality to the style of *Heike Monogatari*.

Heike Monogatari marks the height of *wakan konkōbun* writing, and similar tales were written in the same style from the end of the Kamakura period through the Muromachi period, such as *Soga Monogatari* (Tale of the Soga Brothers) at the end of the Kamakura period, *Taiheiki* (Chronicle of Grand Pacification) in 1370?, and *Gikeiki* (Record of Yoshitsune) in the middle of the Muromachi period. They are not comparable to *Heike Monogatari* for their literary quality, but the influence of these tragic war tales, including *Heike Monogatari*, on the later period was extensive, particularly in the performing arts.

The genres of literature which were most influenced by these *gunki monogatari* in the Muromachi period are Nō plays and *kōwakamai*, or *kōwaka* dance. *Kōwakamai*, its name coming from the boyhood name of Momoi Naoakira (1393–1470), is basically one type of *katarimono*, and has a third-person narration to the accompaniment of a hand drum. The performance involved certain physical movements which indicate its origin as a dance. Most of the 50 extant *kōwakamai* tales are from *gunki monogatari*, and they were popular entertainment among common people, especially among warriors. While *kōwakamai* never developed beyond a primitive theatrical production, Nō became refined as a theatrical art in the Muromachi period.

Nō is a theatrical performance which originated from primitive and local performing arts practiced for years among common people and perfected by Kan'ami (1333–84) and his son Zeami (1363–1443) in this period. (See Reading Selection 20.) Since Kan'ami and Zeami were patronized by the shogun Ashikaga Yoshimitsu (1358–1408), these talented masters were able to concentrate on the refinement of Nō as an art; it includes chanting accompanied with various instruments and stylized acting as well as dancing.

Since Nō was performed on stage, the written materials for Nō were primarily scripts. The Nō plays, of which there are approximately 2000 extant, are naturally more varied than *kōwakamai*. They include tales from *gunki monogatari* and *Genji Monogatari*, as well as from other Heian tales. However, the appearance of a traveling priest in the majority of Nō scripts, together with the frequent appearance of spirits of the dead, indicates that the tales were not taken directly from the written sources, but taken from the stories people related. The traveling priest symbolizes the transmitter of the legend, who listens to the legend told often by the spirit of a dead person, which appears in one of various incarnations first and reveals its true identity later. Since the characters use a first-person narration, Nō achieves a more dramatic effect than the earlier *katarimono*.

The Nō scripts are called *yōkyoku-bon* (books for chanting), since all the scripts were written only for chanting. It was the tradition for a master to give directions on acting, dancing, and playing instruments orally to a disciple, who was usually a younger member of the master's family. Although the entire language of *yōkyoku* is highly stylized, it can be divided into two categories: a narrative part which is chanted by a chorus or by an actor to music, and a dialogue part, which is also chanted rhythmically by the actors who play the role of first-person narrator.

The dialogue part of Nō follows the tradition of *gunki monogatari*'s style and uses *sōrō* as an honorific ending of sentences. The use of *sōrō* is believed to have declined in the spoken language of the latter half of the fourteenth century and the beginning of the fifteenth century, when Zeami wrote his scripts, which remain essentially unchanged today. The narrative part of Nō may be called one type of verse, since it has a strong rhythm, of basically seven and five syllables, and uses refrains very often. It uses highly sophisticated classical language, distinct from the spoken language of the period. Considering the fact that *kyōgen* (comic interludes for Nō) use the spoken language of the period, it must be true that, for the masters, the artistic refinement of Nō meant the use of elegant classical language.

From the first half of the fifteenth century to the first half of the sixteenth century more Nō masters appeared and wrote scripts. However, they followed the earlier masters' style in script writing and performance, and to this day Nō has not changed very much. At the end of the sixteenth century, when *yōkyoku* became a popular pastime among nonprofessionals, many copies of scripts were made for chanting lessons for amateurs. At this time Nō was considered a completely classical theater, and it also influenced new *katarimono* and drama in the Edo period. Since it has maintained its traditions so well, it is believed that some pronunciations in *yōkyoku*, as chanted by Nō players today, retain the fifteenth-century pronunciation.

3. *Kanbun* and the Influence of Zen

In the Kamakura period, since the responsibility for writing official documents fell to the warriors, who did not have the same education as the aristocrats of the Heian period, the writing of official documents in *kanbun* declined. Generally, the warriors were not in a position to aspire to write *jun-kanbun*, an impractical style that did not represent the spoken language at all. However, some of them were compelled to learn the formalities of official communication and mastered *hentai kanbun*, which was used for private documents in the Heian period. Thus with the Kamakura shogunate's adoption of *hentai kanbun* for official documents, the distinction between the styles of official and private documents disappeared.

Azuma Kagami (Mirror of the Eastland), written by unknown authors in 1266, is the representative work for *hentai kanbun* writing of this period. It is a chronicle of the Kamakura shogunate, and it does not contain honorific terms, but contains some *yamato kotoba* of the contemporary spoken language written in *kanji*, such as *omoshiroshi* (interesting), *itooshi* (pitiful), *kaerigoto* (response), and *hikidemono* (gift). Some of the characters for these *yamato kotoba* were used with complete disregard for the meaning of the characters, as when they used the characters for "thread," 糸 (*kun* reading is *ito*), and "regrettable," 惜 (*kun* reading is *oshi*), to write *itooshi*. This kind of *ateji*, the usage of characters for *kun* reading without regard for their meanings, had been seen in the period of *Man'yōshū* but was not practiced in Heian *kanbun* writing. Now it began to reappear and influenced the other styles of writing.

The Muromachi shogunate followed the practice of writing in *hentai kanbun* set in the Kamakura period, and some of the documents were even written in *sōrōbun*, which was used only for letter writing in the earlier periods. The use of *hentai kanbun* for official documents thus became established in these periods, and it was maintained by the shogunate of the Edo period.

The aristocrats in Kyoto continued to study *kanbun*, and records of parties for composing *kanshi* in the Kamakura and Muromachi periods survive. It should be noted that parties for *waka* and parties for *kanshi* were often held in succession on the same day at the court or one of the poets' residences, with the same poets participating. A number of noted *Shin-Kokinshū* poets also composed *kanshi*. Teika's diary, *Meigetsuki* (Bright Moon Diary), written from 1180 through 1235 in *hentai kanbun* depicts the activities of the poets and aristocrats, as well as the relationship between the court and shogunate.

However, it was Buddhist priests who made the greatest contribution to the field of *kanbun* writing in this period. Various sects of Buddhism flourished in this period, and the priests were extremely active in preaching and writing. Although they wrote various works in *kanamajiribun* for the broader scope of readers, who did not read *kanbun*, most of them wrote their major works in *jun-kanbun*, especially academic studies of the doctrines. In addition to these studies, the poetry composed by Zen priests marked an epoch in the history of Japanese literature in Chinese.

The Zen sect was brought into Japan from China in the beginning of the Kamakura period and patronized by the Kamakura shogunate. Following the Chinese model, the shogunate chose the five highest ranking temples in Kamakura, and later in the Muromachi period five temples each in Kamakura and Kyoto were designated as the most important Zen temples. These temples with their highly educated priests attracted talented young priests, making the temples ivory towers. These designated temples, which belong to the Rinzai sect of Zen, are called *gozan* (five mountains) and the literature produced within *gozan* is called *gozan bungaku* (five mountain literature). The other important sect of Zen, Sōtō, spread provincially and concentrated on meditation.

Gozan priests produced numerous collections of *kanshi*, which were influenced by the poetry of the Sung dynasty, as well as by Zen philosophy. The most representative poet-priests are Gidō Shūshin (1325–88) and Zekkai Chūshin (1336–1405), both of whom were disciples of Musō Soseki (1275–1351). Gidō's poems are collected in *Kūgeshū* (Collection of Illusions) and Zekkai's in *Shōkenkō* (Draft of Zekkai's poems); the superior quality of their poetry is widely recognized. With the termination of the patronage of the shogunate, the literary activity of *gozan* priests declined at the end of the Muromachi period. However, the study of *shushigaku* (a school of Confucianism from Sung China), which was also conducted by *gozan* priests, continued and flourished in the Edo period.

The influence of Zen is not found only in the priests' writings, but also in various other aspects of the culture of the Kamakura and Muromachi periods. *Waka* was also influenced by Zen, and new schools of painting and calligraphy developed under the influence of Zen. Flower arrangement and tea ceremony, both of which emerged in the Muromachi period, and new styles of architecture and landscape gardening can be called products of Zen influence.

The many priests who went to China to study Zen and Confucianism and the Chinese priests who came to Japan introduced a new pronunciation of Chinese characters. This new reading of characters based on the pronunciation brought in during this period is called *sōon* (Sung pronunciation) or *tōon* (Chinese pronunciation). However, the *sōon* reading of characters did not replace *go'on* and *kan'on* readings of characters, since these readings already were firmly established and had a long history in Japan. *Sōon* may have been used more in the Zen temples when it was newly imported. However, only a small number of new words, mostly the names of newly introduced objects, such as *futon* (quilt), *chōchin* (paper lantern), and *manjū* (bean-jam bun), assimilated into the Japanese language with *sōon* readings of the characters.

Also written in this period were a number of textbooks on how to compose a letter. The most representative one of them is *Teikin Ōrai* (Household Teaching on Correspondence) written by an unknown author in the early part of the Muromachi period, which was the authoritative textbook for letter writing in *hentai kanbun* in this period. In the Edo period it was published many times, with annotations. There were some textbooks of this kind written in the Heian period too, but a greater number of them were written in the Kamakura and Muromachi periods, suggesting that a larger number of people who needed textbooks aspired to write letters in *hentai kanbun.*

4. Written Materials in the Spoken Language

Although *wabun, wakan konkōbun,* and *hentai kanbun* reflected some elements of the spoken language, they were largely styles using the written language. The syntax of *wabun* writing was no longer the same as that of the spoken language, and *wakan konkōbun* also became stylized and lost its capacity to reflect new elements of the language. In the middle of the Muromachi period the distance between the spoken language and these written languages was very wide. This separation, which began gradually from the end of the Heian period, is called *genbun nito* (two different languages for the written and spoken), and lasted for many centuries until modern writers at the end of the nineteenth century advocated that the written and spoken language should be identical.

However, it does not mean that the Japanese made no effort at all to write in the spoken language for some 500 years. On the contrary, a new type of material written with complete disregard for the existing written styles began to appear. From the fourteenth century to the end of the sixteenth century there are three different categories of material written in the spoken language of the period.

The first category, so-called *shōmono* (annotations on Chinese writings), which began to appear in the latter half of the fourteenth century, is the transcriptions of lectures given by priests, mainly Zen priests, and some scholars on Confucianism or Shinto. The lectures were based on textbooks written in *kanbun,* and so the *shōmono* writing naturally contains a number of *kango* that came from these texts. The earlier *shōmono* were written in a style similar to *senmyōgaki* using *katakana,* but later *shōmono,* which were written from the latter half of the fifteenth century on, used more *katakana* than *kanji* and were written largely in the spoken language.

The language found in *shōmono* is similar to the two other

categories of written materials in the spoken language, the language of *kyōgen*, comic interludes of Nō, and some *kirishitan bungaku*, literature written by Catholic missionaries. But it is a more informal and relaxed style of the spoken language with vocabulary and expressions peculiar to academic circles. The lectures must have been conducted in everyday language and *shōmono* written without anticipation of any other readers. Therefore, it was written in a most lively language, with little influence from written languages. *Zo*, a spoken-language sentence-ending particle, and *nari*, a sentence-ending auxiliary verb in the written language, are both used to end declarative sentences in *shōmono*.

Although scholars still have reservations on how much the general spoken language was reflected in *shōmono*, it is obviously the language of a limited circle of people, since the audience for this type of lecture consisted of scholars and priests. However, the language in *shōmono* reveals the pronunciation of the spoken language of the Muromachi period and most extensively the changes that had taken place in the spoken language in this period.

Kyōgen developed as an interlude between Nō plays in the fourteenth century and is still performed as such on the Nō stage, even though it may be also performed independently today. (See Reading Selection 21.) Both Nō and *kyōgen* are performed in the classical language today, but *kyōgen* language is more easily understood by today's audience. This is because the language used in *kyōgen* is based on the spoken language of around the sixteenth century, while the language of Nō is older; furthermore, *kyōgen* involves more lively acting and articulation of the dialogues. The characters in *kyōgen* are commoners, the type of people one might meet in a town or village; some are more ignorant than others and some are brighter. Since the majority of Nō plays have a tragic tone, these comical interludes provide light entertainment for the audience.

It is difficult to date the language of *kyōgen*, since writing of *kyōgen* scripts came into the picture much later. The first recording of *kyōgen* plays is *Tenshō Kyōgenbon* (Kyōgen Book of the Tenshō Era) written in the latter half of the sixteenth century, probably around 1578. Close examination of *Tenshō Kyōgenbon* reveals that the plays were not recorded in dialogue style, in which most of the later *kyōgen* scripts were written. It merely briefly recorded the outlines of the plays. We can conclude from this that *kyōgen* actors did not use written scripts in this period, but spoke extemporaneously in the language of the time. The instructions on acting were given orally by a master to a disciple, who were usually two generations of the same family, and were handed down from generation to generation.

Writing of *kyōgen* scripts in the dialogue style began in the seventeenth century, when the eight volumes of *Toraakirabon* (Kyōgen Book by Toraakira) were written by Ōkura Toraakira (1597–1662) in 1642. In the preface he claims that his writing was an accurate transcription of what was handed down for generations. However, he was not referring to accuracy in transcribing the dialogues, since there are some discrepancies between the wording of the dialogues in *Toraakirabon* and those of eight written scripts left by his father, Ōkura Torakiyo (1566–1646). This indicates that in the beginning of the Edo period the oral transmission of *kyōgen* did not observe strict control over the phrasing and wording of dialogues.

This late appearance of the first scripts of *kyōgen* makes the dating of the language in *kyōgen* difficult. However, we assume that this was the beginning stage of the loss of spontaneity in the acting and dialogue, and once the scripts were written down the performance of *kyōgen* began to be fixed. The language of *kyōgen* may have become fixed and obsolescent in this period, and this was one of the reasons why *kyōgen* scripts were written down. A comparative study of *Toraakirabon* and later *Torahirobon* (Kyōgen Book by Torahiro), written in 1792 by Ōkura Torahiro (1758–1805), reveals the following aspects:

(1) There is no new element in the contents and themes of *kyōgen* in *Torahirobon* in comparison with *Toraakirabon*, leading us to believe that there were no new developments in *kyōgen* after 1642.

(2) The language in *Toraakirabon* appears to represent a freer and livelier conversational style, obviously influenced by spoken language of the early Edo period.

(3) The language in *Torahirobon* is far more stylized, creating a special stage language for *kyōgen*. The process of stylization and

refinement of *kyōgen* took place between 1642 and 1792, and thus, *Torahirobon* contains an artificial stage language based on what appears to be the spoken language of the sixteenth century.

For the study of the spoken language *Toraakirabon* offers us the best material, written in the spoken language of the sixteenth and seventeenth centuries. The characters that appear in *kyōgen* are common people; thus, the language used in *kyōgen* dialogues is the language of commoners. However, *kyōgen* masters were cautious not to use excessively vulgar expressions on stage. This is especially true with the artistically polished *kyōgen* language of *Torahirobon*. The careful examination of *kyōgen* scripts handed down in three different schools, Ōkura, Izumi, and Sagi, all of which have their own scripts written in the Edo period, would be beneficial to the study of the Edo-period language, as well as make it possible to determine to what extent the language of the sixteenth century is retained.

Comparative studies of the language of *kyōgen* with *shōmono* and *kirishitan bungaku* reveal various aspects of the spoken language of the late Muromachi and Azuchi–Momoyama periods. The spoken language had indeed changed since the end of the Heian period, becoming almost entirely different from what was recorded in *wabun* writing of the Heian period. Various grammatical rules had changed, and the inflections of verbs, auxiliary verbs, and adjectives had become more like those of modern Japanese. However, *kyōgen*, which maintained its traditions faithfully through the Edo period, still retains the pronunciation of the period for some words and expressions today.

One of the significant aspects of the *kyōgen* language is the abundant use of onomatopoeia, since *kyōgen* was, and still is, performed with a minimum use of stage settings and properties. The dialogue, together with acting, often helps provide mental images in the stead of settings and properties by the use of onomatopoeia. Some of the onomatopoeic expressions may have been created specially for *kyōgen*, but since theater is very often the source of the popularization of vogue-words, we can assume that they belonged to the spoken language of the period. *Shōmono* and *kirishitan bungaku* also use onomatopoeia frequently, and it appears that the more materials written in the spoken language of common people appear, the more onomatopoeia are used.

Kirishitan bungaku (Christian literature) is another area in which the language of the sixteenth century is accurately reflected. It was produced by Jesuit missionaries who began to arrive in Japan from the mid-sixteenth century. They imported a printing machine for their own publications in 1590 and various written materials began to be published in Japanese starting in 1591, both in the Latin alphabet using Portuguese spelling and in *kanji* and *hiragana*. *Kirishitan bungaku* includes publications on Catholic doctrine, dictionaries, grammar books for the study of the Japanese language and literature, and textbooks for the missionaries and for Japanese people. Most of the publications on Catholic doctrine were written in the classical written style, while the textbooks for Japanese language study were written in the spoken language.

These Portuguese missionaries were extremely earnest in their study of the Japanese language, since they had to preach in Japanese, as well as hear confessions of the Japanese converts. One of the missionaries, João Rodriguez (1561–1634), who was well versed in Japanese and wrote books on Japanese grammar, said in one of his books that a foreign missionary had to learn the spoken language well enough to convert pagans and to master the written language well enough to write doctrine. All of them were fully aware of the difficulties in mastering the language, of the complexity of the spoken language, with its dialects and honorific terms, and of the difference between the spoken and written languages.

Catholic doctrine was written in a style using *kanamajiribun*, following the *bukkyō setsuwa*'s style, for the purpose of converting educated Japanese. In fact, Francisco de Xavier (1506–52), one of the founders of the Society of Jesus, who came to Japan in 1549, entertained the idea of producing the doctrine in Chinese to convert both Chinese and Japanese, since he was aware that educated Japanese could read Chinese. Beginning in 1587, when the prohibition of Christianity was first proclaimed by Toyotomi Hideyoshi (1536–98), the ruler of Japan from 1582 until his death, the missionaries' activities, such as preaching and traveling, were restricted, so they needed the doctrine published in Japanese to spread their faith among Japanese. As their linguistic ability became more adequate, they published quite actively from the end of the sixteenth century to the beginning of the seventeenth century. Some of their publications stand as monumental works in the study of the Japanese language.

One in this caliber is *Arte da Lingoa de Iapam*, written by Rodriguez between 1604 and 1608, which discusses Japanese grammar in comparison with Latin. This is the first book that uses Western terminology to describe Japanese grammar. It mainly discusses the grammar of the spoken language, but also includes verses and expressions from the written language. Since this book was published in three volumes with specialized terminology, he published a smaller book, an introduction to Japanese grammar, in 1620 in Macau (Macao).

Vocabvlario da Lingoa de Iapam is a Japanese-Portuguese dictionary and is very often cited for the study of the spoken language of this period. It was compiled by several missionaries at Nagasaki in Kyūshū between 1603 and 1604. It contains over 32,000 words of the period, mainly from the spoken language and some from the written language, including Buddhist terms, dialects, slang, and women's vocabulary. Thus, the first bilingual dictionary of the Japanese language and one of the European languages was published by the Portuguese missionaries. Since the missionaries often traveled from Kyūshū to the Kyoto area, they were quite aware of differences in dialects. Although most of the publications were made in Kyūshū, they apparently considered the language spoken in the Kyoto area as standard and treated pronunciations and expressions that differed from those of Kyoto as dialecticisms.

Two language books published for the missionaries were written in the spoken language: *Esopo no Fabulas*, a collection of Aesop's fables together with an account of Aesop's life, published in 1593, and *Feiqe no Monogatari*, a translation of *Heike Monogatari* into colloquial Japanese, published in 1592. (See Reading Selections 22 and 23.) Since both of them were published in the Latin alphabet using Portuguese spelling, they accurately reveal the phonetic state of the language, which otherwise was obscured in *kana* writing. For instance, the writing of certain syllables as *sa*, *xi*, *su*, *xe*, and *so* reveal more about their pronunciation than does writing them in *hiragana* or *katakana*.

In writing *Feiqe no Monogatari*, which is also called *Amakusabon Heike* (Amakusa Version of Heike) since it was published at Amakusa in Kyūshū, the writer, a Japanese Zen-monk-turned-Catholic known as Fabian, applied a dialogue style to relate the tale, with a listener encouraging a narrator to continue the tale. Although we cannot determine the exact copy of *Heike Monogatari* he translated from, we can discern his efforts to change the phrasing completely into the contemporary spoken language without changing the tale itself. Since it was written in a dialogue style, the manner of narration became more personalized and Buddhist philosophy was somewhat played down.

Heike Monogatari was translated not only for the study of the language, but also for the study of the history of the late twelfth century. But the translation of Aesop's fables was done solely for linguistic purposes. Perhaps the choice of the fables was due to the nature of the vocabulary as well as the proverb in each fable, both of which could be useful for the language of preaching. The Jesuits also published a dictionary of Chinese characters, *Rakuyōshū* (Collection of Fallen Leaves), in 1598 and a textbook for teaching Japanese poetry (using an extract from *Wakan Rōeishū*) and letter writing for the education of Japanese Catholics. The extensive writings and publications by the Jesuits reveal their high scholarly standards and the seriousness of their mission. However, they were expelled from Japan and their activities completely brought to an end in the beginning of the Edo period.

Thanks to the materials written in the spoken language in this period, the changes that had taken place in the spoken language are readily observed. The most significant change was the weakening of *kakari musubi*, which was a prominent feature of old Japanese, and in some materials *kakari musubi* almost disappeared. The changes in inflections of verbs, adjectives, and auxiliary verbs were extensive, resulting in more simplified forms. The use of auxiliary verbs became simpler, e.g., the stative auxiliary verb *tari* changed into *ta*, and indicated past tense, and was used in place of several other auxiliary verbs. Together with the simplification of auxiliary verbs, new honorific terms appeared, such as *oryaru* (come or go) and *marasuru* (do), and they changed into new forms in the next period. Because of these extensive changes, the spoken language of this period is considered to be the transitional stage from old Japanese to modern Japanese.

One factor which played an obvious role in the changes was the influence of dialects. Due to the great mobility in the society of the Kamakura, Muromachi, and Azuchi–Momoyama periods, the language of the Kantō area influenced the language of the Kyoto area which had been the center of culture. For instance, we begin to see an auxiliary verb for negation, *nai*, which came from Kantō dialect, used extensively in place of *zu*, an auxiliary verb for negation of the Heian period. In the Heian period there were fragmentary, derogatory observations on dialects, but there were no descriptions of them. However, in this period, in addition to the descriptions in *kirishitan bungaku*, there are some records of dialects in such material as *Kanginshū* (Collection of Leisure Songs), a collection of songs by an unknown compiler in 1518.

A large number of *kango* were assimilated into the spoken language in this period, some of them with Japanized meanings, e.g., *mushin* meaning "innocent" or "natural" was used for "begging," and some of them with a confusion between two *kango*, e.g., *saisai* meaning "in detail" was used for "often," which should be *saisan*. Together with the wider use of *ateji*, these confused uses of *kango* were carried into the next period.

Another new element in the vocabulary of this period, in addition to the new Chinese vocabulary imported with Sung pronunciation, was the assimilation of some European vocabulary, such as from Latin, Portuguese, and Spanish. However, since most terms were Catholic terminology, they disappeared from the language as Christianity vanished from society in the Edo period. A few words such as *pan* (bread), *karuta* (playing cards), and *tabako* (tobacco), which are not related to Catholicism, survived through the Edo period.

The marks for *dakuon*," or ··· , and *han-dakuon* (*p* sound), °, for *kana* writing also began to appear in this period, although their use was still very limited. It started in the field of Chinese studies for marking the reading of characters, and some Nō scripts have *dakuon* marks and some *kirishitan bungaku* materials have *han-dakuon* marks. But the usage of the marks did not become popular until the Edo period.

IV

THE DIVERSIFICATION OF WRITTEN STYLES

The Edo Period (1603–1867)

1. *Kanabun* and the Influence of *Zokugo*

After the establishment of the shogunate by Tokugawa Ieyasu in 1603 in Edo, the present city of Tokyo, peace was maintained in Japan for about 250 years, while various powerful daimyo retained autonomy in their local areas under the guidance of the shogunate. Social order was maintained by the establishment of a hierarchy headed by the warrior class, followed by the farmer, artisan, and merchant classes. Confucianism was patronized by the shogunate and employed to strengthen the social hierarchy and the family system, in which the head of the household held authority over the family members and servants. Thus, the entire country was organized hierarchically, with everyone obeying one's superior.

Warriors were no longer required to fight, but rather than return to farming, they became government officials, or more precisely, armed officials. While only the upper-class warriors had been able to read and write in the Kamakura, Muromachi, and Azuchi–Momoyama periods, in the beginning of the Edo period, the shogunate and local daimyo established official schools to teach Confucianism to sons of warriors. Since the warriors had more time to study and were encouraged to do so by government policy, most warriors became literate in the Edo period. As for private schools for children of merchants, artisans, and farmers, a number of *terakoya* (the name coming from an earlier practice in which the temples educated children) began to appear in the beginning of this period. Although *terakoya* taught only practical subjects, such as reading, writing, and arithmetic, as their number increased, more common people were able to read *hiragana*, *katakana*, and some *kanji*.

The use of currency was generalized by the establishment of a coin-minting system in Japan, permitting the rise of a merchant class, some of whom gained great wealth in the seventeenth century. Merchants and artisans were called *chōnin* (townsmen), since they lived in cities. Affluent *chōnin* participated in various cultural activities, and writers and artists were to emerge from this class at the end of the seventeenth century. The two cities which prospered most in this period were Kyoto, from the sixteenth century on, and Osaka, which prospered from the mid-seventeenth century on. Although the center of politics moved to Edo, where the shogun resided, the center of culture remained in Kamigata, the Kyoto–Osaka area, for the first half of the Edo period.

Printing techniques advanced rapidly after the importation of a printing press from Korea in 1593, and a number of publishers began to publish various books in Kyoto to meet the demands of new readers, making books far more available than in earlier periods when they could be reproduced only by copying by hand. Also, book-lenders made books available to those who could not afford to buy them. The term *kanazōshi* (books written in *kana*) is used for the various illustrated books published in Kyoto in the beginning of the Edo period for less sophisticated readers. They were not written entirely in *kana*, *katakana* being particularly rare, but used some *kanji*, usually together with *furigana* (small *kana* alongside *kanji* to indicate their readings).

Kanazōshi deal with diversified topics including Confucian teachings, etiquette, and letter writing; some contain humor, descriptions of famous places, or information about actors or courtesans; and some are love stories or mysteries. *Kanazōshi* can be classified into three categories: books written for didactic purposes, for entertainment, and for practical information for less-educated readers. Although some *kanazōshi* have no literary value, most contributed to the later development of Edo literature, which is more sophisticated and of greater literary value.

The style of writing in *kanazōshi* generally followed the style of *otogizōshi* with its influence of the spoken language of the period. The degree of the spoken language's influence and the number of characters used vary to a great extent depending on the topic and author. *Kanazōshi* were written neither in the spoken language nor a classical style, but in a style called *kanabun* (style of writing using *kana*), which employs a simplified *wabun* grammar, influenced by the spoken language. The term *kanabun* is used by some scholars in a broader sense to include the *wabun* writing of the Heian period or the Kamakura and Muromachi periods, but refers here to the literature produced in the Edo period for readers with only a limited knowledge of *kanji*.

Considering that some materials were written in the spoken language at the end of the sixteenth century, we may wonder why *kanazōshi* were not written in the spoken language entirely, especially for the unsophisticated reader. Perhaps it was because the tradition of writing in classical styles was so entrenched for writers with education that they thought that writing in the spoken language was too unsophisticated. Since many authors of *kanazōshi* did not sign their manuscripts nor receive remuneration for them, it is difficult to determine who the authors of some of the publications were. However, those authors whose identities are known were still of the educated class: upper-class warriors, retired warriors, scholars, priests, or aristocrats.

Representative *kanazōshi* of literary value include the following: *Uraminosuke* (The Tale of Uraminosuke) in 1612?, *Tsuyudono Monogatari* (The Tale of Tsuyunosuke) in 1626?, *Chikusai* (The Tale of Chikusai) in 1636?, *Nise Monogatari* (The Imitation Tale) in 1640? were all written by anonymous authors, and *Ukiyo Monogatari* (The Tale of the Floating World) attributed to Asai Ryōi (1612?–91) and written in 1665?. *Uraminosuke* and *Tsuyudono Monogatari* are love stories that follow the medieval-tale pattern in their theme and written style. *Nise Monogatari* is a humorous parody of *Ise Monogatari* of the Heian period, and it is more representative of *kanazōshi* of this period than the first two. (See Reading Selection 24.) *Chikusai* is the story of quack doctor Chikusai's journey from Kyoto to Edo and includes parodies of Heian *waka*. *Ukiyo Monogatari* is the life story of a merchant's son and is famous for including a definition of *ukiyo* (floating world) as the positive acceptance of hedonism in this world, in contrast to the medieval Buddhist idea of *ukiyo* as "grieving world."

Collections of humorous tales, such as *Kinō wa Kyō no Monogatari* (The Tale of Yesterday is Today), an anonymous work written after 1615, and *Seisuishō* (Sobering Laughter), written by Anrakuan Sakuden (1554–1642) in 1623, are more influenced by the spoken language than other *kanazōshi*, since these humorous tales were trasmitted orally before they were written down. (See Reading Selection 25.) The style of *kanabun* in these works is almost entirely that of the spoken language, with little influence from *wabun* writing. Both works were written extensively in *hiragana*, including most of the few *kango* that obviously belonged to the spoken language. These collections contributed to the emergence of professional storytellers, who entertained the common people in cities with tales of humor and mystery. *Otogibōko* (Companion Maid), written in 1666 by Asai Ryōi, is also a source book for storytellers and one of the books strongly influenced by new Chinese fiction, such as *Chien-teng Hsin-hua* (New Tales by the Trimmed Lamp), a Ming-dynasty collection of mysterious tales.

Although the spoken language reflected in most *kanazōshi* is the language of Kamigata, there are a few works that include dialecticisms from certain other areas. *Oan Monogatari* (The Tales Told by Oan), which was written in the early seventeenth century by one of the people who heard an oral version of the tales, reflects the language of Ōmi and Tosa provinces; *Mikawa Monogatari* (The Tales of Mikawa Province) written between 1625 and 1626 by Ōkubo Hikozaemon (1560–1639), reflects the language of warriors from the Mikawa province; and *Zōhyō Monogatari* (The Tales of Miscellaneous Footmen), compiled in the middle of the seventeenth century, reflects the language of the lowest-ranked warriors from the Kantō area.

While *kanazōshi* were entertaining and educational for new readers of the Edo period, the genre of literature in which the common people began to participate was *haikai*, derived from the humorous linked verse, *haikai no renga. Haikai no renga* was on the wane at the end of the sixteenth century, but it was taken up by less-educated people in the beginning of the Edo period because this type of verse was easy for them to compose without a knowledge of classical poetry.

The essence of *haikai* was its use of *haigon*, which consists of *zokugo* and the *kango* used in the daily language of the common people. This distinguished *haikai* from *renga*, since *waka* and serious *renga* excluded the use of *zokugo* and *kango*, and *haikai no renga* did not require the use of these words in every verse. *Haikai* of this period emphasized vocabulary and is full of plays on words, such as puns or associated words, and the linking of verses became completely dependent on words, rather than images. Although it is not highly appreciated in literary value, it held great meaning for its participants, for whom it was a first literary activity and a novel group activity.

However, the masters of *haikai* included the educated class, such as the representative master of the early seventeenth century, Matsunaga Teitoku (1571–1653), an upper-class warrior, who compiled *Enokoshū* (Puppy Collection) in 1633. *Enokoshū* is a collection of *haikai* composed by a large number of people from various localities, even though the center of the Teitoku school was in Kyoto. Decentralization of *haikai* is observed in *Enokoshū*, and in the mid-seventeenth century *haikai* poets lived in various localities of Japan.

Another school of *haikai* poets began to be very active in Osaka in the mid-seventeenth century, under the leadership of Nishiyama Sōin (1605–82), a retired warrior. The poets in this prosperous city of merchants began to exhibit a new trend in *haikai*, free from the word play of the Teitoku school, and with great energy composed larger numbers of verses by one poet or at one session than before. The new trend freely depicted the contemporary customs and manners by emphasizing the speed and enjoyment of composing *haikai* as an entertainment, but it placed less importance on its quality.

A *haikai* verse is short, either seventeen or fourteen syllables, and might consist of nothing but nouns or nouns and particles. Its extensive use of *haigon*, or contemporary *zokugo*, gives the impression that *haikai* were composed entirely in the spoken language. In fact, it was not completely free of the classical language until the twentieth century, but the use of *haigon* contributed to the appearance of everyday language in more sophisticated forms of literature at the end of the seventeenth century, including *haikai* itself and *ukiyozōshi* (stories of the floating world).

Haikai attained its peak through the work of the eminent poet Matsuo Bashō (1644–94), who spent most of his life in Edo or on journeys. While he was young, Bashō also participated in composing *haikai* with the poets of the Teitoku and Sōin schools. He and his followers established poetic values for *haikai*, by going through stages of being influenced by Chinese poetry first and then by traditional Japanese poetry. Bashō was an admirer of the twelfth-century priest Saigyō, a wandering *waka* poet who renounced the world. A number of Bashō's journeys, following Saigyō's pattern, were for the sake of deep observations of nature, and varieties of human life, observations that are reflected in his *haikai*, which before his time did not dwell on such themes.

The representative *haikai* collections by Bashō and his group are the following seven collections: *Minashiguri* (Hollow Chestnuts) in 1683, *Fuyu no Hi* (A Winter Day) in 1686, *Haru no Hi* (A Spring Day) in 1686, *Hisago* (Gourd) in 1690, *Sarumino* (The Monkey's Straw Raincoat) in 1690, *Sumidawara* (Charcoal Bag) in 1694, and *Zoku-Sarumino* (The Monkey's Straw Raincoat Continued) in 1694. These collections show traces of the development of their *haikai* from the period when the Chinese influence was still strong to the period of its maturity as poetry. (See Reading Selection 26.)

Bashō also wrote several accounts of trips, such as *Nozarashi Kikō* (Weathering Journey) in 1685, *Oi no Kobumi* (Traveler's Notebook) in 1688, and *Oku no Hosomichi* (The Narrow Road to the Far North) in 1694; these are prose works although they contain a number of Bashō's verses. His prose established a style of writing called *haibun*, a style of writing influenced by *haikai*. *Haibun* used the *haikai* technique of association of imagery, with the use of *zokugo* and *kango*, within the framework of classical grammar. It employs a poetic rhythm to depict everyday life with a certain dignity and elegance.

Both *haikai* and *haibun* declined in artistic quality after Bashō's death. However, *haikai* became more popular among common people as a hobby and claimed numerous poets in the eighteenth and nineteenth centuries. Among them the most noted poets are Yosa Buson (1716–83), also a noted painter, and Kobayashi Issa (1763–1827), and their poetry represented the two sides of *haikai*, namely, the poetic elegance of Buson's picturesque verses and the refined plainness of those of Issa, who was of the farmer class. Of the *haibun* written in these centuries, *Uzuragoromo* (Patched Clothes) by Yokoi Yayū (1702–83) and *Oraga Haru* (My Spring) by Issa are the most noted.

Ihara Saikaku (1642–93), the best *ukiyozōshi* writer, was one of the Osaka *haikai* poets notorious for composing *haikai* with inordinate speed. Saikaku became a fiction writer with the publication of his first story, *Kōshoku Ichidai Otoko* (The Life of an Amorous Man). The term *ukiyozōshi* is applied to stories written and published over an 80-year period beginning with *Kōshoku Ichidai Otoko* in 1682. They are different from *kanazōshi* stories in the sense that they reflect the manners and customs of the period better than *kanazōshi* did and are completely free of medieval influence on the writers' philosophy or written style. They appealed to the taste of affluent townsmen, and in fact, Saikaku himself was a wealthy Osaka merchant.

Kōshoku Ichidai Otoko is in a sense a parody of *Genji Monogatari*, but Saikaku established himself as a writer by publishing successively the following amorous fiction: *Kōshoku Nidai Otoko* (The Life of an Amorous Man, the Second Generation) in 1684, *Kōshoku Gonin Onna* (Five Women Who Loved Love) in 1686, and *Kōshoku Ichidai Onna* (The Life of an Amorous Woman) in 1686. He also published collections of *setsuwa*-type stories, such as *Shokoku-banashi* (Tales from the Provinces) in 1685, but his collections were entertaining and avoided the didactic and moralistic tone of *setsuwa*. However, Saikaku's talent is best seen in his later works depicting the world of merchants, such as *Nihon Eitaigura* (The Eternal Storehouse of Japan), published in 1688, *Yorozu no Fumihōgu* (Myriad Scraps of Old Letters), written between 1690 and 1691 and published in 1696, *Seken Mune San'yō* (This Scheming World), published in 1692, and his last, *Okimiyage* (The Parting Present), published in 1694. (See Reading Selection 27.)

Although Saikaku's early writings differ somewhat in style from his later works, it is generally characterized by a strong *haikai* influence, including the uses of puns, associated words, and allusions. His style, using simplified *wabun* grammar, is one type of *kanabun* with a rich use of *zokugo*. In his writing, the shifts from one phrase to another are extremely free, skillfully employing the associations of imagery. Thus, the distinction between dialogue and narrative parts is blurred, except that the dialogue is more influenced by the spoken language than the narrative parts. Even though Saikaku did not write in the spoken language per se, some scholars call his style conversational, meaning that shifts from one phrase to another are similar to those in conversation. We may see Saikaku's efforts here to bring his writing as close to the spoken language as possible within the framework of tradition.

Saikaku's prose style may be considered as a prosification of his *haikai*, which did not attain poetic refinement, and is different from the *haibun* of this period, which is also derived from *haikai*. Saikaku's contemporary, Bashō, once criticized his style for going into too much detail. *Haibun* aimed at poetic elegance, and, therefore, reflected little of the spoken language, while Saikaku's writing aimed at a faithful description of everyday life within the framework of fiction and was elevated to artistic level by his talent.

Ukiyozōshi prospered and became more commercialized in the first half of the eighteenth century, when Hachimonjiya, the leading publisher-bookstore in Kyoto, published over 200 books by its commissioned writers. The most successful of these writers for Hachimonjiya, Ejima Kiseki (1667–1736), emphasized entertainment more than artistry in his writings in order to appeal to readers; his best-known works are so-called *katagimono* (character sketches), such as *Seken Musuko Katagi* (Characters of Worldly Young Men) published in 1715, *Seken Musume Katagi* (Characters of Worldly Young Women) published in 1717, and *Ukiyo Oyaji Katagi* (Characters of Fathers of the Floating World) published in 1718. These *ukiyozōshi* were increasingly influenced by the spoken language, although they were still not completely free of the classical grammar of the written language.

Theatrical arts developed to a great extent in the seventeenth century, resulting in the establishment of both Kabuki and *ningyō jōruri* (puppet theater with chanted narrative), also known as Bunraku. Nō and *kyōgen* of the medieval period continued, but since they became classical and aristocratic, appealing only to those with classical education, Kabuki and *ningyō jōruri* gained a great popularity among less-educated people. Although *ningyō jōruri* and Kabuki influenced each other in their developmental stages, and share many dramas in their repertoires, they originated from different performing arts and the histories of their script writing are different.

Jōruri (chanted narrative) of *ningyō jōruri* started as *katarimono* accompanied by the music of the *shamisen* (samisen), which was imported from Okinawa at the end of the sixteenth century. This *jōruri* began to be performed initially with simple puppet shows and became established as *ningyō jōruri* in the seventeenth century. Whereas *ningyō jōruri* began with storytelling using written scripts from the outset, Kabuki has its beginnings in dance with musical accompaniment in the beginning of the Edo period. Its development as drama was slower than that of *ningyō jōruri*, and Kabuki used no scripts in the early stage, since actors could speak extemporaneously when the drama was still undeveloped.

Kabuki scripts were written in the latter half of the seventeenth century, but none of them survive. One reason for the loss of these Kabuki scripts was the lack of esteem for script-writing in the Kabuki world. Kabuki performance in this period was very much actor-oriented, and scripts were rewritten by different writers many times at the request of actors. However, a number of *eiri kyōgenbon* (Kabuki books with illustrations), synopses of Kabuki performances, sold for promotion of the theater, survive. They were generally written in a style similar to *kanazōshi*, and even though they were not written for performance, they include dialogues strongly influenced by the spoken language. Kabuki scripts from the mid-eighteenth century on survive, when script writing became more important, and this will be discussed below together with the written materials of the latter half of the Edo period.

In *jōruri*, a single narrator, who used different tones of voice for dialogues by different puppet characters in a drama, needed a script to read from the outset. In the beginning of the Edo period *jōruri* narrators used *Jōrurihime Monogatari* (The Tale of Princess Jōruri), from which the name of *jōruri* came, and tales from *otogizōshi* and *kōwakamai*, all of which were medieval stories. They expanded their repertoire by adding Buddhist sermon plays and hero stories of ancient warriors, together with a variety of chanting techniques and improved musical accompaniment and achieved a great popularity in the cities of Kyoto, Osaka, and Edo in the middle of the seventeenth century.

Ningyō jōruri reached its peak from the end of the seventeenth to the beginning of the eighteenth century, when the eminent writer, Chikamatsu Monzaemon (1653–1724) wrote masterpieces of *jōruri* for the noted narrator Takemoto Gidayū (1651–1714), who founded his own theater in Osaka in 1684, and his son, Takemoto Gidayū the Second. Chikamatsu, who was of the warrior class, also wrote Kabuki scripts, which do not survive, for the noted actor Sakata Tōjūrō (1645–1709), but from 1705 on he concentrated on writing *jōruri* only and established his fame in this field.

Chikamatsu's *jōruri* plays are famous for their double suicide themes, found in such plays as *Sonezaki Shinjū* (The Love Suicides at Sonezaki), which was a great success in 1703, and *Shinjū Ten no Amijima* (The Love Suicides at Amijima), written in 1720. (See Reading Selection 28.) He also wrote historical dramas, which were the major theme of the theater in this period, found in such plays as *Shusse Kagekiyo* (Kagekiyo Victorious), which lead to further joint work of Chikamatsu and Gidayū in 1685, and *Kokusen'ya Kassen* (The Battles of Coxinga), which had a long run for 17 months starting in 1715.

Jōruri scripts written by Chikamatsu exhibit a unique style; they applied the spoken language of common people quite freely in dialogues, since many of his protagonists were common people, while the narrative parts used elegant rhetoric, with puns, associative words, and allusions to classical works. They are known for their *michiyukibun*, beautiful passages that blend scenery and the intense feelings of lovers eloping or on their way to commit love suicide. *Jōruri* scripts of the early stage were influenced by the styles of *otogizōshi* or *kōwakamai*, but Chikamatsu's narrative parts are strongly influenced by the narrative parts of Nō scripts. They have a rhythm of repetitions of five- and seven-syllable phrases, accompanied with *shamisen* music.

The scripts include certain instructions for chanting and music, and small punctuation circles to end phrases and sentences. Modern punctuation had not been developed yet, and the fact that the scripts had one punctuation method for both phrases and sentences may have contributed to the style of *jōruri*, in which sentences are often very long without a clear distinction between dialogue and narrative parts. The style of *jōruri* had achieved artistic elegance and became established in this period, and influenced later written materials in the latter half of the Edo period.

The period from the late seventeenth century through the beginning of the eighteenth century, especially the era known as Genroku (1688–1703), is known for the richness of the flourishing Kamigata culture. Literature and theater in the Kamigata region attained their pinnacles in this era, with Saikaku's *ukiyozōshi*, Bashō's *haikai*, and Chikamatsu's *ningyō jōruri*. This flourishing of Kamigata culture coincided with that of the Kamigata cities of Kyoto and Osaka, where affluent *chōnin* participated in various cultural activities with great energy and enthusiasm. The spoken language used in the theater, as well as in *kanazōshi* and *ukiyozōshi*, reflected the language of Kamigata, which is the basis of the Kamigata language of today. In the eighteenth century, however, Kamigata gradually lost its cultural dominance over the city of Edo, when different kinds of literature were produced there.

2. *Kanbun* and Confucian Studies

The Tokugawa shogunate established by Tokugawa Ieyasu used *hentai kanbun* for official documents, including *sōrōbun* for letter writing. Public announcements by the shogunate were written in *kanamajiribun* for those who could not read *hentai kanbun*. After peace had been established in the country, the shogunate promoted the study of Confucianism by hiring Hayashi Razan (1583–1657), a scholar of *shushigaku*, a neo-Confucian school originated by Chu Hsi of the Sung dynasty, thus making *shushigaku* the official doctrine. Local daimyo established educational institutions for their warriors, and private schools began to emerge under noted scholars.

In contrast to the aristocrats of the Nara and Heian periods and Zen priests of the medieval period, those who contributed to the flourishing study of Chinese in the Edo period were new intellectuals, scholars of neo-Confucian schools, who were mostly of the warrior class, but also of the priest, merchant, and farmer classes. With the emergence of private schools and public lectures by noted scholars, common people had opportunities to be exposed to books in Chinese and study them, even if they did not become scholars. As a result, the study of Chinese and the composition of *kanshi* thrived to a great extent in the Edo period, and the latter half of the period is considered another peak for composition of *kanshi* in the history of literature in Chinese.

Although most Confucian scholars in the Edo period composed *kanshi*, those of the first half of the period were generally more known for their scholarly writings and their theories than for their poetry. The famous scholars of this period are Fujiwara Seika (1561–1619) and his noted disciples: Hayashi Razan; Hori Kyōan (1585–1642); Matsunaga Sekigo (1592–1657), a son of Matsunaga Teitoku; and Nawa Katsusho (1597–1650); and Matsunaga Sekigo's disciples: Kinoshita Jun'an (1621–98) and Kaibara Ekiken (1630–1714), who is also known as a scholar of medicinal herbs. Nakae Tōju (1608–48) and Kumazawa Banzan (1619–91) were noted scholars of *yōmeigaku*, a Confucian school of Wang Yang-ming of the Ming dynasty. Another school called *kogaku* (school of ancient studies), specializing in studying the classics of Confucius and Mencius, produced such scholars as Yamaga Sokō (1622–85); Itō Jinsai (1627–1705); his son, Itō Tōgai (1670–1736); Ogyū Sorai (1666–1728) and his disciples: Dazai Shundai (1680–1747) and Hattori Nankaku (1683–1759).

These scholars studied the Confucian classics and neo-Confucian theories, as well as other Chinese writings including poetry. Their studies stressed the interpretation of the philosophy of the classics, thus resulting in varieties of interpretations among different schools. Confucian studies were put to practical use by applying their interpretations in evaluation of government policy, the social system, and the morals of the period. *Kun* reading was de-emphasized, and they made efforts to read the classics in Chinese. However, the system of *kaeriten* (reading-order marks), some of which were used in the earlier period, was perfected in this period, and used extensively in *kanbun* publications, for the sake of those readers who depended on reading by *kun*. *Kaeriten* are still used today for the study of *kanbun*.

The study of Japanese history was also pursued, and historical accounts were compiled. The study of history, along with the study of the Chinese classics, led to the emergence of another field, the study of Japanese classics, which will be discussed in Chapter 3. Tokugawa Mitsukuni (1628–1700) began compilation of *Dai Nihonshi* (Great History of Japan) in 1657, which a large number of scholars brought to completion with the 397th volume in 1906. Arai Hakuseki (1657–1725), a scholar of *shushigaku* as well as a historian, wrote important history books: *Tokushi Yoron* (Lessons from History) in 1712 and *Koshitsū* (Through Ancient History) in 1716.

Ogyū Sorai advocated the importance of the composition of *kanshi*, and the composition of *kanshi* reached its pinnacle in the latter half of the Edo period, starting in the middle of the eighteenth century. Among numerous poets, most of whom were also Confucian scholars, the following are representative of the period: Emura Hokkai (1713–88); Kan Sazan (1748–1827); Rai San'yō (1780–1813), considered to be the greatest; and Yanagawa Seigan (1789–1857); all of these poets produced several personal anthologies. Their *kanshi* are considered to be of high quality, demonstrating a complete mastery of the medium of Chinese poetry, which only employed classical Chinese language. The composition of *kanshi* survived and the study of Chinese classics was highly esteemed by intellectuals until the early twentieth century.

Writing *kanshi* itself did not affect the spoken and written languages of the period, but the increasing popularity of reading or studying Chinese did influence vocabulary and *kanji* usage. The use of *kango* increased in many publications for a wide readership, suggesting that those *kango* had assimilated into the spoken language and the use of *kanji* increased in publications for educated readers, with or without *furigana*, in the latter half of the period.

In addition to the fact that the study of Chinese classics and poetry enriched the cultural activities of the Edo period as a whole, modern Chinese romances influenced literary works. Chinese books of the Ming and Ch'ing dynasties were imported to Japan by

Chinese merchants who periodically came to Nagasaki, the only port officially open for trade with Dutch and Chinese when the country was under the shogunate's isolation policy. Among them, there were Chinese romances written in the colloquial language, in contrast to the written style of the classics. They were received with enthusiasm by some scholars, and similar stories were written in *kanbun*, and also in different styles of writing other than *kanbun*.

One of the most successful writers who wrote stories under the influence of modern Chinese fiction is Ueda Akinari (1734–1809) who was of the Osaka merchant class. Akinari was a *haikai* poet who also published some *ukiyozōshi*, but later studied Japanese classics and became a *waka* poet. Like many other scholars and intellectuals of the late eighteenth century, Akinari was able to read and write *kanbun*, and his *Ugetsu Monogatari* (Tales of Moonlight and Rain), published in 1776, shows a strong influence of Chinese fiction. (See Reading Selection 29.) *Ugetsu Monogatari*, one of the most highly regarded literary works of the Edo period, was written in an elegant classical style of writing, *wabun*, a unique choice as other writers wrote similar stories either in *kanbun* or *wakan konkōbun*. Many tales in *Ugetsu Monogatari* are skillful adaptations of Chinese stories, especially stories from *Chien-teng Hsin-hua*, mysteries with supernatural elements; thus, their style was influenced by *kanbun* rhetoric and vocabulary.

Adaptations of Chinese stories, with or without the necessary sophistication to make them works of literature, characterizes a genre of publications called *yomihon* (books for reading), mostly written in *wakan konkōbun* from the mid-eighteenth century on. The term *yomihon* is used in contrast to books with more illustrations than writing, which were popular among the less-educated readership. *Harusame Monogatari* (Tales of the Spring Rain), written by Akinari and published after his death, as well as *Ugetsu Monogatari* are included in the *yomihon* genre, even though they were not written in *wakan konkōbun*. Both *wakan konkōbun* and *wabun* had become classical written styles by the Edo period, using simplified Heian grammar, with very little influence from the spoken language.

Another highly successful *yomihon* writer was Takizawa Bakin

(1767–1848), who did not surpass Akinari's works in literary quality, but in the prolonged popularity of his works he surpassed all other Edo writers. Bakin, who lived in Edo, wrote more than 300 works in *wakan konkōbun* strongly influenced by Chinese romantic stories in theme, plot, and vocabulary. Before he became a successful *yomihon* writer, he wrote stories of vendettas or love suicides, which indicate the influence of the contemporary theater, and stories based on legends. Bakin's representative works are *Chinsetsu Yumiharizuki* (A Camellia Tale of the Waxing Moon), written over the period from 1806 to 1810, and *Nansō Satomi Hakkenden* (The Eight Retainers of Satomi), written over the period from 1814 to 1841. (See Reading Selection 30.) Most of his works including these two are of considerable length, with a grand scale of plot, a technique he learned from Chinese fiction. Bakin's stories often have a historical figure as protagonist, and his knowledge of Japanese history is apparent, but his stories go beyond the frame of history into the romantic world of imagination.

Bakin's fiction has a didactic theme of the good rewarded and the evil punished, mixed with the Buddhist concept of karma; this theme accommodated the government's policy and made his *yomihon* popular among the contemporary readership. Bakin's writings contain *kango* and *kanji* extensively, including new vocabulary from Chinese fiction. All *kanji* were printed with *furigana*, many of which comprise *yamato kotoba* written beside *kango* with an equivalent meaning, e.g., the character for "sky" or "heaven," which is read "*ten*" in Japanese, has *furigana* "*sora*" (sky). The use of *furigana* promoted the use of *ateji* to a great extent in this period.

Sōrōbun was very popular for letter writing in the Edo period, even though the use of *sōrō* completely disappeared from the spoken language. *Hentai kanbun sōrōbun*, following the examples in *Teikin Ōrai*, was written by men with *kanbun* education, mostly of the warrior class, while others with less education wrote their letters in *kanamajiri sōrōbun*, about which numerous books were published, and some of these were used as textbooks in *terakoya*. Women also wrote *kanamajiri sōrōbun*, using more *yamato kotoba* and *hiragana* than *kango* and *kanji*. Letter writing was perhaps the area in which the largest segment of the population participated, and it is interesting to observe that these new writers, members of classes which had never written before, wrote in the already antiquated *sōrōbun*. This practice continued to some extent to the early twentieth century.

3. The Revival of *Wabun* and the Influence of *Kokugaku*

Alongside the study of Confucianism and Japanese history, the latter also being conducted under the influence of Confucian philosophy, another field of study called *kokugaku* (national learning) emerged in the Edo period, and some *kokugaku* scholars produced important works on Japanese classics. The term *kokugaku* has a broad meaning which includes the study of Japanese classics, Shintoism, Japanese history, philology, and Japanese language. The study of Japanese history and Shintoism were very often conducted under the influence of nationalistic philosophy. Theories and studies of *kokugaku* also led to the revival of *waka* composition and *wabun*-style writing.

The general philosophy of *kokugakusha* (*kokugaku* scholars) promoted the restoration of the ancient spirit, idealizing Shintoism and the early periods of Japan, and they denounced all foreign influences, such as Buddhism and Confucianism. Noted *kokugakusha* of the early stage of *kokugaku* were the priest Keichū (1640–1701), who wrote important works on *Man'yōshū* and *Kokinshū*, and Kada no Azumamaro (1669–1736), a Shinto priest and *waka* poet, who advocated the study of Japanese classics in order to clarify the ancient spirit. In the eighteenth century *kokugaku* was fully established and the best-known *kokugakusha* are Kamo no Mabuchi (1697–1769), who was a disciple of Azumamaro, and Motoori Norinaga (1730–1801), a disciple of Mabuchi, who were succeeded by Hirata Atsutane (1776–1843), whose thought eventually influenced the philosophy which urged the Meiji Restoration of the imperial regime.

Mabuchi studied the classics of early periods, especially *Man'yōshū*, and wrote *Man'yō-kō* (Thoughts on *Man'yōshū*) in 1760. His view on Japanese poetry is seen in *Kai-kō* (Thoughts on the Meaning of Poetry) and *Niimanabi* (New Studies) written in

1756. He advocated the restoration of the style of *waka* found in *Man'yōshū*, which is free of the techniques and ideas of *waka*'s later development, and denounced the medieval and aristocratic tradition of *waka*, in which the style of Fujiwara no Teika was considered the supreme example. In his later years, he composed *waka* in *man'yō* style, the style of poetry in *Man'yōshū*. Among his disciples of *waka*, the writer Ueda Akinari followed the master's style, but Katō Chikage (1735–1808) and Murata Harumi (1746–1811), both of whom were noted *waka* poets of the city of Edo, composed in the more elegant *shin-kokin*-style, the *waka* style in *Shin-Kokinshū*.

Motoori Norinaga was not talented as a poet but is eminent for his accomplishments as a *kokugakusha*. The most representative works by him are *Kojiki-den* (Annotated *Kojiki*) in 48 volumes, completed in 1798, and *Genji Monogatari Tama no Ogushi* (The Precious Comb to Unravel the Tale of Genji) written in 1796. *Kojiki-den* is known as the first comprehensive commentary on *Kojiki*, and its study of mythology reveals Norinaga's belief in Shintoism. Norinaga regarded emperors as descendants of gods and mythology as a part of history, an idea that was maintained in later *kokugaku* and motivated the restoration of the emperor's regime at the end of the Edo period. Confucian scholar-historians did not share Norinaga's views on mythology, and they kept it separate from history. *Genji Monogatari Tama no Ogushi* is highly regarded by literary scholars because it contains Norinaga's enlightened views on *monogatari*, advocating that literary criticism of classical *monogatari* should be freed from Buddhist and Confucian ideas and that *monogatari* should express *mono no aware*, human emotions. His views on *monogatari* are unique in the Edo period, when Confucianism was the dominant philosophy of governmental policy, contemporary mores, and literary criticism.

Since *kokugakusha* denounced foreign influence and advocated the use of pure Japanese, they rejected the use of *kango*, which are of foreign origin, and revived *wabun*-style writing. The style of *wabun* written by *kokugakusha* starting in the mid-eighteenth century is called *gikobun* (a style of writing modeled after *wabun* of the Heian period), and it sometimes includes the vocabulary of the Nara period. *Gikobun* employs *kango* only when unavoidable, such as in the titles of books; Mabuchi once went so far as to translate some of them into *yamato kotoba*, e.g., *Furukotobumi* (A Book of Ancient Events) for *Kojiki* and *Yamatobumi* (A Book on Japan) for *Nihon Shoki*.

However, *gikobun* contains some *kanji* with *furigana* in *yamato kotoba*, and some *kanji* without *furigana*, which were intended to be read as *yamato kotoba*. (See Reading Selection 31.) This device of *furigana* was not new in the middle of the eighteenth century, since it had been used in many other publications for a wide readership from the beginning of the Edo period. *Kokugakusha* writings did not have a broad readership, and therefore, their use of *furigana* was not extensive, but the number of *kanji* for the same *yamato kotoba furigana* became extensive. Since many *yamato kotoba* have broad meanings, it is possible to use one *yamato kotoba* for several *kango* or *kanji*; an example found in *gikobun* is: the *furigana* of *fumi* (sentence, letter, book, history, etc.) was used for the following *kanji*: 文 (sentence or letter), 書 (book or writing), 典 (book or important book), 籍 (book or recording), 史 (recording or recording of history), 記 (recording or memory), and 紀 (recording or history).

In other publications, *furigana* was used to provide the reading of *kanji* for readers who could not read them otherwise, but the *furigana* in *kokugaku* writings was not for readers who could not read the *kanji*, but provided readers with a particular *yamato kotoba* reading, while utilizing the meaning of *kanji*, which was ambiguous in *yamato kotoba*. There are a very few chapters of *gikobun* written by Norinaga, in which he tried "*furi-kanji*," *kanji* written beside the word written in *hiragana*, e.g., beside the word *kami* (hair) written in *hiragana*, the *kanji* for "hair" was written to prevent possible confusion with homonyms: *kami* for "paper," "god," and "above."

Most *kokugakusha* studied *kanbun* writing and encouraged others to do so, but at the same time they refused to read *kanji* in *on* reading, using *kanji* only to clarify the meaning of *yamato kotoba*. It is apparent that *yamato kotoba* alone was insufficient to express the ideas of the Edo period; by the eighteenth century the assimilation of *kango* and the use of *kanji* had reached such proportions in the language and thinking of the population that it was not possible to revive the language of the early Heian period. In fact, Ueda Akinari, who can be also considered as a *kokugakusha* and who wrote excellent *gikobun* with a strong Chinese influence, did not refuse to use *kango* or *kanji*, nor did later *kokugakusha* at the end of the Edo period, such as Hirata Atsutane, who was concerned with more urgent issues than writing style.

The restricted use of *kango* by *kokugakusha* did not affect writing in any other areas, but the use of *furigana* found in *kokugaku* writings encouraged the expanded use of *ateji* in such writings as *yomihon* of the nineteenth century, wherein much Chinese vocabulary was written in *kanji* but with *furigana* providing *yamato kotoba* readings which were not widely accepted. Since *yomihon* were popular through the end of the nineteenth century, the expanded use of *ateji* continued until the Meiji era.

The emergence of *kokugakusha* and their literature in *gikobun* extended the use of *wabun* outside the literary field, since their writings were academic theories and discussions on topics of their choice. Norinaga's terse style of *gikobun* was an especially useful example for writing essays and theories at the end of the Edo period and in the Meiji era, though writers used more *kango* then than Norinaga did.

Motoori Norinaga is also known for his studies on the Japanese language and in this field had noted disciples, such as Suzuki Akira (1764–1837), Ishizuka Tatsumaro (1764–1823), and Motoori Haruniwa (1763–1828), Norinaga's son. Fujitani Nariakira (1738–79), who wrote *Kazashishō* (Description of Ornamental Phrases) in 1767 and *Ayuishō* (Description of Binding Words) in 1773, and the priest Gimon (1786–1843), who wrote *Wago no Setsuryakuzu* (Illustration of Japanese Word Conjugation) in 1833, are also well-known scholars of the language in this period. Since the study of the language was originally motivated by the study of Japanese classics and poetry, the language which these scholars first attempted to describe was the classical language, in which they also wrote. The contemporary spoken language was neither their topic of study nor their means of writing.

In the nineteenth century a noted *waka* poet Kagawa Kageki's (1768–1843) style replaced Mabuchi's *man'yō* style and the traditional style of the aristocrats in Kyoto in the composition of *waka*. However, the priest Ryōkan (1757–1831) and Hiraga Motoyoshi (1799–1865) supported Mabuchi's idea and composed *man'yō*-style *waka*. At the end of the Edo period Ōkuma Kotomichi (1798–1868) and Tachibana Akemi (1797–1868), both of the merchant class, composed *waka* using more everyday vocabulary than their forerunners did. However, *waka* did not become as free as *haikai* in the use of *zokugo* and remained rather aristocratic, being only popular among educated people.

4. The Use of the Colloquial Language in Edo *Gesaku*

The city of Edo was rather small in comparison to the cities of Kyoto and Osaka in the beginning of the Edo period. The population of Kyoto consisted largely of merchants and artisans, with a small percentage of aristocrats, and Osaka was on the way to becoming a prosperous city of merchants in the seventeenth century, but Edo was largely populated by warriors. Half of the Edo population consisted of warriors throughout the Edo period, due to the fact that a large number of them moved there to serve the shogunate or to serve their local lords under the system of *sankin kōtai*, under which each daimyo was forced to spend every other year in Edo and to leave his family there when he returned to his fief. The Tokugawa family was originally from the Mikawa province, and the warriors who moved to Edo with the Tokugawa shogunate in the beginning of the period brought their Mikawa dialect, and those who came to serve their local lords brought their own dialects from all over Japan.

Merchants from various localities also moved to Edo with the hope of opening a new business or, in the case of already established Kamigata merchants, expanding their trade. Unlike Kyoto, Edo had no traditional culture; it was a new city and as Japan's new political center rapidly expanded into the largest city in Japan in the late seventeenth century. However, Kamigata trade, culture, and language were a strong influence in Edo during the first half of the period, and Edo did not produce a distinct culture until the middle of the eighteenth century. For instance,

Kamigata publishers established branch offices in Edo for the distribution of their books, but in the latter half of the eighteenth century these branches began to publish more books than their main offices, thus moving the center of the publishing business to Edo.

Although the Kantō dialect was spoken in Edo, because the city's new population brought many dialects with them, the spoken language lacked homogeneity in the beginning of the period. The slow development of Edo culture was partially due to the lack of uniformity of the language and to its provincial nature. The language of Kamigata was considered superior, being the language of traditional culture and the direct descendant of the classical language. *Haikai* was the first Kamigata literary form to become popular in Edo, owing to its short, colloquial nature. Confucian studies, initiated by the shogunate, and *kokugaku* also thrived, as these studies were not hampered by the spoken language. Prose literature was the area most affected by the spoken language, and Edo did not produce any important works and writers in it until the latter half of the eighteenth century.

Illustrated books for children began to be published in Edo in the latter half of the seventeenth and first half of the eighteenth centuries. *Akahon* (cinnabar-cover books), with stories for children, began to appear around 1670, and from around 1740 *kurohon* (black-cover books) and *aohon* (green-cover books) appeared, both of which were oriented to older children and thus more sophisticated than *akahon*. As the *ukiyozōshi* of Kamigata declined in popularity, a new prose literature, considered as *gesaku* (popular fiction), emerged and began to entertain the citizens of Edo.

The literature that thrived in Edo from around 1770 until the 1790s, when some *gesaku* works were banned by the shogunate under the Kansei reforms (1789–93), can be grouped into four genres, including two of poetry: *kyōka* (humorous poetry in *waka* form); *sharebon* (pleasure-quarters books); *kyōku* (humorous poems in *haikai* form), also known as *senryū*; and *kibyōshi* (yellow-cover books).

Although *kyōka* was popular much earlier in Kamigata, the *kyōka* of Edo began around 1770 as a pastime among intellectual warriors and established itself as a literary genre in the 1780s, when the noted poets Karagoromo Kisshū (1742–1802), Yomo no Akara (1749–1823, also known as Shokusanjin), and Akera Kankō (1739–1800) published collections of *kyōka* in 1783: *Wakabashū* (Young Grasses), compiled by Karagoromo Kisshū, and *Manzai Kyōkashū* (The Kyōka Omnibus), compiled by Yomo no Akara and Akera Kankō. *Kyōka* spread first among intellectual warriors and then among *chōnin*, and most poets wrote under humorous and witty pseudonyms to conceal their identities and to indicate that their compositions were written in a light vein.

Kyōka of this period is full of social satire written in a facetious manner, in *waka* form, and it served as literary catharsis for the intellectual warriors. Writing in a humorous and witty manner, both prose and poetry, is characteristic of Edo *gesaku* literature (*gesaku* literally means "jesting writing"), and most writers of *sharebon* and *kibyōshi* composed *kyōka*. Since *kyōka* described contemporary society, it integrated the vocabulary of everyday life, *zokugo*, into the traditional frame of *waka*. Because of the caricatures in *kyōka* of contemporary government policy and its officials, this form of verse was banned by the Kansei reforms in the 1790s, and its major poets, who were warriors in active service, were prevented from further writing. *Kyōka* did survive after this for some time but without its characteristic satirical manner.

Sharebon, devoted exclusively to witty descriptions of the pleasure quarters, emerged around the same time as *kyōka* did, and, catering to the specific tastes of the people of Edo, it thrived until the 1790s. Literature describing these quarters had previously been written in *kanbun* following the Chinese model pleasure-quarters literature, and similar works containing dialogue were also written in *kanamajiribun* in the mid-eighteenth century. However, it was the publication of *Yūshi Hōgen* (Rake's Dialect) by Inakarōjin Tadanojijii in 1770? and *Tatsumi no Sono* (Garden of the Southeast) by Muchūsanjin Negotosensei in 1770 that established *sharebon* as a realistic short story depicting activities inside the pleasure quarters with the esthetic sensibilities of the Edo citizen. (See Reading Selection 32.) The real names of the authors are not known, as is the case with many *sharebon* authors, since they concealed their true identities under humorous pseudonyms, such as Inakarōjin Tadanojijii, which means "a mere old man of the provinces," and Muchūsanjin Negotosensei, which means "a master nonsense talker in dreams."

Along with the flourishing of pleasure quarters in large cities and in post towns, a large number of *sharebon* were published to the delight of the reading public. The most successful writer of *sharebon* was Santō Kyōden (1761–1816), of the merchant class, who was already a successful *kibyōshi* writer and *ukiyoe* (genre picture) artist under the pseudonym Kitao Masanobu when he began to write *sharebon* in the 1780s. His *Tsūgen Sōmagaki* (Stars of the Brothel) in 1787 and *Keiseikai Shijūhatte* (Forty-eight Hands at Commerce with Courtesans) in 1790 are the best known. Kyōden's works were so popular that his last three works published in 1791 attracted the attention of the shogunate and were banned, and he stopped writing *sharebon* after being punished for the offense of inciting people to frequent the immoral pleasure quarters.

Most *sharebon* works from 1770 on were written in a dialogue style, with short narrative insertions, which was established by *Yūshi Hōgen*. *Sharebon* writers of this period were citizens of Edo, so they used the colloquial language of Edo in the dialogues. *Kibyōshi* also used dialogue written mostly in the spoken language, but it did not have the same emphasis on dialogue as *sharebon*, in which dialogue was an important means of depicting characters. Thus, *sharebon* is significant in the history of the written language in the sense that it was the first prose literature to employ the colloquial language of Edo, especially the language of courtesans and their customers.

The dialogue style of *sharebon* was probably influenced by Kabuki scripts, since it is written like a script, with the name of the character preceding each dialogue. The narrative in *sharebon* is usually a short description of the scene and the characters—their appearance, especially details on their dress. Although the narrative portions show the influence of classical grammar, they may also be, depending on the writer, strongly influenced by the spoken language. Since *sharebon's* topics are limited to the activities within the pleasure quarters, the spoken language used in it is limited in scope. However, its lively conversations, often including special terms unique to the pleasure quarters, are important materials for the study of Edo language, which already had overcome its lack of uniformity and provincialism of the earlier period.

While both *kyōku* and *kibyōshi* were popular around the time *kyōka* and *sharebon* thrived, *kyōku* was even more popular among less-educated people than *kyōka*. *Kyōku* had been composed along with *haikai*, as humorous variations of it, from the time *haikai* started, but it was recognized as a literary genre when Karai Senryū (1718–90) published the first *Yanagidaru* (Sake Cask), a series of 167 *kyōku* collections published between 1765 and 1838. *Kyōku* are also known as *senryū* for this reason.

Although the 17-syllable first verse, the *hokku*, of a *haikai* linked verse composition could sometimes stand alone as a poetic composition, it was the *kyōku* that really established the 17-syllable composition as a verse form. While early collections of *kyōku* included an introductory 14-syllable phrase to give the situation under which the following 17-syllable verse was composed, by the time the first issue of *Yanagidaru* was published, it was no longer regarded as having poetic value. The grammar used in *kyōku* was that of the spoken language, and *kyōku* had no requirements of seasonal words or *haigon*. The verses of social satire were also composed in *kyōku* form in the 1780s due to the influence of *kyōka* which was at its pinnacle until the Kansei reforms took place. *Kyōku*, with its humorous depictions of everyday life, enjoyed a stronger base among the people than *kyōka*, with the result that it survives today as a poetry of the common people.

Kibyōshi, in which illustrations played a key role, contained broader topics than *sharebon* and were very popular among less-educated people. Since they derived from *aohon*, illustrated books written mainly for juveniles, they have large illustrations on every page with only a little text within the illustration. *Kibyōshi* developed into books for adults when *Kinkin-sensei Eiga no Yume* (The Dream of Splendor of Master Gold), written and illustrated by Koikawa Harumachi (1744–89), one of the most successful *kibyōshi* writers, was published in 1775. Like Harumachi, some successful writers of *kibyōshi* were also *ukiyoe* artists who illustrated their own and other writers' stories for *kibyōshi*.

It was the influence of *kyōka*, *kyōku*, and *sharebon* on *kibyōshi* that turned it into adult literature. (Koikawa Harumachi, the author of *Kinkin-sensei Eiga no Yume*, also wrote *kyōka* poetry under the name of Sakenoue no Furachi.) *Kibyōshi* were not restricted to pleasure-quarter topics, and people found the humorous, often nonsensical stories entertaining. Over 2000 *kibyōshi* were published from 1775 to 1806; the most successful writers were Koikawa Harumachi; Hōseidō Kisanji (1735–1813), also known as *kyōka* poet Tegara no Okamochi, who wrote *Nagaiki Mitaiki* (A Search for Long Life) in 1783; Shiba Zenkō (1750–93), also known as *kyōgen* actor Yamamoto Tōjūrō, who wrote *Daihi no Senroppon* (The Thousand and Six Radish-Handed Buddha of Mercy) in 1785; and Santō Kyōden, who wrote and illustrated *Edo-umare Uwaki no Kabayaki* (A Wanton Edo Born) in 1785.

Because *kibyōshi* relies heavily on illustrations, the stories are quite sketchy, and its language is an odd mixture of spoken language and simplified classical grammar, though the influence of the classical language varies depending on the author and the topic. Since dialogues in *kibyōshi* are not as important as those in *sharebon* and not written in the colloquial language to the same degree, *kibyōshi* does not offer valuable materials for the study of the Edo language as *sharebon* does.

Kibyōshi was also affected by the Kansei reforms. Some *kibyōshi* caricatured government policy, and such writers as Hōseidō Kisanji and Koikawa Harumachi, warriors on active duty, stopped writing. After the Kansei reforms, those writers who continued to write turned to more serious topics, including vendettas and Confucian teachings advocating loyalty and filial piety, so that they would not offend the shogunate, but *kibyōshi* did not long survive the loss of humor.

From the end of the eighteenth century to the beginning of the nineteenth century, *kokkeibon* (humor books) and *ninjōbon* (books of sentiment) succeeded the declining *kibyōshi* and *sharebon*. *Kokkeibon* inherited humor from *sharebon* and *kibyōshi*, and the sentimental love stories of *ninjōbon* began to appeal to women readers. Since social satire was prohibited by shogunate policy, *kokkeibon* depicted the everyday life of commoners with a great sense of humor, but uncritically. *Kokkeibon* also inherited the dialogue style of *sharebon*, and offer rich material for the study of the spoken language of the nineteenth century.

The best-known *kokkeibon* writers are Jippensha Ikku (1765–1831), who wrote the bestseller *Tōkaidōchū Hizakurige* (A Shank's Mare Tour of the Eastern Sea Road) from 1802 to 1809, and Shikitei Sanba (1776–1822), who wrote *Ukiyoburo* (Bath House of the Floating World) from 1809 to 1812 and *Ukiyodoko* (Barber Shop of the Floating World) from 1811 to 1823. (See Reading Selection 33.) The success of these works was due to the taste of the populace for humor, which also resulted in the prosperity of variety houses of this period, where people were entertained with humorous stories. *Tōkaidōchū Hizakurige*, which contains a number of *kyōka*, entertained readers not only with its humor, but also with local color and information about various places from Edo to Osaka, while *Ukiyoburo* and *Ukiyodoko* were enjoyed for their depiction of urban Edo life through the conversations of common people at the bath house or barber shop.

Ikku and Sanba also wrote *kibyōshi* and *sharebon*, which were written mainly for the citizens of Edo, but the popularity of *Tōkaidōchū Hizakurige* carried the enthusiasm for *kokkeibon* beyond the limits of Edo. In fact, Ikku's book was so successful that he become one of the few writers in this period to earn his livelihood strictly from his royalties. *Tōkaidōchū Hizakurige* contains various local scenes with dialogue in dialect, while the main characters are from Edo. *Ukiyoburo* and *Ukiyodoko* also contain some representations of dialects in the conversations of characters. However, the major part of these works were written in the colloquial language of Edo, which by this period was established as the center of culture.

Kokkeibon established the dialogue style of writing and employed far more varieties of the colloquial language, since the characters that appear in *kokkeibon* are more varied than those in *sharebon*. The characters were depicted by the use of dialogue full of slang, gags, and terms of abuse. The characters in *Ukiyoburo*, for instance, are men and women of all ages, who come not merely to bathe, but also to gossip and quarrel, and especially to play games and drink tea on the second floor of the bath house, which was where commoners did their socializing. Sanba wanted his readers to identify easily with the characters in his books, and so he did not change the language in his writing from that actually spoken.

While *yomihon* was popular among serious readership and *kokkeibon* provided readers with laughter, *ninjōbon* began to entertain a less-educated readership, including women, from the end of the eighteenth century through the first half of the nineteenth century. *Ninjōbon* had the nickname of *nakihon* (books for crying); the stories were of sentimental love affairs with subthemes of filial duty and women's virtue. The term *ninjōbon* comes from the fact that a successful writer, Tamenaga Shunsui (1789–1843), signed himself as "the first *ninjōbon* writer" in his successful work, *Shunshoku Ume-goyomi* (Plum Calendar of Spring) written from 1832 to 1835.

Since *ninjōbon* did not depend on a plot to the extent *yomihon* did, it was possible for several writers, or ghostwriters, to write different chapters of one story, which was edited and published by one famous writer. Drama scripts in the Edo period were very often written under a similar system, each act or scene being written by a different writer, since writers' rights and importance were not recognized yet in the field of theater. Tamenaga Shunsui was known to be an author who published books written originally by his disciples as his own, but his written style is distinct in *Shunshoku Ume-goyomi* and *Harutsugedori* (Harbinger of Spring), published in 1837, where his writing talent is apparent. (See Reading Selection 34.)

The written style of *ninjōbon* is much more elegant and descriptive than that of *kibyōshi*, and although they have some illustrations, as all *gesaku* works do, *ninjōbon* do not rely on the illustrations to compensate for insufficient prose like *kibyōshi* did. In fact, another term for *ninjōbon* is *eiri yomihon* (illustrated books for reading); the narrative employs a simple but elegant classical grammar, while the dialogue is written in colloquial language. Since *ninjōbon* were intended to be read by women of various social standing, the colloquial language used in them is very polite. Although *ninjōbon* were disdained by contemporary intellectuals, the refined style of writing in *ninjōbon* was praised by later writers in the Meiji era. *Ninjōbon* declined in the middle of the nineteenth century, when some of them were banned for their descriptive love scenes.

In the field of theater, the system of collaboration in script writing was common after Chikamatsu Monzaemon's death. Also, scripts were always rewritten to take advantage of new theatrical techniques or to stay attuned to the changing tastes of the audience. In the beginning of the eighteenth century, while Kabuki was in a state of decline, *ningyō jōruri* was still thriving in Kamigata, and a number of great works were produced under the system of collaboration. Takeda Izumo (1691–1756) and Chikamatsu Hanji (1725–83), a son of Chikamatsu Monzaemon's close friend, were noted as writers and organizers of *jōruri* theater. Well-known works produced under Izumo's name are *Sugawara Denju Tenarai Kagami* (The Exemplary Mirror of the Sugawara), first performed in 1746, *Yoshitsune Senbonzakura* (A Thousand Cherry Trees of Yoshitsune) in 1747, and *Kanadehon Chūshingura* (The Exemplary Loyal Retainers) in 1748, all of which were performed in both *ningyō jōruri* and Kabuki. As for Hanji's works, *Honchō Nijūshikō* (Twenty-four Filial Sons of Japan) in 1766, *Imoseyama Onna Teikin* (Imoseyama Teaching for Women) in 1771, and *Shinpan Utazaimon* (New Song-Prayer) in 1780 are famous and still performed today.

While *ningyō jōruri* waned after Chikamatsu Hanji's death for lack of a successful script writer, Kabuki, which often borrowed *jōruri* scripts when no one was writing any Kabuki scripts, underwent a revival at the end of the eighteenth century in Edo and reached its pinnacle in the beginning of the nineteenth century. The success of Edo Kabuki in this period owes to the famous writer Tsuruya Nanboku (1755–1829), who established its style by appealing successfully to the tastes of the nineteenth-century audience. His plays are famous for including the roles of a ghost and a wicked woman and for depicting the life and language of the people living in the lowest social and economical stratum. His representative works are *Tenjiku Tokubei Ikokubanashi* (Tenjiku Tokubei's Story of a Foreign Land) in 1804, *Iroeiri Otogizōshi* (A Story Book with Colored Pictures) in 1808, and *Tōkaidō Yotsuya Kaidan* (A Ghost Tale of Yotsuya) in 1825.

Kabuki scripts written in Edo were naturally written in the colloquial language of Edo, except the narrative parts chanted with musical accompaniment. Kawatake Mokuami (1816–93) of the late Edo period contributed to the refinement of dialogues in Kabuki scripts with his detailed depiction of manners and customs, often using monologues in seven-five-syllable rhythm. Characters in Mokuami's works include the lowest class of people, especially thieves; he depicted the dark side of the society with poetic elegance. His famous works are *Tsuta Momiji Utsunoya Tōge* (Scarlet Ivy on the Pass of Utsunoya), first performed in 1856, and *Sannin Kichisa Kuruwa no Hatsugai* (The Thieves) in 1860. Manboku, who contributed to the last bloom of Edo Kabuki, continued to write in the Meiji era without much success. The style and theatrical techniques of Kabuki were established and fixed so firmly, based on the esthetic tastes of the Edo period, that Kabuki did not have the creativity to cope with the demands of a new era. It has survived as a classical theater since then.

Although freedom of writing was very often interrupted by the shogunate, the latter half of the Edo period also produced a great number of publications, and Edo-centered culture thrived from the end of the eighteenth century through the first half of the nineteenth century. To recapitulate the written materials and styles of this period, there were *kanshi* at its height, *wabun* written by *kokugakusha*, *wakan konkōbun* written by *yomihon* writers, *sōrōbun* for letter writing, and various *gesaku* genres influenced to different degrees by the Edo language. Although the entire population was organized into a hierarchical class order and language differed depending on social status and locality, writers represented a much broader scope of society and people from more parts of society were able to read and write than in earlier periods.

Because of the increasing discrepancies in the backgrounds and education of both readers and writers, the use of *ateji* became so varied that some *ateji* became impossible to read without *furigana*. For instance, the combination of the characters 活 and 業, meaning "vocation," could be read in several different ways: *shōbai* (business), *itonami* (work), *tatsuki* (means for livelihood), *nariwai* (vocation), and *sugiwai* (vocation). Naturally, the use of *furigana*, which was popular throughout the Edo period for books for broad readership, contributed greatly to extension of the *ateji* usage of characters.

The colloquial language recorded in *gesaku* writings, especially in *sharebon* and *kokkeibon*, is the language known as the Edo dialect, with a characteristic assimilation of some sounds still heard today in the Tokyo dialect. *Gesaku* works employed the language whenever it was the best means to appeal to readers. However, all *gesaku* writers maintained the attitude that their writing was not a serious occupation, even thought it was a major source of income for some writers like Ikku. The appearance of classical grammar in some *gesaku* works and in the preface of most works gives the impression that the use of colloquial language had not been fully accepted as written language. The written language per se was still in the classical style, using a grammar somewhat similar to that of the Heian period. In fact, the colloquial language was not really accepted as a written language until writers in the Meiji era advocated that the written and spoken languages should be identical.

V
THE SEARCH FOR A WRITTEN STYLE
The Meiji Era (1868–1911)

In the early Meiji era, when the imperial regime was restored and Emperor Meiji moved to Tokyo, formerly Edo, Japan resumed its relations with other countries of the world, and Western civilization poured into Japan. Japanese intellectuals became more and more aware of the differences in the reading and writing systems of other cultures. The study of Chinese, which dominated the study of foreign culture and language up to the end of the Edo period, was not as important as the Japanese had thought, and writing in *kanbun* need not have the authoritative status it had before. Written and spoken languages were similar in the case of Western languages, and the written languages appeared to be understood by the majority of speakers of the languages, if they had any education at all. Writers did not have to choose whether they should write in a written language or in the spoken language, as they did in Japan.

Japanese men continued to read books in *kanbun*, especially Chinese philosophy and literature, as a part of their academic training, but the writing of *kanbun* lost its authority. Imperial rescripts were written in *kanamajiribun*, using *katakana*, at the end of the Edo period and in the Meiji era. Thus, official documents were all written in *katakana* and *kanji*; still the influence of *kanbun* was very much present, since these were drafted by officials educated in *kanbun*. *Kanshi* writing continued, not on a national scale, but for mental training and as a pastime for educated men. Private diaries and letters may have been written in *sōrōbun* or *hentai kanbun* in early Meiji, but the general trend was to discontinue writing in a style and language which were not understood widely.

In spite of the decline in Chinese studies in this period, the fact that most intellectuals had a knowledge of *kanbun* played an important role when they studied European languages. Just as all the Japanese scholars who studied Dutch in the Edo period (when only the study of natural science was permitted by the shogunate) knew Chinese, so did the Meiji intellectuals who studied European languages. The knowledge of *kanbun* assisted their study in two ways: understanding the syntax of Western languages was naturally easier, after the experience of studying the syntax of Chinese, which is different from that of Japanese; and when there was no suitable vocabulary in Japanese for translating Western languages, similar vocabulary was often found, or sometimes created, in *kango*. In fact, for the purpose of translating Western languages, a large number of new *kango* were created in Japan, as well as in China, around this period, and assimilated into the Japanese language.

As the government's compulsory education system broadened the nation's readership base and improved printing methods made books readily available, Meiji intellectuals came to realize that uniformity in written styles was necessary so that the broad readership would have equal opportunities to read. Society was no longer divided into four classes, and although there existed some feeling of class distinction between aristocrats, the former warrior class, and commoners, the equality of all people was also advocated. Therefore, writers were faced with the task of choosing a written style which could be read easily by the broadened readership.

However, the choice and establishment of the right style of writing was not accomplished in a short period of time. The written style used in the early Meiji era in official documents, academic writings, newspapers, and magazines is called *kanamajiribun* or *wakan konkōbun*, which was written in simple classical grammar with a large amount of *kango* vocabulary, with which the writers displayed their education. Except for some sporadic use of the colloquial language in a few articles in newspapers and magazines, *kanamajiribun* was used for most articles, which contained *kango* vocabulary which was quite difficult, especially for general readers of newspapers.

Fiction writers of this period selected their own styles from among the styles used by the Edo writers. For instance, Kanagaki Robun (1829–94) chose *kokkeibon* style, freely using the colloquial language of the early Meiji era, for *Seiyōdōchū Hizakurige* (A Shank's Mare Tour of the Western Countries), written between 1870 and 1876, and *Aguranabe* (Idle Talks in the Sukiyaki House), written between 1871 and 1872. The translation of *Earnest Maltravers* and *Alice* by Edward George Earle Bulwer Lytton (1803–73), as *Karyū Shunwa*, by Niwa Jun'ichirō (1851–1919) between 1878 and 1879, which is considered to be the first translation of a Western novel, was done in *kanamajiribun* with *katakana*. The noted writer and translator Tsubouchi Shōyō (1859–1935) translated Shakespeare's *Julius Caesar* into the style of *jōruri* scripts in 1884, and wrote *Tōsei Shosei Katagi* (Characters of Modern Students) in 1885 in a mixed style of *ninjōbon*, Bakin's *wakan konkōbun* and *jōruri* scripts. San'yūtei Enchō (1839–1900), a noted storyteller in variety houses, published the transcription of his stories, *Kaidan Botandōrō* (Ghost Story: The Peony Lantern) in 1884, entirely in the colloquial language.

The discussions of *genbun itchi* (unity of the written and spoken languages) was begun by such enlightened thinkers of the early Meiji era as Maejima Hisoka (1835–1919), who advocated the abolishment of the use of *kanji* and of writing in *kana* only, and Nishi Amane (1829-97), who advocated the use of the Latin alphabet to write Japanese. Many intellectuals and writers participated in the discussion and experimentation to determine in what style Japanese prose should be written as well as which writing system should be used. The proposal to write Japanese entirely in *kana* or the Latin alphabet did not convince many people, but the use of *kanji* and *kango*, which often exceeded the knowledge of less-educated commoners, was once reviewed by the participants of the *genbun itchi* movement. Fukuzawa Yukichi (1835–1901), a noted educator and the author of *Gakumon no Susume* (Encouragement of Learning), written between 1872 and 1876, advocated the restriction of number of *kanji* for general use. In his book for children, *Moji no Oshie* (A Lesson on Writing), in 1873, he proposes limiting these to two or three thousand and includes his selection of 938 essential *kanji*. (See Reading Selection 35.) Although he was neither a linguist nor a novelist, he was an advocator of the equality of people and concerned with their education, and his proposal that the number of *kanji* be limited was surprisingly farsighted, considering the fact that about 2000 *kanji* were selected for practical use by the Ministry of Education after the Second World War.

Genbun itchi movement discussions of written styles, which were continued to the end of the nineteenth century by many novelists and intellectuals, came to advocate roughly two types of written style: a compromise between the classical and the colloquial languages, called *futsūbun* (ordinary style of writing), in which a simple classical grammar and colloquial vocabulary were used; and a written style totally based on colloquial grammar and vocabulary, which was called *zokubun* (written style of colloquial language) or *kōgobun* (written style in the spoken language). Newspapers, magazines, and academic writers chose *futsūbun* and began writing in this style in the 1880s; language textbooks in elementary schools also followed this trend.

However, for novelists of the Meiji era, being exposed to Western novels made the selection of a written style even harder. In fact, they were searching for a new type of novel in a new style of writing. For many of them, the styles applied by *gesaku* writers in the Edo period were not elegant, serious, and terse enough to write a contemporary novel influenced by Western novels. In an attempt to establish a new style for novels, Futabatei Shimei (1864–1909), who also translated Russian novels, Yamada Bimyō (1868–1910), and Saganoya Omuro (1862–1947), began to write in the colloquial language in the 1880s.

Futabatei Shimei's *Ukigumo* (Floating Cloud), written between 1887 and 1889, and his translations of Turgenev's novels, *Aibiki* (Rendezvous) and *Meguriai* (A Chance Meeting) in 1888, were written with sentences ending with *da* (copula). (See Reading Selection 36.) Futabatei, being a talented writer, demonstrated the possibility of writing in colloquial language with poetic elegance and convinced many writers of the period. While Yamada Bimyō wrote *Fūkin Shirabe no Hitofushi* (A Melody of a Hand Organ) and *Musashino* (Musashi Plain) in 1887, *Natsu Kodachi* (Summer Grove) in 1888, and *Kochō* in 1889, establishing his style ending sentences with *desu* (copula), Saganoya Omuro wrote *Hakumei no Suzuko* (Suzuko, the Ill-Fated) in 1888 and *Nozue no Kiku* (Wild Chrysanthemums) in 1889, establishing his style ending sentences with *de aru* (copula) or *de arimasu* (copula), though he has one successful work, *Hatsukoi* (The First Love) in 1889, written in a style ending sentences with *da*. (See Reading Selection 37.)

There were writers who were against writing in colloquial language, especially among conservatives such as Kōda Rohan (1867–1947), who wrote *Fūryūbutsu* (The Stylish Buddha) in 1889 and *Gojū no Tō* (Five-Storied Pagoda) in 1891, and Ozaki Kōyō (1867–1903), who wrote *Kyara Makura* (The Perfumed Pillow) in 1890; both of them were influenced by Saikaku's style of the seventeenth century. Also, the noted writer, translator, and medical doctor Mori Ōgai (1862–1922) wrote *Maihime* (The Dancing Girl) in 1890 using classical grammar. (See Reading Selection 38.) These writers were supporters of *futsūbun*, claiming that *kōgobun* did not have sufficient elegance for their novels.

However, Ozaki Kōyō began writing in the colloquial language for his *Ninin Nyōbō* (Two Ladies) between 1891 and 1892 and also his successful novel, *Tajō Takon* (Tears and Regrets) in 1896. The success of these works, which were written in *de aru* ending sentences, brought other writers of this period to adopt the *de aru* style, in which sentences end with *de aru*. Izumi Kyōka (1873–1936), who wrote *Kōya Hijiri* (The Sage of Mount Kōya) in 1900 and *Onna Keizu* (A Woman's Destiny) in 1907, and Shimazaki Tōson (1872–1943), who wrote *Hakai* (Broken Commandment) in 1906, *Haru* (Spring) in 1908, and *Ie* (Family) in 1910, wrote in *de aru* style, which began to be established as the style for using the colloquial language. Since ending sentences with *desu* or *de arimasu* was considered to be too polite and personal, and ending with *da* too rough, the *de aru* ending came to be considered as the equivalent of *nari* in classical grammar.

Linguists also promoted writing in *kōgobun*. Ueda Kazutoshi (1867–1937), for instance, advocated writing in "standard Japanese," which should be based on the Tokyo dialect, thus introducing the idea of "standard Japanese," and *Gengogaku*

Zasshi (Magazine: Linguistics), published by the Association for Linguistics established in 1900, also discussed the practical use of the language and supported *kōgobun* by publishing articles in it.

The last stage of the *genbun itchi* movement was marked by the promotion of *shaseibun*, writing which tried to sketch directly from life, and by the literary movement of naturalism. *Shaseibun* was first advocated by a *haiku* poet, Masaoka Shiki (1867–1902), who used the term *haiku* for *haikai*, and it attracted *haiku* poets. The noted writer, Natsume Sōseki (1867–1916) was a contributor to the *haiku* magazine *Hototogisu* (The Cuckoo) founded by Masaoka Shiki, when he wrote *Wagahai wa Neko de aru* (I am a Cat) between 1905 and 1906. (See Reading Selection 39.) Sōseki's terse style in *kōgobun* was applauded by the supporters of *kōgobun*, and writing novels in *kōgobun* peaked in 1908, when the naturalist approach to writing novels was popular among writers. The representative writers are Tayama Katai (1871–1930), who wrote *Futon* (The Quilt) in 1907, Masamune Hakuchō (1879–1962), who wrote *Jin'ai* (Dirt) in 1907, and Kunikida Doppo (1871–1908), who wrote *Unmei* (Destiny) in 1906, all of whom wrote in *kōgobun*, establishing the *de aru* style as the style for writing novels.

Thus, *genbun itchi* succeeded in achieving its goal, the identity of the spoken and written languages, in the field of literature at the end of the Meiji era. However, all the Meiji writers had *kanbun* education, e.g., Natsume Sōseki's *kanshi* are well known, and their *kōgobun* tended to be influenced by their education, such as in the choice of vocabulary. A written style completely free of *kanbun* writing was established by such writers as Mushanokōji Saneatsu (1885–1976), who wrote *Omedetaki Hito* (God's Fool) in 1911, Arishima Takeo (1878–1923), who wrote *Aru Onna* (A Certain Woman) in 1911, and Shiga Naoya (1883–1971), who wrote *Kōjinbutsu no Fūfu* (A Good-natured Couple) in 1917 and *Kozō no Kamisama* (A Young Man's God) in 1920, in the Taishō era (1912–26). (See Reading Selection 40.)

Literary magazines began publishing mostly articles in *kōgobun*, while free-style poetry, engendered by the influence of Western poetry in the middle of the Meiji era began to be written in the colloquial language at the end of Meiji. Editorials in large newspapers kept using *futsūbun* until the 1920s, the last *futsūbun* articles appearing in Tokyo Asahi Shinbun (Tokyo Asahi Newspaper, the present Asahi) in December of 1921. Official and legal documents and imperial rescripts did not change to *kōgobun* until after World War II, when the number of *kanji* for practical use was limited and the *kana* spelling, for which the Meiji government adopted the seventeenth-century *kokugakusha* Keichu's spelling system for elementary school education, was finally changed in accordance with contemporary pronunciation in 1946.

Vocabulary from Western languages began to appear in writing, as well as in the spoken language. This vocabulary which originally came from Western languages and assimilated into Japanese is called *gairaigo* (loan words), and the Meiji writers often attempted to write equivalent *kango* with *furigana* giving *gairaigo* readings. For instance, *teregarafu* was written in *kana* beside the characters, 伝信機 (telegraphic instrument), and *garasu* beside the characters, 硝子 (glass). Both *hiragana* and *katakana* were used for the *furigana*, as well as for writing *gairaigo* without *kanji*, since it was only after World War II that *katakana* was prescribed for *gairaigo*. Another influence of Western languages on the writing of Japanese was the use of punctuation marks. In the middle of the Meiji era, the ends of sentences and phrases were marked with a small circle, *maru*, and a dot, *ten*, respectively.

The history of the Japanese written language is marked by two important periods: one when Chinese culture poured into Japan, or into the Japanese court, in the sixth, seventh, and eighth centuries, and one when Western culture was imported and studied in the latter half of the nineteenth century. We have discussed how the Japanese coped with written language at these times. Thanks to the Meiji writers and intellectuals, the written language is today as similar as possible to the spoken language, although the finishing touches of *genbun itchi* were achieved by the government only after World War II, when all official and legal documents were required to be written in the spoken language. Also, the reduction of the number of *kanji* for general use and the *kana* spelling reforms virtually eliminated illiteracy in Japan. The written language, however, does have older expressions and phrases than the contemporary spoken language as is true in any written language with a long history. The use of *kanji* for a large amount of homonymous vocabulary in written Japanese creates problems in these days of the computer, but this is beyond the discussion of this book.

BIBLIOGRAPHY

概　説　General

岩波講座「日本語 10　文体」. 岩波書店, 1977.

講座国語史 3「語彙史」. 大修館, 1972.

講座国語史 6「文体史・言語生活史」. 大修館, 1972.

国語学会編「国語学辞典」. 東京堂, 1955.

佐藤喜代治. 「日本文章史の研究」. 明治書院, 1966.

佐伯梅友・馬淵和夫. 「古語辞典」. 講談社, 1969.

築島裕. 「国語の歴史」. 東京大学出版会, 1977.

日本古典文学研究必携（別冊国文学）. 学燈社, 1979.

日本語講座第六巻「日本語の歴史」. 大修館, 1977.

日本語の歴史 1「民族のことばの誕生」. 平凡社, 1963.

日本語の歴史 2「文字とのめぐりあい」. 平凡社, 1963.

日本語の歴史 3「言語芸術の花ひらく」. 平凡社, 1964.

日本語の歴史 4「移りゆく古代語」. 平凡社, 1964.

日本語の歴史 5「近代語の流れ」. 平凡社, 1964.

林巨樹・池上秋彦. 「国語史辞典」. 東京堂, 1979.

Keene, Donald. *Anthology of Japanese Literature*. New York: Grove Press, Inc., 1955.

Putzar, Edward. *Japanese Literature*. Tucson: University of Arizona Press, 1973.

奈良時代　Nara Period

図説日本文化史大系 2「飛鳥時代」. 小学館, 1957.

日本古典文學大系「懐風藻・文華秀麗集・本朝文粋」. 岩波書店, 1964.
日本古典文學大系「古事記・祝詞」. 岩波書店, 1958.
日本古典文學大系「日本書紀上」. 岩波書店, 1967.
日本古典文學大系「萬葉集一, 二, 三, 四」. 岩波書店, 1958–62.
山岸徳平. 「日本漢文学史論考」. 岩波書店, 1974.

平安時代 Heian Period

角川源義. 「語り物文芸の発生」. 東京堂, 1975.
古典遺産の会「将門記　研究と資料」. 新読書社, 1963.
小松茂美. 「かな」. 岩波書店, 1968.
日本古典文學大系「源氏物語一」. 岩波書店, 1958.
日本古典文學大系「古今和歌集」. 岩波書店, 1958.
日本古典文學大系「今昔物語五」. 岩波書店, 1959.
日本古典文學大系「竹取物語・伊勢物語・大和物語」. 岩波書店, 1957.
日本古典文學大系「土左日記 ・ かげろふ日記・和泉式部日記・更級日記」岩波書店, 1957.
日本古典文學大系「日本靈異記」. 岩波書店, 1967.
日本古典文學大系「保元・平治物語」. 岩波書店, 1961.
日本古典文學大系「枕草子・紫式部日記」. 岩波書店, 1958.
日本語の世界 5. 築島裕. 「仮名」. 中央公論社, 1981.
山口久雄. 「平安朝の漢文学」. 吉川引文館, 1981.

鎌倉・室町時代 Kamakura–Muromachi Periods

岩井良雄. 「日本語法史　室町時代編」. 笠間書院, 1973.
亀井高孝・阪田雪子翻字. 「平家物語」. 吉川弘文館, 1966.
藝能史研究會「日本の古典芸能 4　狂言」. 平凡社, 1970.
永山勇. 「仮名づかい」. 笠間書院, 1978.
日本古典全書「吉利支丹文学集下」. 朝日新聞社, 1960.
日本古典文學大系「宇治拾遺物語」. 岩波書店, 1960.
日本古典文學大系「狂言上」. 岩波書店, 1960
日本古典文學大系「五山文学・江戸漢詩集」. 岩波書店, 1966.

日本古典文學大系「沙石集」. 岩波書店，1966.

日本古典文學大系「新古今和歌集」. 岩波書店，1958.

日本古典文学大系「平家物語上・下」. 岩波書店，1959, 1960.

日本古典文學大系「方丈記・徒然草」. 岩波書店，1959.

日本古典文學大系「謠曲集上」. 岩波書店，1960.

Watson, Burton. *Japanese Literature in Chinese,* 2 vols. New York: Columbia University Press, 1975.

江戸時代 Edo Period

池上禎造. 岩波講座日本文学史「文体の変遷」. 岩波書店，1959.

講座日本近世史 9「近世思想論」. 有斐閣，1981.

杉本つとむ.「近代日本語の成立」. 桜楓社，1961.

暉峻康隆・郡司正勝.「江戸市民文学の開花」. 至文堂，1967.

暉峻康隆・郡司正勝.「元禄文芸復興」. 至文堂，1966.

日本古典文學全集「洒落本・滑稽本・人情本」. 小学館，1971.

日本古典文學全集「東海道中膝栗毛」. 小学館，1975.

日本古典文學全集「連歌俳諧集」. 小学館，1974.

日本古典文學大系「上田秋成集」. 岩波書店，1959.

日本古典文學大系「江戸笑話集」. 岩波書店，1966.

日本古典文學大系「假名草子」. 岩波書店，1965.

日本古典文學大系「黄表紙・洒落本集」. 岩波書店，1958.

日本古典文學大系「西鶴集下」. 岩波書店，1960.

日本古典文學大系「近松浄瑠璃集上」. 岩波書店，1958.

日本古典文學大系「椿説弓張月上」岩波書店，1958.

日本思想大系「近世神道論・前期國學」. 岩波書店，1972.

日本思想大系「本居宣長」. 岩波書店，1978.

日野龍夫.「徂徠学派」. 筑摩書房，1975.

松村明.「近代の国語　江戸から現代へ」. 桜楓社，1982.

明治時代 Meiji Era

大島田人・河村清一郎・八角真編.「資料　近代文章史」. 桜楓社，1980.

現代日本文學全集 1「坪内逍遙・二葉亭四迷集」. 筑摩書房, 1956.

杉本つとむ.「近代日本語」. 紀伊國屋書店, 1981.

日本現代文學全集「夏目漱石集(一)」. 講談社, 1961.

日本現代文學全集「森鷗外集」. 講談社, 1962.

日本現代文學全集「山田美妙・広津柳浪・川上眉山・小栗風葉集」. 講談社, 1968.

山本正秀.「言文一致の歴史論考」. 桜楓社, 1971.

INDEX

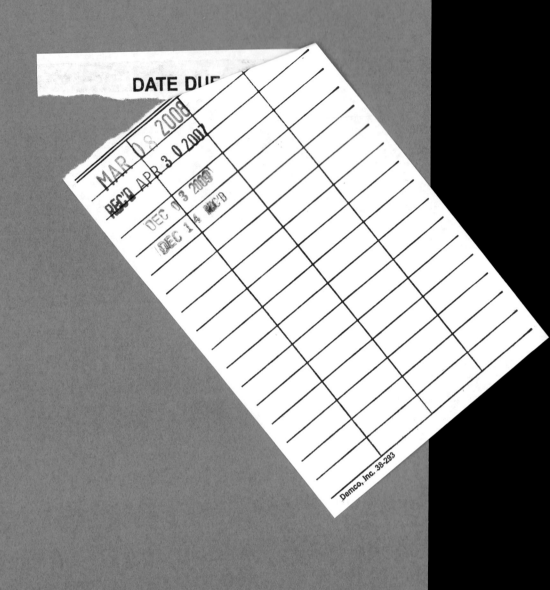

VI
READING SELECTIONS IN JAPANESE

凡例

一、歌には国歌大観の番号を付けた。

二、底本の漢字、仮名遣いはほとんど改めてないが、新字体のある漢字は、読みやすいように、新字体に改めた。

三、一から二十九までは、句読点、カッコ、濁点を加えたものを使用した。

四、二十二、二十三はローマ字を仮名交り文に直したものを使用した。

五、二十四から四十までのふりがなは、元の版本、出版本に付いていたものである。

六、十九の促音は、底本にはないが、異本を参照し、カッコの中に入れた。

七、二十一と二十八は現在も上演される関係上、促音、拗音を入れたものを使用した。

八、三十二は、底本の話し手の名前は□の中に入っているが、それを取ってカギカッコを付け、他と同じ形式に統一した。

一、憲法十七条（日本書紀）

一曰、以和為貴、無忤為宗。人皆有党。亦少達者。是以、或不順君父。乍違于隣里。然上和下睦、諧於論事、則事理自通。何事不成。

二曰、篤敬三宝。三宝者仏法僧也。則四生之終帰、万国之極宗。何世何人、非貴是法。人鮮尤悪。能教従之。其不帰三宝、何以直枉。

四曰、群卿百寮、以礼為本。其治民之本、要在乎礼。上不礼、而下非齊。下無礼、以必有罪。是以、群臣有礼、位次不乱。百姓有礼、国家自治。

十曰、絶忿棄瞋、不怒人違。人皆有心。心各有執。彼是則我非。我是則彼非。我必非聖。彼必非愚。共是凡夫耳。是非之理、詎能可定。相共賢愚、如鐶无端。是以、彼人雖瞋、還恐我失。我独雖得、従衆同挙。

十四曰、群臣百寮、無有嫉妬。我既嫉人、人亦嫉我。嫉妬之患、不知其極。所以、智勝於己則不

悦。才優於己則嫉妬。是以、五百之乃今遇賢。千載以難待一聖。其不得賢聖。何以治国。

十六曰、使民以時、古之良典。故冬月有間、以可使民。従春至秋、農桑之節。不可使民。其不農何食。不桑何服。

十七曰、夫事不可独断。必与衆宜論。少事是軽。不可必衆。唯逮論大事、若疑有失。故与衆相弁、辞則得理。

日本古典文學大系「日本書紀上」より

二、上野国山名村碑文

辛巳歳集月三日記、佐野三家定賜健守命孫黒売刀自、此新川臣児斯多々弥足尼孫大児臣娶生児長利僧、母為記定文也、放光寺僧

図説日本文化史大系2「飛鳥時代」より

三、古事記

故、所避追而、降出雲国之肥河上、名鳥髪地。此時箸従其河流下。於是須佐之男命、以為人有其河上而、尋覓上往者、老夫与老女二人在而、童女置中泣。爾問賜之汝等者誰。故、其老夫答言、僕者国神、大山津見神之子焉。僕名謂足名椎、妻名謂手名椎、女名謂櫛名田比売。亦問汝哭由者何、答白言、我之女者、自本在八稚女。是高志之八俣遠呂智、(此三字以音。)毎年来喫。今其可来時。故泣。爾問其形如何、答白、彼目如赤加賀智而、身一有八頭八尾。亦其身生蘿及檜椙、其長度谿八谷峡八尾而、見其腹者、悉常血爛也。(此謂赤加賀知者、今酸醤者也。)

爾速須佐之男命、詔其老夫、是汝之女者、奉於吾哉、答白恐不覚御名。爾答詔、吾者天照大御神之伊呂勢者也。(自伊下三字以音。)故今、自天降坐也。爾足名椎手名椎神、白然坐者恐。立奉。爾速須佐之男命、乃於湯津爪櫛取成其童女而、刺御美豆良、告其足名椎手名椎神、汝等、醸八塩折之酒、亦作廻垣、於其垣作八門、毎門結八佐受岐、(此三字以音。)毎其佐受岐置酒船而、毎船盛其八塩折酒而待。故、随告而如此設備待之時、其八俣遠呂智、信如言来。乃毎船垂入己頭飲其酒。於是飲酔留伏寝。爾速須佐之男命、抜其所御佩之十拳剣、切散其蛇者、肥河変血而流。故、切其中尾時、御刀之刃毀。爾思怪以御刀之前、刺割而見者、在都牟刈之大刀。故、取此大刀、思異物而、白上於天照大御神也。是者草那芸之大刀也。(那芸二字以音。)

故是以其速須佐之男命、宮可造作之地、求出雲国。爾到坐須賀此二字以音。下效此。地而詔之、吾来此地、我御心須賀須賀斯而、其地作宮坐。故、其地者於今云須賀也。茲大神、初作須賀宮之時、自其地雲立騰。爾作御歌。其歌曰、

夜久毛多都　伊豆毛夜幣賀岐　都麻碁微爾　夜幣賀岐都久流　曾能夜幣賀岐袁

於是喚其足名椎神、告言汝者任我宮之首、且負名号稲田宮主須賀之八耳神。

日本古典文學大系「古事記・祝詞」より

四、懐風藻

五言　於宝宅宴新羅客　一首 賦得烟字

左大臣正二位長屋王

高旻開遠照
遥嶺靄浮烟
有愛金蘭賞
無疲風月筵
桂山余景下
菊浦落霞鮮

莫謂滄波隔
長為壮思篇

五言　初春侍宴　一首

従二位大納言大伴宿禰旅人

寛政情既遠
迪古道惟新
穆穆四門客
済済三徳人
梅雪乱残岸
煙霞接早春
共遊聖主沢
同賀撃壌仁

五言　詠月　一首

文武天皇

月舟移霧渚
楓檝泛霞浜

台上澄流耀
酒中沈去輪
水下斜陰砕
樹除秋光新
独以星間鏡
還浮雲漢津

五言 春苑言宴 一首

大津皇子

開衿臨霊沼
遊目歩金苑
澄清苔水深
晻曖霞峰遠
驚波共絃響
哢鳥与風聞
群公倒載帰
彭沢宴誰論

日本古典文學大系「懐風藻・文華秀麗集・本朝文粋」より

五、万葉集

額田王歌

8 熟田津尓　船乗世武登　月待者　潮毛可奈比沼　今者許芸乞菜

天皇遊獦蒲生野時　額田王作歌

20 茜草指　武良前野逝　標野行　野守者不見哉　君之袖布流

大津皇子贈石川郎女御歌一首

107 足日木乃　山之四付二　妹待跡　吾立所沾　山之四附二

石川郎女奉和歌一首

108 吾乎待跡　君之沾計武　足日木能　山之四附二　成益物乎

柿本朝臣人麻呂　従石見国別妻上来時歌

131 石見之海　角乃浦廻乎　浦無等　人社見良目　滷無等　一云、礒無等　人社見良目　能咲八師　浦者無

友　縦画屋師　滷者（一云、礒者）　無鞆　鯨魚取　海辺乎指而　和多豆乃　荒礒乃上尓　香青生　玉藻
息津藻　朝羽振　風社依米　夕羽振流　浪社来縁　浪之共　彼縁此依　玉藻成　依宿之妹乎
（一云、波之伎余思妹之手本乎）　露霜乃　置而之来者　此道乃　八十隈毎　万段　顧為騰　弥遠尓　里者放奴　益
高尓　山毛越来奴　夏草之　念思奈要而　志怒布良武　妹之門将見　靡此山

反歌二首

132 石見乃也　高角山之　木際従　我振袖乎　妹見都良武香

133 小竹之葉者　三山毛清尓　乱友　吾者妹思　別来礼婆

山上憶良臣　罷宴歌一首

337 憶良等者　今者将罷　子将哭　其彼母毛　吾乎将待曾

大宰師大伴卿讃酒歌

338 験無　物乎不念者　一坏乃　濁酒乎　可飲有良師

348 今代尓之　楽有者　来生者　虫尓鳥尓毛　吾羽成奈武

笠女郎贈大伴宿祢家持歌

607 皆人乎　宿与殿金者　打礼杼　君乎之念者　寐不勝鴨

608 不相念　人乎思者　大寺之　餓鬼之後尓　額衝如

山部宿祢赤人反歌二首

924 三吉野乃　象山際乃　木末尓波　幾許毛散和口　鳥之声可聞

925 烏玉之　夜乃深去者　久木生留　清河原尓　知鳥数鳴

志貴皇子懽御歌一首

1418 石激　垂見之上乃　左和良妣乃　毛要出春尓　成来鴨

岡本天皇御製歌一首

1511 暮去者　小倉乃山尓　鳴鹿者　今夜波不鳴　寐宿家良思母

詠水江浦嶋子一首

1740 春日之　霞時尓　墨吉之　岸尓出居而　釣船之　得乎良布見者　古之　事曾所念　水江之　浦嶋児之　堅魚釣　鯛釣矜　及七日　家尓毛不来而　海界乎　過而榜行尓　海若　神之女尓　邂尓　伊許芸趍　相誂良比　言成之賀婆　加吉結　常代尓至　海若　神之宮乃　内隔之　細有殿尓　携

二人入居而　耆不為　死不為而　永世尓　有家留物乎　世間之　愚人乃　吾妹児尓　告而語久
須臾者　家帰而　父母尓　事毛告良比　如明日　吾者来南登　言家礼婆　妹之答久　常世辺　復
変来而　如今　将相跡奈良婆　此篋　開勿勤常　曾己良久尓　堅目師事乎　墨吉尓　還来而　家
見跡　宅毛見金手　里見跡　里毛見金手　恠常　所許尓念久　従家出而　三歳之間尓　垣毛無
家滅目八跡　此筥乎　開而見手歯　如本　家者将有登　玉篋　小披尓　白雲之　自箱出而　常世
辺　棚引去者　立走　叫袖振　反側　足受利四管　頓　情消失奴　若有之　皮毛皺奴　黒有之
髪毛白斑奴　由奈由奈波　気左倍絶而　後遂　寿死祁流　水江之　浦嶋子之　家地見

1883 百礒城之　大宮人者　暇有也　梅乎插頭而　此間集有

2119 恋之久者　形見尓為与登　吾背子我　殖之秋芽子　花咲尓家里

3373 多麻河泊尓　左良須弖豆久利　佐良左良尓　奈仁曾許能児乃　己許太可奈之伎

3384 可都思加能　麻末能手児奈乎　麻許登可聞　和礼尓余須等布　麻末乃弖胡奈乎

4399 宇奈波良尓　霞多奈妣伎　多頭我祢乃　可奈之伎与比波　久尓弊之於毛保由

4400 伊弊於毛負等　伊乎祢受乎礼婆　多頭我奈久　安之弊毛美要受　波流乃可須美尓

右　十九日　兵部少輔大伴宿祢家持作之

日本古典文學大系「萬葉集一、二、三、四」より

六、祝　詞（延喜式）

祈　年　祭

集侍神主・祝部等、諸聞食登宣。（神主・祝部等、共称唯。余宣准此。）

高天原爾神留坐、皇睦神漏伎命・神漏弥命以、天社・国社登称辞竟奉、皇神等能前爾白久、今年二月爾、御年初将賜登為而、皇御孫命宇豆能幣帛乎、朝日能豊逆登爾称辞竟奉久登宣。

御年皇神等能前爾白久、皇神等能依左志奉牟奥津御年乎、手肱爾水沫画垂、向股爾泥画寄弖、取作牟奥津御年乎、八束穂能伊加志穂爾、皇神等能依左志奉者、初穂乎波千穎八百穎爾奉置弖、瓱閉高知、瓱腹満雙弖、汁爾母穎爾母称辞竟奉牟。大野原爾生物者、甘菜・辛菜、青海原住物者、鰭能広物・鰭能狭物、奥津藻葉・辺津藻葉爾至弖爾、御服者、明妙・照妙・和妙・荒妙爾、称辞竟奉牟。御年皇神能前爾、白馬・白猪・白鶏、種々色物乎備奉弖、皇御孫命能宇豆乃幣帛乎、称辞竟奉久登宣。

大御巫能辞竟奉、皇神等能前爾白久、神魂・高御魂・生魂・足魂・玉留魂・大宮乃売・大御膳都神・辞代主登、御名者白而、辞竟奉者、皇御孫命御世乎、手長御世登、堅磐爾常磐爾斎比奉、茂御世爾幸閉奉故、皇吾睦神漏伎命・神漏弥命登、皇御孫命能宇豆乃幣帛乎、称辞竟奉久登宣。

座摩乃御巫乃辞竟奉、皇神等能前爾白久、生井・栄井・津長井・阿須波・婆比支登、御名者白弖、辞竟奉者、皇神能敷坐、下都磐根爾宮柱太知立、高天原爾千木高知弖、皇御孫命乃瑞能御舎乎仕奉弖、天御蔭・日御蔭登隠坐弖、四方国乎安国登平久知食故、皇御孫命能宇豆乃幣帛乎、称辞竟奉久登宣。

御門能御巫能辞竟奉、皇神等能前爾白久、櫛磐間門命・豊磐間門命登、御名者白弖、辞竟奉者、四方能御門爾、湯都磐村能如塞坐弖、朝者御門開奉、夕者御門閉奉弖、疎夫留物能自下往者下乎守、自上往者上乎守、夜能守日能守爾守奉故、皇御孫命能宇豆乃幣帛乎、称辞竟奉久登宣。

生嶋能御巫能辞竟奉、皇神等能前爾白久、生国・足国登、御名者白弖、辞竟奉者、皇神能敷坐嶋能八十嶋者、谷蟆能狭度極、塩沫能留限、狭国者広久、峻国者平久、嶋能八十嶋堕事无、皇神等能依志奉故、皇御孫命能宇豆乃幣帛乎、称辞竟奉久登宣。

辞別、伊勢爾坐天照大御神能大前爾白久、皇神能見霽志坐四方国者、天能壁立極、国能退立限、青雲能靄極、白雲能堕坐向伏限、青海原者、棹柁不干、舟艫能至留極、大海爾舟満都都気弖、自陸往道者、荷緒縛堅弖、磐根木根履佐久弥弖、馬爪至留限、長道无間久立都都気弖、狭国者広久、峻国者平久、遠国者八十綱打挂弖引寄如事、皇大御神能寄奉波、荷前者、皇大御神能大前爾、如横山打積置弖、残乎波平聞看。又皇御孫命御世乎、手長御世登、堅磐爾常磐爾斎比奉、茂御世爾幸閉奉故、皇吾睦神漏伎・神漏弥命登、宇事物頸根衝抜弖、皇御孫命能宇豆乃幣帛乎、称辞竟奉久登宣。

御県爾坐皇神等乃前爾白久、高市・葛木・十市・志貴・山辺・曾布登、御名者白弖、此六御県爾生出、甘菜・辛菜乎持参来弖、皇御孫命能長御膳能遠御膳登聞食故、皇御孫命能宇豆乃幣帛乎、称辞竟奉久登宣。

山口坐皇神等能前爾白久、飛鳥・石寸・忍坂・長谷・畝火・耳无登、御名者白弖、遠山・近山爾生立留大木・小木乎、本末打切弖、持参来弖、皇御孫命能瑞能御舎仕奉弖、天御蔭・日御陰登隠坐弖、四方

国乎、安国登平久知食須我故、皇御孫命能宇豆乃幣帛乎、称辞竟奉久登宣。水分坐皇神等能前爾白久、吉野・宇陀・都祁・葛木登、御名者白弖、辞竟奉者、皇神等能寄志奉牟奥都御年乎、八束穂能伊加志穂爾寄志奉者、皇神等爾、初穂波、穎爾毛汁爾母瓱閉高知、瓱腹満雙弖、称辞竟奉弖、遺乎波皇御孫命能朝御食・夕御食能加牟加比爾、長御食能遠御食登、赤丹穂爾聞食故、皇御孫命能宇豆乃幣帛乎、称辞竟奉久登、諸聞食登宣。

辞別、忌部能弱肩爾太多須支取挂弖、持由麻波利仕奉礼留幣帛乎、神主・祝部等受賜弖、事不過捧持奉登宣。

日本古典文學大系「古事記・祝詞」より

七、古今集

仁和のみかど、みこにおましましける時に、人にわかなたまひける御うた

21 きみがため春の野にいでてわかなつむ我衣手に雪はふりつゝ

はつせにまうづるごとに、やどりける人の家に、ひさしくやどらで、程へて後にいたれりければ、かの家のあるじ、かくさだかになんやどりはあると、いひいだして侍りければ、そこにた

てりける梅の花ををりてよめる　つらゆき
42 ひとはいさ心もしらずふるさとは花ぞむかしのかにゝほひける
なぎさのゐんにてさくらをみてよめる　在原業平朝臣
53 世中にたえてさくらのなかりせば春の心はのどけからまし
花ざかりに京をみやりてよめる　素性法師
56 みわたせば柳桜をこきまぜて宮こぞ春の錦なりける
さくらの花のちるをよめる　きのとものり
84 久方のひかりのどけき春の日にしづ心なく花のちるらむ
はるのうたとてよめる　つらゆき
94 みわ山をしかもかくすか春霞人にしられぬ花やさくらむ
題しらず　小野小町
113 花の色はうつりにけりないたづらに我身世にふるながめせしまに

秋立つ日よめる　藤原敏行朝臣
169 あききぬとめにはさやかに見えねども風のをとにぞおどろかれぬる

これさだのみこの家の哥合によめる　大江千里
193 月みればちゞにものこそかなしけれわが身ひとつの秋にはあらねど

これさだのみこの家の哥合のうた　たゞみね
214 山里は秋こそことにわびしけれしかのなくねにめをさましつゝ

よみ人しらず
215 奥山に紅葉ふみわけ鳴く鹿のこゑきく時ぞ秋はかなしき

冬の哥とてよめる　源宗于朝臣
315 山ざとは冬ぞさびしさまさりける人めも草もかれぬとおもへば

やまとのくににまかれりける時に、雪のふりけるをみてよめる　坂上これのり
332 あさぼらけありあけの月とみるまでによしののさとにふれるしら雪

題しらず　読人しらず
343 わがきみは千世にやちよにさゞれいしのいはほとなりてこけのむすまで

題しらず　　　　　　　　　　　　　　　　　　　　読人しらず

469 ほとゝぎすなくやさ月のあやめぐさあやめもしらぬこひもする哉

題しらず　　　　　　　　　　　　　　　　　　　　小野小町

552 思ひつゝぬればや人のみえつらん夢としりせばさめざらましを

やまひしてよはくなりにける時よめる　　　　　　なりひらの朝臣

861 つゐにゆく道とはかねてきゝしかどきのふけふとはおもはざりしを

日本古典文學大系「古今和歌集」より

八、伊勢物語

むかし、おとこありけり。そのおとこ、身をえうなき物に思なして、京にはあらじ、あづまの方にすむべきくにもとめにとてゆきけり。もとより友とする人ひとりふたりしていきけり。みちしれる人もなくて、まどひいきけり。みかはのくに、やつはしといふ所にいたりぬ。そこをやつはしといひけるは、水ゆく河のくもでなれば、はしをやつわたせるによりてなむやつはしといひける。そのさはのほとりの木のかげにおりゐて、かれいひくひけり。そのさはにかきつばたいとおもしろく

さきたり。それを見て、ある人のいはく、かきつばたといふいつもじをくのかみにすへて、たびの心をよめといひければ、よめる。

　から衣きつゝなれにしつましあればはる〴〵きぬるたびをしぞ思

とよめりければ、みな人、かれいひのうへになみだおとしてほとびにけり。

ゆき〳〵て、するがのくににいたりぬ。うつの山にいたりて、わがいらむとするみちは、いとくらうほそきに、つたかえではしげり、物心ぼそく、すゞろなるめを見ることと思ふに、す行者あひたり。かかるみちはいかでかいまするといふを見れば、見しひとなりけり。京に、その人の御もとにとて、ふみかきてつく。

　するがなるうつの山べのうつゝにもゆめにも人にあはぬなりけり

ふじの山を見れば、さ月のつごもりに、雪いとしろうふれり。

　時しらぬ山はふじのねいつとてかかのこまだらにゆきのふるらん

その山は、こゝにたとへば、ひえの山をはたちばかりかさねあげたらんほどして、なりはしほじりのやうになんありける。

猶ゆき〳〵て、武蔵のくにとしもつふさのくにとの中に、いとおほきなる河あり。それをすみだ河といふ。その河のほとりにむれゐておもひやれば、かぎりなくとをくもきにけるかなとわびあへるに、わたしもり、はやふねにのれ、日もくれぬといふに、のりてわたらんとするに、みな人物わびしくて、京に思ふ人なきにしもあらず。さるおりしも、しろきとりのはしとあしとあかき、しぎのおほきさなる、みづのうへにあそびつゝいををくふ。京には見えぬとりなれば、みな人見しらず。わたしもりにとひければ、これなん宮こどりといふをきゝて、

名にしおはばいざ事とはむ宮こ鳥わがおもふ人はありやなしやと
とよめりければ、舟こぞりてなきにけり。

日本古典文學大系「竹取物語・伊勢物語・大和物語」より

九、土佐日記

をとこもすなる日記といふものを、をむなもしてみんとてするなり。それのとしのしはすのはつかあまりひとひのひのいぬのときに、かどです。そのよし、いささかにものにかきつく。
あるひと、あがたのよとせいつとせはてて、れいのことどもみなしをへて、げゆなどとりて、すむたちよりいでて、ふねにのるべきところへわたる。かれこれ、しるしらぬ、おくりす。としごろよくくらべつるひとぐ〵なん、わかれがたくおもひて、日しきりにとかくしつゝ、のゝしるうちによふけぬ。

廿七日。おほつよりうらどをさしてこぎいづ。かくあるうちに、京にてうまれたりしをんなご、くににてにはかにうせにしかば、このごろのいでたちいそぎをみれど、なにごともいはず。京へかへるに、をんなごのなきのみぞかなしびこふる。あるひとぐ〵もえたへず。このあひだに、あるひとのかきていだせるうた、

みやこへとおもふをもののかなしきはかへらぬひとのあればなりけり

また、あるときには、

あるものとわすれつゝなほなきひとをいづらととふぞかなしかりける

といひけるあひだに、かこのさきといふところに、かみのはらから、またことひと、これかれさけなにともておひきて、いそにおりゐて、わかれがたきことをいふ。かみのたちのひと〴〵のなかに、このきたるひと〴〵ぞ、こころあるやうにはいはれほのめく。かくわかれがたくいひて、かのひと〴〵のくちあみももろもちにて、このうみべにて、になひいだせるうた、

をしとおもふひとやとまるとあしがものうちむれてこそわれはきにけれ

といひてありければ、いといたくめでて、ゆくひとのよめりける、

さをさせどそこひもしらぬわたつみのふかきこゝろをきみにみるかな

といふあひだに、かぢとりもののあはれもしらで、おのれしさけをくらひつれば、はやくいなんとて、しほみちぬ、かぜもふきぬべし、とさわげば、ふねにのりなんとす。このをりに、あるひと〴〵、をりふしにつけて、からうたども、ときににつかはしきいふ。また、あるひと、にしぐになれど、かひうたなどいふ。かくうたふに、ふなやかたのちりもちり、そらゆくくももたゞよひぬ、とぞいふなる。こよひうらどにとまる。ふぢはらのときざね、たちばなのすゑひら、ことひと〴〵おひきたり。

日本古典文學大系「土左日記・かげろふ日記・和泉式部日記・更級日記」より

十、日本霊異記

沙門誦持方広大乗沈海不溺縁

諸楽京有一大僧。名未詳也。僧常誦於方広経典、即俗貸銭、蓄養妻子。一女子嫁、別住夫家。帝姫阿陪天皇代之時、聟任於奥国椽。則舅僧貸銭廿貫、為装束、向於所任之国。歴歳余、識銭一倍、僅償本銭、未償利銭。弥逕年月、猶徴乞之。聟竊懐嫌而作是念、求便殺舅。々不知、猶平心而乞。聟語舅曰、将共奥。舅聞之往、乗船度奥。聟与船人、同心謀悪、縛僧四枝、擲陥海中、往語妻曰、汝之父僧、欲瞬汝面、率共度来。忽値荒浪、駅船沈海、大徳溺流、救取無便。終漂沈亡、但我僅活耳。其女聞之、大哀哭言、無幸亡父、片図失宝。我別知之。能見父儀、寧視底玉、亦得父骨。哀哉痛哉。僧沈海、至心読誦方広経、海水凹開、踞底不溺。逕二日二夜後、他船人向於奥国而度。見之縄端泛、有於海而漂留。船人取縄牽之、忽僧上。形色如常。於是船人大怪問之、汝誰。答之、我某、我遭賊盗、繋縛陥海。又問、師何有要術故、沈水不死。答、我常誦持方広大乗。其威神力、何更疑之。唯聟姓名、向他不顕。具我泊奥。船人随冀、送之於奥。彼聟奥国而為陥舅、聊備斎食、供於三宝。舅僧展転乞食、偶値法事、有於白度之例、匿面而居、受其供養。聟椽自捧於布施、献於衆僧。於是於海中僧、申手受施行。椽見之、目漂青面赫然、驚恐而隠。法師含咲、不瞋而忍、終後不顕乎彼悪事。是沈海水汚不溺、毒魚不呑、身命不亡。誠知、大乗威験、諸仏加護。賛曰、美哉不挙

彼悪、猶能忍之。寔斯法師、鴻立忍辱高行。所以長阿含経云、以怨報怨、如草滅火、以慈報怨、如水滅火者、其斯謂歟矣。

日本古典文學大系「日本靈異記」より

十一、枕草子

にくきもの　いそぐ事あるをりにきてながごとするまらうど。あなづりやすき人ならば、後にとてもやりつべけれど、さすがに心はづかしき人、いとにくくむつかし。すずりにかみのいりてすられたる。また、すみの中に、いしのきしきしときしみなりたる。

俄かにわづらふ人のあるに、げんざもとむるに、れいある所にはなくて、ほかに尋ねありくほど、いと待ちどほに久しきに、からうじてまちつけて、よろこびながらかぢせさするに、この頃もののけにあづかりて、こうじにけるにや、ゐるままにすなはちねぶりごゑなる、いとにくし。

なでふことなき人の、ゑがちにて物いたういひたる。火をけの火、すびつなどに、手のうらうち返しうち返し、おしのべなどしてあぶりをる者。いつかわかやかなる人など、さはしたりし。おいばみたる者こそ、ひをけのはたにあしをさへもたげて、物いふままにおしすりなどはすらめ。さやうのものは、人のもとにきて、ゐんとする所を、まづあふぎしてこなたかなたあふぎちらして、ちりはきすて、ゐもさだまらずひろめきて、かりぎぬのまへまきいれてもゐるべし。かかることは、

いふかひなき者のきはにやとおもへど、すこしよろしきもののしきぶのたいふなどいひしがせしなり。

また、酒のみてあめき、くちをさぐり、ひげあるものはそれをなで、さかづきこと人にとらするほどのけしき、いみじうにくしとみゆ。また、のめといふなるべし、身ぶるひをし、かしらふり、くちわきをさへひきたれて、わらはべのこふ殿にまゐりてなどうたふやうにする、それはしも、まことによき人のし給ひしを見しかば、心づきなしとおもふなり。

物うらやみし、身のうへなげき、人のうへいひ、つゆちりのこともゆかしがり、きかまほしうして、いひしらせぬをばゑんじ、そしり、また、わづかにききえたることをば、我もとよりしりたることのやうに、こと人にもかたりしらぶるもいとにくし。

物きかむと思ふほどになくちご。からすのあつまりてとびちがひ、さめきなきたる。

しのびてくる人見しりてほゆるいぬ。あながちなる所にかくしふせたる人の、いびきしたる。また、しのびくる所に、ながえぼうしして、さすがに人に見えじとまどひいるほどに、物につきさはりて、そよろといはせたる。いよすなどかけたるにうちかづきて、さらさらとならしたるも、いとにくし。もかうのすは、まして、こはじのうちおかるるおといとしるし。それも、やをらひきあげているは、さらにならず。やり戸をあらくたてあくるもいとあやし。すこしもたぐるやうにしてあくるは、なりやはする。あしうあくれば、さうじなどもごほめかしうほとめくこそしるけれ。

ねぶたしとおもひてふしたるに、かのほそごゑにわびしげになのりて、かほのほどにとびありく。はかぜさへその身のほどにあるこそいとにくけれ。

きしめく車にのりてありく者。みみもきかぬにやあらんといとにくし。わがのりたるは、その車

のぬしさへにくし。また、物語するに、さし出でして我ひとりさいまくる者。すべてさしいでは、わらはもおとなもいとにくし。あからさまにきたるこども・わらはべを、みいれらうたがりて、をかしきものとらせなどするに、ならひて常にきつつ、ゐ入りててうどうちちらしぬる、いとにくし。

家にても宮づかへ所にても、あはでありなんとおもふ人のきたるに、そらねをしたるを、わがもとにあるもの、おこしによりきて、いぎたなしとおもひがほにひきゆるがしたる、いとにくし。いままゐりのさしこえて、物しりがほにをしへやうなる事いひうしろみたる、いとにくし。

わがしる人にてある人の、はやう見し女のことほめいひ出でなどするも、程へたることなれど、なほにくし。まして、さしあたりたらんこそおもひやらるれ。されど、なかなかさしもあらぬなどもありかし。

はなひてずもんする。おほかた、人の家のをとこしゅうならでは、たかくはなひたる、いとにくし。のみもいとにくし。きぬのしたにをどりありきてもたぐるやうにする。いぬのもろ声にながながとなきあげたる、まがまがしくさへにくし。

あけていでいる所たてぬ人、いとにくし。

日本古典文學大系「枕草子・紫式部日記」より

十二、源氏物語

わらはやみにわづらひたまひて、よろづに、まじなひ・かぢなど、まゐらせたまへど、しるしなくて、あまたゝびおこりたまへば、ある人、「きたやまになむ、なにがしでらといふところに、かしこきおこなひ人侍る。こぞのなつも、世におこりて、ひとぐ〳〵、まじなひわづらひしを、やがて、とゞむるたぐひ、あまた侍りき。しゝこらかしつる時は、うたて侍るを、とくこそ心みさせ給はめ」など、きこゆれば、めしにつかはしたるに、「おいかゞまりて、むろの外にもまかでず」と、申したれば、「いかゞはせむ。いとしのびてものせん」と、の給ひて、御ともに、むつましき四五人ばかりして、まだ暁に、おはす。やゝ、ふかういる所なりけり。三月のつごもりなれば、京の花ざかりは、みなすぎにけり。山の桜は、まださかりにて、入もておはするまゝに、霞のたゝずまひも、をかしう見ゆれば、かゝるありきも、ならひ給はず、所せき御身にて、めづらしうおぼされけり。

寺のさまも、いとあはれなり。みねたかく、ふかきいはの中にぞ、ひじり入ゐたりける。のぼり給ひて、たれともしらせ給はず、いと、いたうやつれ給へれど、しるき御さまなれば、「あな、かしこや。ひとひ、めし侍りしにや、おはしますらん。いまは、この世の事をおもひたまへねば、げむがたのおこなひも、すてわすれて侍るを、いかで、かうおはしましつらむ」と、おどろきさわぎ

て、うちゑみつゝ見たてまつる。いとたふときだいとこなりけり。さるべきものつくりて、すかせたてまつり、かぢなどまゐるほど、日たかくさしあがりぬ。すこしたちいでつゝみわたしたまへば、たかきところにて、こゝかしこ、そう坊ども、あらはにみおろさる。「たゞ、このつゞらをりのしもに、おなじこしばなれど、うるはしうしわたして、きよげなるや・らうなどつゞけて、こだちいとよしあるは、なに人のすむにか」と、とひたまへば、御ともなる人、「これなん、なにがしそうづの、このふたとせこもり侍るかたに侍りける」「こゝろはづかしき人、すむなるところにこそあなれ、あやしうも、あまりやつしけるかな。きゝもこそすれ」などの給ふ。きよげなるわらはなど、あまたいできて、あかたてまつり、花をりなどするも、あらはにみゆ。

日も、いとながきに、つれ〴〵なれば、ゆふぐれのいたうかすみたるにまぎれて、かのこしばがきのもとにたちいで給ふ。人々は、かへし給ひて、これみつのあそむと、のぞきたまへば、たゞ、このにしおもてにしも、ぢ仏すゑたてまつりておこなふ、あまなりけり。すだれすこしあげて、花たてまつるめり。中のはしらによりゐて、けふそくのうへにきやうをおきて、いと、なやましげによみゐたるあま君、たゞ人とみえず。四十余ばかりにて、いとしろうふくらかに、まみの程、かみのうつくしげにそがれたるすゑも、「中〳〵、ながきよりも、こよなう、いまめかしきものかな」と、あはれに見給ふ。きよげなるおとなふたりばかり、さては、わらはべぞ、いでいりあそぶ。中に、「十ばかりにやあらむ」と見えて、しろききぬ、山ぶきなどの、なれたるきて、はしりきたる女ご、見えつるこどもに、にるべうもあらず、いみじく、おひさき見えて、うつくしげなるかたち

なり。かみは、あふぎをひろげたるやうに、ゆら〳〵として、かほは、いとあかくすりなしてたてり。「なに事ぞや。わらはべと、はらだち給へるか」とて、あま君の、みあげたるに、すこし、おぼえたる所あれば、「子なめり」と、見給ふ。「すゞめのこを、いぬきがにがしつる、ふせごのうちに、こめたりつるものを」とて、「いとくちをし」とおもへり。此、ゐたるおとな、「れいの、心なしの、かゝるわざをして、さいなまるゝこそ、いと心づきなけれ。いづかたへか、まかりぬる。いと、をかしう、やう〳〵なりつるものを。からすなどもこそ、見つくれ」とて、たちてゆく。かみゆるゝかにいとながく、めやすき人なめり。少納言のめのとゝぞ、人いふめるは、此子のうしろみなるべし。あま君、「いで、あな、をさなや。いふかひなう、ものし給ふかな。おのが、かく、けふ、あすにおぼゆるいのちをば、なにともおぼしたらで、すゞめしたひ給ふほどよ。「つみうることぞ」と、つねにきこゆるを。心うく」とて、「こちや」といへば、ついゐたり。つらつき、いとらうたげにて、まゆのわたり、うちけぶり、いはけなくかいやりたるひたひつき、かむざし、いみじううつくし。「ねびゆかむさま、ゆかしき人かな」と、めとまり給ふ。さるは、「かぎりなう、心をつくしきこゆる人に、いとようにたてまつれるが、まもらるゝなりけり」と、おもふにも涙ぞおつる。あま君、かみをかきなでつゝ、「けづる事をうるさがり給へど、をかしの御ぐしや。いと、はかなうものし給ふこそ、あはれに、うしろめたけれ。かばかりになれば、いと、かゝらぬ人もあるものを。こ姫君は、十二にて殿におくれ給ひし程、いみじう、ものは、おもひしり給へりしぞかし。たゞいま、おのれ、見すてたてまつらば、いかで、世におはせむとすらむ」とて、いみじくなくを、見給ふも、すゞろにかなし。をさな心ちにも、さすがに、うちまもりて、ふしめになりてうつぶし

たるに、こぼれかゝりたるかみ、つやつやとめでたう見ゆ。

おひたたむありかもしらぬわか草をおくらす露ぞきえむそらなき

又、ゐたるおとな、「げに」と、うちなきて、

はつ草のおひゆく末もしらぬまにいかでか露のきえむとすらん

ときこゆるほどに、僧都、あなたよりきて、「こなたは、あらはにや侍らむ。けふしも、はしにおはしましけるかな。此、かみのひじりの坊に、源氏中将、わらはやみまじなひに、ものし給ひけるを、たゞいまなむ、ききつけ侍る。いみじう、しのび給ひければ、しり侍らで、こゝに侍りながら、御とぶらひにもまうでざりけるに」と、の給へば、「あな、いみじや。いと、あやしきさまを、人やみつらん」とて、すだれおろしつ。「この世に、のゝしり給ふひかる源氏。かゝるついでに、見たてまつり給はんや。世をすてたるほふしの心ちにも、いみじう、よのうれへわすれ、よはひのぶる、人の御ありさまなり。いで、御せうそこきこえむ」とて、たつおとすれば、かへり給ひぬ。

日本古典文學大系「源氏物語一」より

十三、今昔物語

身貧男去妻成摂津守妻語第五

今昔、京ニ極テ身貧キ生者有ケリ。相知タル人モ無ク、父母・類親モ無クテ、行宿ル所モ无カリケレバ、人ノ許ニ寄テ被仕ケレドモ、其レモ聊ナル思モ無カリケレバ、若シ宜キ所々モ有ルト、所々ニ寄ケレドモ、只同様ニノミ有ケレバ、宮仕ヘヲモ否不為デ、可為キ様モ無クテ有ケルニ、其ノ妻年若クシテ形チ・有様宜クテ、心風流也ケレバ、此貧キ夫ニ随テ有ケル程ニ、夫万ニ思ヒ煩テ、妻ニ語ヒケル様、「世ニ有ラム限ハ、此テ諸共ニコソハ思ツルニ、日ニ副テハ貧サノミ増ルハ、若シ共ニ有ルガ悪キカト、各テ試ムト思フヲ何ニ」ト云ケレバ、妻、「我レハ更ニ然モ不思ハズ。只前ノ世ノ報ナレバ、互ニ餓死ナム事ヲ可期シ、ト思ツレドモ、其ニ、此ク云フ甲斐无クノミ有レバ、実ニ共ニ有ルガ悪キカト、別レテモ試ヨカシ」ト云ケレバ、男、「現ニ」ト思テ、互ニ云契テ、泣々ク別レニケリ。

其ノ後、妻ハ年モ若ク形チ・有様モ宜カリケレバ、□ノ□ト云ケル人ノ許ニ寄テ被仕ケル程ニ、女ノ心極テ風流也ケレバ、哀レニ思テ仕ケル程ニ、其ノ人ノ妻失ニケレバ、此ノ女ヲ親ク呼ビ仕ケル程ニ、傍ニ臥セナドシテ思不㥁カラズ思エケレバ、然様ニテ過ケル程ニ、後ハ偏ニ此ノ女ヲ妻トシテ有ケレバ、万ヲ任セテノミゾ過ケル。

而ル間、摂津ノ守成ニケリ。女弥ヨ微妙キ有様ニテナム年来過ケルニ、本ノ夫ハ妻ヲ離レテ試ムト思ケルニ、

其ノ後ハ弥ヨ身弊クノミ成リ増テ、遂ニ京ニモ否不居デ、摂津ノ国ノ辺ニ迷ヒ行テ、偏ニ田夫ニ成テ人ニ被仕ケレドモ、□ニ下衆ノ為ル田作リ・畠作リ・木ナド伐ナド様事ヲモ、不習ヌ心地ナレバ、否不為デ有ケルニ、仕ケル者、此ノ男難波ノ浦ニ葦ヲ苅ニ遣タリケレバ、行テ葦ヲ苅ケルニ、彼ノ摂津ノ守、其ノ妻ヲ具シテ摂津ノ国ニ下ケルニ、難波辺ニ車ヲ留メテ逍遥セサセテ、多ク郎等・眷属ト共ニ、物食ヒ酒呑ナドシテ遊ビ戯ケルニ、其ノ守ノ北ノ方ハ車ニシテ、女房ナドゝ共難波ノ浦ノ可咲ク謚キ事ナド見興ジケルニ、其ノ浦ニ葦苅ル下衆ドモ多カリケリ。其ノ中ニ下衆ナレドモ故有テ哀レニ見ユル男一人有リ。

守ノ北ノ方此レヲ見テ吉ク護レバ、恠ク「我ガ昔ノ夫ニ似タル者カナ」ト思フニ、僻目カ□思テ強ニ見レバ、「正シク其レ也」ト見ル。奇異キ姿ニテ葦ヲ苅立テルヲ、尚、「心踈クテモ有ケル者カナ。何ナル前ノ世ノ報ニテ此ルラム」ト思フニモ、涙泛レドモ、然ル気无クテ人呼テ、「彼ノ葦苅ル下衆ノ中ニ、然ゝ有ル男召セ」ト云ケレバ、使走リ行テ、「彼ノ男御車ニ召ス」ト云ケレバ、男思ヒモ不懸ネバ、奇異クテ仰ギ立テルヲ、使、「疾ク参レ」ト音ヲ高クシテ恐セバ、葦ヲ苅リ弃テ、鎌ヲ腎ニ着シテ、車ノ前ニ参タリ。

北ノ方近クテ吉ク見レバ、現ニ其レ也。土ニ穢テタ黒ナル袖モ无キ麻布ノ帷ノ膕本ナルヲ着タリ。帽子様ナル烏帽子ヲ被テ、顔ニモ手足ニモ土付テ、穢気ナル事無限シ。膕・脛ニハ蛭ト云フ物食付テ血肉也。北ノ方此レヲ見ルニ、心踈ク思エテ、人ヲ以テ物食ハセ、酒ナド呑スレバ、車ニ指向テ糸吉ク食居ル顔糸心踈シ。然テ車ニ有ル女房ニ、「彼葦苅ル下衆共ノ中ニ、此レガ故有テ哀レ気ニ見エツルニ、糸惜ケレバ也」トテ、衣ヲ一ツ、車ノ内ヨリ「此レ彼ノ男ニ給ヘ」トテ取スルニ、紙ノ端ニ此ク書テ、衣ニ具シテ給フ、

アシカラジトヲモヒテコソハワカレシカ、ナドカナニハノウラニシモスム　ト。

男衣ヲ給ハリテ、思ヒ不懸ヌ事ナレバ、「奇異」ト思テ見レバ、紙ノ端ニ被書タル物ノ有リ。此ヲ取テ見ルニ、此ク被書タレバ、男、「早ウ、此ハ我ガ昔ノ妻也ケリ」ト思ニ、「我ガ宿世糸悲ク耻カシ」ト思エテ、「御硯ヲ

給ハラム」ト云ケレバ、硯ヲ給ヒタレバ、此ク書テナム奉タリケル、

キミナクテアシカリケリトオモフニハ、イトヾナニハノウラゾスミウキ　ト。

北ノ方此レヲ見テ、弥ヨ哀ニ悲ク思ケリ。然テ男ハ、葦不苅ズシテ走リ隠レニケリ。其ノ後、北ノ方、此ノ事ヲ此彼人ニ語ル事無クテ止ニケリ。

然レバ皆、前ノ世ノ報ニテ有ル事ヲ不知シテ、愚ニ身ヲ恨ル也。

此レハ其ノ北ノ方、年ナド老テ後ニ語ケルニヤ。其レヲ聞継テ世ノ末ニテ此ク語リ伝ヘタルヲトヤ。

日本古典文學大系「今昔物語五」より

十四、保元物語

父為義が立たる跡に居かはりて、畏てぞ候ひける。其気色まことにあたりを払てぞみえし。新院母屋の御簾を引ほころばして叡覧あり。竜顔頗醫にいたらせ給。左大臣殿大床に候ひ給ひけるが、はるかにみいだして咲まけて、「為朝既に参りて候。誠にまことにゆゝしく候。一人当千とは是をこそ申らめ」とて、もつての外にぞ御感ありける。「為朝合戦の次第はからひ申せ」と仰くださる。畏て申上けるは、「為朝幼少より鎮西に居住つかまつりて、合戦にあふこと既二十度あまり卅度に及べり。或は敵を落し、或は敵におとされ、しかる間毎度かつにのる先蹤をかんがふるに、夜うちにしかず。天の明ざらんさきに、内裏高松殿に押寄て、三方より火をかけ、一方よりせめむずる

に、火をのがるるものは矢をのがるべからず。矢をのがるゝものは火をのがるべからず。舎兄にて候義朝計こそていたく防候はむずれ。それをば為朝まんなか仕ていとをしなん。其外の奴原をば、太刀引ぬきてまんなかにかけ入、とをからんものをば、さしおよびて手打にきつてはとをし、なぎおとし、はらひおとし、ちかきものをは、かひつかむでひつさげて、さげきりにきつておとし、きつてはすて、或はくびねぢきり、かいなを引ぬき、ひきさきなどしてはせめぐらば、行疫神はいさしらず、誰かは面をむくべき。まして又清盛などがへろ〳〵矢はものゝかずにてや候べき。その時定て行幸他所へなり候はんずらん。御こしに矢をまいらすべし。是為朝がはなつ矢にて候まし。天照太神・正八幡宮のはなたせ給ふ御矢也。駕輿丁矢におそれて御こしを打捨たてまつりにげちりなむ。その時行幸を御所へなしたてまつる事をめぐらすべからず」とことばをはなちものげもなく申ければ、左大臣殿、「此条あらぎなり。臆持なし。若気のいたす処か。夜うちなどいふ事は、十騎廿騎のわたくしいくさなどの事也。さすがに主上・上皇のくにあらそひに、夜うちなんどしかるべからず。就中今度の合戦に、源平両家の名を得たる兵共、数をつくして両方に引わかるゝ。故実を存、互に思慮をめぐらすべし。用意おろかにしてははなはだ叶べからず。凡合戦といふは、はかりことをもつてほんとし、勢をもつて先とす。しかるに今院中にめさるゝ所の軍兵共、もつていくばくならず。卒尓に発向せむ事、しかるべきともおぼえず。そのうへ南都の衆徒、信実・玄実以下、吉野十津河のさし矢三町、遠矢八丁のものども、すでに千余騎にて今夜富家殿の見参に入。明日卯辰の時に此御所へまいるべし。しからばかのともがらを相具して、ゆきむかつて合戦あるべし。物さはがしきはかならずこうくわひあるべき也。又明日院司・公卿・殿上人もよほして且はまつりことをおこなはせべし。もしまいらざらん輩におゐては、速にめしとりて死罪におこなふべし。かう

べを刎事両三人におよばんか、などか参らざらん。夜のほど此御所を能々守護して、南都の衆徒をあいまつべし」とおほせられければ、為朝うけたまはりあへず罷出けるが、「信実・玄実をまたんこと、勢をとゝのへて御らんせんか。勝負をけつせんには時剋あひのぶべし。義朝はさしも合戦に心得たるものにてあるものを。それも人に上手えられんとはよもおもはじ。夜うちにせんとぞはからふらん。明日までものぶべくはこそ、指矢三丁も大切ならめ。いさかひはてゝのちぎり木にてぞあらん。あはれ節会・印奏・除目なんど公事の奉行にははにぬものを。合戦のはかりことをば為朝にまかせ御覧ぜよかし。くちおしきかなや。只今敵におそはれて、御方の兵あはて迷はむよ」とたからかにのゝしり罷出ぬ。

日本古典文學大系「保元・平治物語」より

十五、新古今集

はるたつ心をよみ侍りける　　摂政太政大臣

1 み吉野は山もかすみてしら雪のふりにし里に春はきにけり

五十首歌たてまつりし時　　宮内卿

4 かきくらし猶古郷の雪の中に跡こそみえね春はきにけり

百首歌たてまつりし時　藤原家隆朝臣

17谷川のうち出づる浪も声たてつ鶯さそへ春の山風

詩をつくらせて歌に合はせ侍りしに、水郷春望といふ事を　藤原秀能

26夕着夜塩みちくらし難波江のあしの若葉にこゆるしらなみ

晩霞といふ事をよめる　後徳大寺左大臣

35なごの海の霞のまより詠むればいる日をあらふ奥津白なみ

をのこども、詩を作りて歌に合はせ侍りしに、水郷春望といふ事を　太上天皇

36見渡せば山もと霞むみなせ川夕べは秋と何思ひけん

守覚法親王、五十首歌よませ侍りけるに　藤原定家朝臣

38春の夜の夢のうきはしとだえして嶺にわかるゝよこ雲のそら

百首歌中に　式子内親王

149花は散り其の色となく詠むればむなしき空に春雨ぞふる

入道前関白、右大臣に侍りける時、百首歌よませ侍りける郭公歌　　皇太后宮大夫俊成

201 昔思ふ草の庵のよるの雨になみだなそへそ山郭公

だいしらず　　寂蓮法師

361 さびしさは其の色としもなかりけりまき立つ山の秋のゆふ暮

西行法師

362 心なき身にもあはれはしられけりしぎ立つ沢の秋の夕暮

西行法師、すゝめて、百首歌よませ侍りけるに　　藤原定家朝臣

363 み渡せば花ももみぢもなかりけり浦の苫屋の秋の夕ぐれ

崇徳院に百首歌たてまつりけるに　　左京大輔顕輔

413 秋風にたなびく雲のたえまよりもれいづる月の影のさやけさ

擣衣のこゝろを　　藤原雅経

483 み吉野の山の秋風さ夜深けて古郷さむく衣うつなり

五十首歌たてまつりし時　　寂蓮法師

491 急雨の露もまだひぬ槇の葉に霧立ちのぼる秋の夕ぐれ

百首歌たてまつりし時　摂政太政大臣

518 蛩鳴くや霜夜のさむしろに衣かたしきひとりかもねん

百首歌たてまつりしとき　藤原定家朝臣

617 駒とめて袖打はらふかげもなしさののわたりの雪の夕ぐれ

百首歌の中に忍恋　式子内親王

1034 玉のをよ絶えなばたえねながらへば忍ぶる事のよわりもぞする

題不知　小侍従

1191 待つ宵にふけ行く鐘のこゑきけばあかぬ別れの鳥は物かは

住吉歌合に、山を　太上天皇

1633 おく山のおどろがしたもふみ分けて道あるよぞと人にしらせん

題不知　清輔朝臣

1843 ながらへば又此のごろやしのばれんうしとみしよぞ今は恋しき

日本古典文學大系「新古今和歌集」より

十六、宇治拾遺物語

袴垂合保昌事

昔、袴だれとて、いみじき盗人の大将軍ありけり。十月ばかりに、絹の用なりければ、衣すこしまうけむとて、さるべき所々うかゞひありきけるに、夜中ばかりに、人みなしづまりはてゝのち、月のおぼろなるに、きぬあまたきたりけるぬしの、指貫のそばはさみて、きぬの狩衣めきたるきて、たゞひとり、笛ふきて、行もやらずねりゆけば、あはれ、これこそ、われにきぬえさせむとて出たる人なめりと思て、走かゝりて、きぬをはがむと思ふに、あやしく物のおそろしくおぼえければ、そひて、二三町ばかりいけども、我に人こそつきたれと思たるけしきもなし。いよ〳〵笛を吹ていけば、試むと思て、足をたかくしてはしりよりたるに、笛をふきながらみかへりたるけしき、とりかゝるべくとおぼえざりければ、走のきぬ。

かやうにあまたゝび、とざまかうざまにするに、露ばかりもさはぎたるけしきなし。希有の人かなと思て、十余ちやうばかり、ぐしてゆく。さりとてあらんやはと思ひて、刀をぬきてはしりかゝりたるときに、そのたび、笛を吹やみて、たち帰て、「こはなにものぞ」とゝふに、心もうせて、吾にもあらでつい居られぬ。又、「いかなる者ぞ」とゝへば、今はにぐともよも逃さじとおぼえければ、「ひはぎにさぶらふ」といへば、「何ものぞ」とゝへば、「あざな袴だれとなんいはれさぶらふ」

ところたふれば、「さいふものありときくぞ。あやうげに、希有のやつかな」といひて、「ともにまうでこ」とばかりいひかけて、又おなじやうに、笛吹てゆく。

この人のけしき、今はにぐとも、よもにがさじとおぼえければ、鬼に神とられたるやうにて、ともに行ほどに、家に行つきぬ。いづこぞと思へば、摂津前司保昌といふ人なりけり。家のうちによびいれて、綿あつき衣一を給はりて、「きぬの用あらんときは、参りて申せ。心もしらざらん人にとりかゝりて、汝あやまちすな」とありしこそ、あさましく、むくつけく、おそろしかりしか。いみじかりし人のありさまなり。とらへられて後かたりける。

日本古典文學大系「宇治拾遺物語」より

十七、徒　然　草

第十一段

神無月の比、栗栖野といふ所を過て、ある山里にたづね入事侍しに、遙なる苔のほそ道をふみわけて、心ぼそくすみなしたる庵あり。木の葉にうづもるゝかけ樋のしづくならでは、露おとなふものなし。閼伽棚に菊・紅葉など折ちらしたる、さすがにすむ人のあればなるべし。

かくてもあられけるよと、あはれに見るほどに、かなたの庭におほきなる柑子の木の、枝もたわゝになりたるが、まはりをきびしく囲ひたりしこそ、すこしことさめて、この木なからましかばと

おぼえしか。

第二十二段

なに事もふるき世のみぞしたはしき。今やうは、無下にいやしくこそ成ゆくめれ。かの木の道のたくみのつくれる、うつくしきうつは物も、古代の姿こそをかしと見ゆれ。

文の詞などぞ、昔の反古どもはいみじき。たゞいふ言葉も、口をしうこそなりもてゆくなれ。いにしへは、「車もたげよ」、「火かゝげよ」とこそいひしを、今やうの人は「もてあげよ」、「かきあげよ」といふ。「主殿寮人数だて」といふべきを、「たちあかししろくせよ」といひ、最勝講の御聴聞所なるをば、「御かうのろ」とこそいふを、「かうろ」といふ、くちをしとぞ、ふるき人はおほせられし。

第百九段

高名の木のぼりといひしをのこ、人をおきてて、たかき木にのぼせて梢をきらせしに、いとあやふくみえしほどはいふ事もなくて、おるゝときに、軒長ばかりに成て、「あやまちすな。心しておりよ」と言葉をかけ侍しを、「かばかりになりては、飛おるともおりなん。如何にかくいふぞ」と申侍しかば、「その事に候。めくるめき、枝あやふきほどは、おのれがおそれ侍れば申さず。あやまちは、やすき所に成て、必仕る事に候」といふ。

あやしき下﨟なれども、聖人のいましめにかなへり。鞠も、かたき所を蹴出してのち、やすくおもへば、必落と侍るやらん。

日本古典文學大系「方丈記・徒然草」より

十八、沙石集

正直ノ女人ノ事

近比奥州ノ或山寺ノ別当ナリケル僧、本尊ヲ造立セント年来思ヒ企テヽ、金ヲ五十両守ノ袋ニ入テ、頸ニカケテ上洛シケル程ニ、駿河国原中ノ宿ニテ、ヒル水アミケル家ニテ、此袋ヲ忘レテ、次日ノ夕方菊河ニテ、思出タリケリ。口惜浅猿シカリケレドモ不及力。「今ハ人ノ物ニゾ成リヌラム。カヘリテ尋ヌトモアラジ」ト、思テ上洛シテ、空下向セムモ本意ナク覚ヘテ、如形本尊ヲ奉書テゾ下ケル。サテ原中ノ宿ニテ、下人ニ、「此家トコソオボユレ」ナド云テ、見入テトヲリケルヲ、家ノ中ニ若キ女人アリテ、「何事ゾ候仰ゾ」ト云。「登リノ時、物ヲ忘レタリシガ、此御宿ト覚候事ヲ申也」ト云。「何ヲ御忘レ候ケル」ト問フ。其時アヤシクテ、馬ヨリヲリテ、「シカ〳〵ノ願ヲ発シテ、金ヲ五十両入テ候ツル守ノ袋ヲ忘レタリ」ト、アリノ儘ニ委ク語リケレバ、此女人、「ワラハコソ、ミツケテ候ヘ」トテ、シタ、メタリシ儘ニテ取出テトラセケレバ、アマリノ事ニテ浅猿カリケリ。「サテ、是ハ失タル物ニテコソ。十両ハ参ラセム」ト云ヘバ、「十両ホシクハ、五十両ナガラコソ、ヒキコメ候ハメ。仏ノ御物ナリ。イカヾスコシモ可給」ト云ケレバ、「中〳〵兎角ノ子細ニ不及。下リニ能々可申旨アリ」トテ、ヤガテ又上洛シテ本尊思ノ如ク造立シテ、下リサマニ此女人ヲ尋テ、「抑イカナル人ニテヲワスルゾ」ナンド、コマヤカニカタライ聞ケレバ、「京ノ物ニテ侍ル

ガ、親キ物モ皆失テ、縁ニフレテ下リ侍ルガ、白地ト思シ程ニ、此宿ニ一両年住ミ侍リ」ト云。「サテハイヅクモ同ジ御旅ニコソ。イザ、セ給ヘ。小所領ナンド知行スル身ナレバ、世間ミウシロミテタベ」ト云バ、「承ヌ」トテ、軈而供セラレテ下テ、世間ウシロミテ、タノシク心安ク当時アリト聞ユ。上古ニハ斯ル様モアリ。当世ニハマメヤカニ難有正直ノ賢人ナリ。去文永年中ノ事ナレバ、無下ニ近キ事也。慥ニ聞伝テ或人語リ侍シガ、随喜ノ心切ニシテ、斯ルタメシ人ニモ普ク聞セ、世ノ末ヘマデモ云伝テ、人ノ心ノ枉ルヲ引ナヲスハシトモセント思テ、此物語書置侍ル志、タヾ此事ニヨリテナム思ハジメ侍ルナリ。

人ハ心直ナルベキモノナリ。此女人モ金ヲ引隠シタラバ、非分ノ事ナレバ、盗賊ニモカスメラレ、無由失フ事モアルベシ。タトヒアリトモ幾程カアラム。当時後見シテ、一期不貧シテ心安クスゴサン事、先ヅ今生モ得分ナリ。後生ハ又仏ヲツクラン功徳ヲウベシ。カタ〴〵難有コソ。若引コメタラバ、今生モタモチガタク、仏物ヲヲカセバ、後生モ苦シカルベシ。正直ノ物ヲバ天是レヲ助ケ、幸ヲエシメ、諂曲ノ物ヲバ冥是レヲ罰シテ、災イヲ与フ。生死ノ稠林ヲ出ルニハ、心ナヲクシテ、出ヤスシト云ヘリ。曲ル木ハ稠林ヲ難出、ナヲキハ出ヤスキガ如クナリ。正直ナレバ神明モ頭ニヤドリ、貞廉ナレバ仏陀モ心ヲ照ス。現当二世無為安楽ナルベキ事、正直ニハスギズ。法花ニモ、「柔和質直者、即皆見我身」ト説テ、心和ニスグナルモノ我身ヲ見ルト、釈尊モ説キ給ヘリ。イカニモ、諂曲ノ心ヲステヽ、正直ノ道ニ入ルベキヲヤ。

日本古典文學大系「沙石集」より

十九、平家物語

敦盛最期

いくさやぶれにければ、熊谷次郎直実、「平家の君達たすけ船にのらんと、汀の方へぞおち給らん。あはれ、よからう大将軍にくまばや」とて、磯の方へあゆまするところに、ねりぬきに鶴ぬうたる直垂に、萌黄の匂の鎧きて、くはがたう(ッ)たる甲の緒しめ、こがねづくりの太刀をはき、きりうの矢おひ、しげ藤の弓も(ッ)て、連銭葦毛なる馬に黄覆輪の鞍をいての(ッ)たる武者一騎、沖なる舟にめをかけて、海へざ(ッ)とうちいれ、五六段ばかりおよがせたるを、熊谷「あれは大将軍とこそ見まいらせ候へ。まさなうも敵にうしろをみせさせ給ふものかな。かへさせ給へ」と扇をあげてまねきければ、招かれてと(ッ)てかへす。汀にうちあがらむとするところに、おしならべてむずとくんでどうどおち、と(ッ)ておさへて頸をかゝんと甲をおしあふのけて見ければ、年十六七ばかりなるが、うすげしやうしてかねぐろ也。我子の小次郎がよはひ程にて容顔まことに美麗也ければ、いづくに刀を立べしともおぼえず。「抑いかなる人にてまし〳〵候ぞ。なのらせ給へ、たすけまいらせん」と申せば、「汝はたそ」ととひ給ふ。「物そのもので候はね共、武蔵国住人、熊谷次郎直実」と名のり申。「さては、なんぢにあふてはなのるまじゐぞ、なんぢがためにはよい敵ぞ。名のらずとも頸をと(ッ)て人にとへ。みしらふずるぞ」とぞの給ひける。熊谷「あ(ッ)ぱれ大将軍や、此人一人うちたてま(ッ)たり共、ま

くべきいくさに勝べき様もなし。又うちたてまつらず共、勝べきいくさにまくることよもあらじ。小次郎がうす手負たるをだに、直実は心ぐるしうこそおもふに、此殿の父、うたれぬときいて、いかばかりかなげき給はんずらん、あはれ、たすけたてまつらばや」と思ひて、うしろをきと(ッ)みければ、土肥・梶原五十騎ばかりでつゞいたり。熊谷涙をおさへて申けるは、「たすけまいらせんとは存候へ共、御方の軍兵雲霞の如候。よものがれさせ給はじ。人手にかけまいらせんより、同くは直実が手にかけまいらせて、後の御孝養をこそ仕候はめ」と申ければ、「たゞとく／＼頸をとれ」とぞの給ひける。熊谷あまりにいとおしくて、いづくに刀をたつべしともおぼえず、めもくれ心もきえはてて、前後不覚におぼえけれども、さてしもあるべき事ならねば、泣々頸をぞかいて(ン)げる。「あはれ、弓矢とる身ほど口惜かりけるものはなし。武芸の家に生れずは、何とてかゝるうき目をばみるべき。なさけなうもうちたてまつる物かな」とかきくどき、袖をかほにおしあててさめ／＼とぞ泣ゐたる。良久うあ(ッ)て、さてもあるべきならねば、よろい直垂をと(ッ)て、頸をつゝまんとしけるに、錦の袋にいれたる笛をぞ腰にさゝれたる。「あないとおし、この暁城のうちにて管絃し給ひつるは、この人々にておはしけり。当時みかたに東国の勢なん万騎かあるらめども、いくさの陣へ笛もつ人はよもあらじ。上臈は猶もやさしかりけり」とて、九郎御曹司の見参に入たりければ、是をみる人涙をながさずといふ事なし。後にきけば、修理大夫経盛の子息に大夫敦盛とて、生年十七にぞなられける。それよりしてこそ熊谷が発心のおもひはすゝみけれ。件の笛はおほぢ忠盛笛の上手にて、鳥羽院より給はられたりけるとぞ聞えし。経盛相伝せられたりしを、敦盛器量たるによ(ッ)て、もたれたりけるとかや。名をばさ枝とぞ申ける。狂言綺語のことはりといひながら、遂に讃仏乗の因となるこそ哀なれ。

日本古典文學大系「平家物語下」より

二十、能

井筒

ワキ　旅僧
シテ　女
アイ　櫟本の者
後シテ　井筒の女
（〽は節をつけて謡う。）

（名ノリ笛）

ワキ「これは諸国一見の僧にて候。われこの程は南都七堂に参りて候。またこれより初瀬に参らばやと存じ候。これなる寺を人に尋ねて候へば、在原寺とかや申し候ふほどに、立ち寄り一見せばやと思ひ候。

ワキ〽さてはこの在原寺は、古業平紀の有常の息女、夫婦住み給ひし石上なるべし。風吹けば沖つ白波竜田山と詠じけんも、この所にての事なるべし。

ワキ〽昔語の跡訪へば、その業平の友とせし、紀の有常の常なき世、妹背をかけて弔はん、妹背をかけて弔はん。

（次第）

シテ〽暁ごとの閼伽の水、暁ごとの閼伽の水、月も心や澄ますらん。

シテ〽さなきだにもののさびしき秋の夜の、人目稀なる古寺の、庭の松風更け過ぎて、月もかたぶく軒端の草、忘れて過ぎし古を、忍ぶ顔にていつまでか、待つ事なくてながらへん、げに何事も思ひ出の、人には残る世の中かな。

シテ〽たゞいつとなく一筋に、頼む仏の御手の糸、導き給へ法の声。

シテ〽迷ひをも、照させ給ふ御誓ひ、照させ給ふ御誓ひ、げにもと見えて有明の、行方は西の山なれど、眺めは四方の秋の空、松の声のみ聞ゆれども、嵐はいづくとも、定めなき世の夢心、何の音にか覚めてまし、何の音にか覚めてまし。

ワキ「われこの寺にやすらひ、心を澄ます折節、いとなまめける女性、庭の板井を掬び上げ花水とし、これなる塚に回向の気色見え給ふは、いかなる人にてましますぞ。

シテ「これはこのあたりに住む者なり。この寺の本願在原の業平は、世に名を留めし人なり。さればその跡のしるしもこれなる塚の蔭やらん、わらはも詳しくは知らず候へども、花水を手向け御跡を弔ひ参らせ候。

ワキ「げにげに業平の御事は、世に名を留めし人なりさりながら、今ははるかに遠き世の、昔語の跡なるを、しかも女性の御身として、かやうに弔ひ給ふ事、その在原の業平に、〽いかさま故ある御身やらん。

シテ「故ある身かと問はせ給ふ、その業平はその時だにも、昔男といはれし身の、ましてや今は遠き世に、故もゆかりもあるべからず。

ワキ〽もつとも仰せはさる事なれども、ここは昔の旧跡にて、主こそ遠く業平の、

シテ〽あとは残りてさすがにいまだ、
ワキ〽聞えは朽ちぬ世語を、
シテ〽語れば今も、
ワキ〽昔男の、
地謡〽名ばかりは、在原寺の跡古りて、在原寺の跡古りて、松も老いたる塚の草、これこそそれよ亡き跡の、一叢薄の穂に出づるは、いつの名残なるらん。草茫々として、露深々と古塚の、まことなるかな古の、跡なつかしき気色かな、跡なつかしき気色かな。
ワキ「なほなほ業平の御事詳しく御物語り候へ。
地謡〽昔在原の中将、年経てここに石上、古りにし里も花の春、月の秋とて住み給ひしに、
シテ〽その頃は紀の有常が娘と契り、妹背の心浅からざりしに、
地謡〽また河内の国高安の里に、知る人ありて二道に、忍びて通ひ給ひしに、
シテ〽風吹けば沖つ白波竜田山、
地謡〽夜半にや君が独り行くらんと、おぼつかなみの夜の道、行方を思ふ心遂げて、よその契りはかれがれなり。
シテ〽げに情知るうたかたの、
地謡〽あはれを述べしも理なり。
地謡〽昔この国に、住む人のありけるが、宿を並べて門の前、井筒に寄りてうなゐ子の、友だち語らひて、互ひに影を水鏡、面を並べ袖をかけ、心の水もそこひなく、移る月日も重なりて、大人しく恥がはしく、互ひに今はなりにけり。その後かのまめ男、言葉の露の玉章の、心の花も

色添ひて、

シテ〽筒井筒、井筒にかけしまろが丈、

地謡〽生ひにけらしな、妹見ざる間にと、詠みて贈りけるほどに、その時女も比べ来し、振分髪も肩過ぎぬ、君ならずして、誰か上ぐべきと、互ひに詠みし故なれや、筒井筒の女とも、聞えしは有常が、娘の古き名なるべし。

地謡〽げにや古りにし物語、聞けば妙なる有様の、あやしや名のりおはしませ。

シテ〽まことはわれは恋衣、紀の有常が娘とも、いさ白波の竜田山、夜半に紛れて来りたり。

地謡〽ふしぎやさては竜田山、色にぞ出づるもみぢ葉の、

シテ〽紀の有常が娘とも、

地謡〽または井筒の女とも、

シテ〽恥かしながらわれなりと、

地謡〽結ふや注連縄の長き世を、契りし年は筒井筒、井筒の蔭に隠れけり、井筒の蔭に隠れけり。

日本古典文學大系「謡曲集上」より

二十一、狂　言

棒　縛

シテ　次郎冠者
アド　太郎冠者
アド　主

主「これはこのあたりに住まい致す者でござる。某所用あって、山一つあなたへ参りまする。それにつきいつも留守になれば、両人の者が酒を盗んで飲みまするによって、今日は両人とも、きっといましめて参ろうと存ずる。まず太郎冠者を呼び出だいて、談合致すことがござる。ヤイヤイ太郎冠者、あるかやい。

太「ハアー。

主「いたか。

太「お前におりまする。

主「念無う早かった。汝を呼び出だすは別なることでもない。ちと思う子細があるによって、次郎冠者をいましめておけ。

太「ハ、お咎のほどは存じませぬが、これは何とぞ御免なされて下されい。

主「イヤイヤ少しのうちじゃによって苦しゅうない。さりながら、あの次郎冠者は、日ごろ心得た者じゃによって、「参るぞ、かかるぞ」ではいましめられまいが、何としてよかろうぞ。

太「まことに何と致いてようござりましょうぞ。イヤそれそれ、よいことがござる。きゃつはこの間棒を稽古致しまする。なかにも夜の棒と申して、秘蔵の棒がござるによって、これを御所望なされ、使うところを、こなたと私と致いて、棒縛りに致しましょうが、何とござろうぞ。

主「これは一段とよかろう。それならば、次郎冠者をこれへ呼び出せ。

太「畏ってござる。
次「なかなか。
太「イヤのうのう、次郎冠者召すは。
次「なんじゃ召す。
太「召すなら召すとおしゃらいで。
次「つっとお出やれ。
次「心得た。
次「ハ、次郎冠者お前に。
主「念無う早かった。汝を呼び出だすは別なることでもない。聞けば汝は、この間棒を稽古すると
な。一手二手使うて見せい。
次「イヤ、私はさようのことは致しませぬ。
主「な隠しそ、太郎冠者が告げた。
次「ヤアヤアわごりょ申し上げたか。
太「なかなか申し上げたほどに使うてお目にかけさしめ。
次「申し上げたことでござらば、使うてお目にかけましょう。
主「それがよかろう。
次「まず棒を取って参りましょう。
主「早う取ってこい。
次「畏ってござる。

太「のうのう早う取っておりゃれ。

次「心得た。

主「ヤイヤイ、よい時分に左右をせい。

太「畏ってござる。

次「イヤ申し申し、この棒でござる。

主「その棒か。

次「まず向こうから打って参れば、こう受けまする。打った太刀なれば引かねばなりませぬ。その引くところを付けて参り、胸板をほうど突き、たじたじたじとするところを、おっ取り直いて両臑を、打って打って打ちなやいてやりまする。

主「さてさていさぎよいことじゃなあ。

太「けなげなことでござる。

主「まだ何とやらいう棒があったが。

次「まずこれまででござる。

主「イヤイヤ何とやらいうた。オオそれそれ、夜の棒をも使うて見せい。

次「わごりょは夜の棒まで申し上げたか。

太「なかなか申し上げたほどに使うてお目にかけさしめ。

次「これは私の秘蔵の棒ではござれども、申し上げたことでござらば、使うてお目にかけましょう。

主「それそれ使うて見せい。

次「総じて我らごときの者は、夜中お使に参ると申しても、見させらるるとおり丸腰でござる。その時、この棒が一本ござれば、こわいことも恐ろしいこともござらぬ。
主「ホオー。
次「まず夜の棒と申すは、かように致いたものでござる。左から打って参れば、こう受けまする。また右から打って参っても、こう受けまする。とかくあと先へ、用心を致いて参れば、こわいことも恐ろしいこともござりませぬ。
主・太「がっきめ、やるまいぞ。と、その両手首を棒にしばりつける
次「これは何となさるる。
主「何とするとは覚えがあろう。
次「何も覚えはござらぬ。太郎冠者何とするぞ。
太「御意じゃ御意じゃ。
主・太「エイエイエイ、ヤットナ。
太「よいなりの、よいなりの。
主「がっきめ。太郎冠者のうしろから両手をしばりつける
太「私は何もお咎はござりますまい。
主「汝も覚えがあろう。
太「覚えはござらぬ。
次「よいなりの、よいなりの。きっといましめてやらせられい。
主「エイエイ、ヤットナ。ヤイヤイ、両人ともよう聞け。某は所用あって、山一つあなたへ行

くほどに、よう留守をせい。
次「何とこの体で、お留守が成るものでござるか。
太「盗人が入っても存じませぬぞ。
主「某はもはや行くぞ。
次「申し、頼うだ人。
太「頼うだお方。
次「頼うだお方。
太「頼うだ人。
次「はや行かせられたそうな。
太「まことに行かせられたそうな。
次「まずこちへおりゃれ。
太「心得た。
次「とてものことに下におりゃれ。
太「心得た。
次・太「エイエイ、ヤットナ。

日本古典文學大系「狂言上」より

二十二、キリシタン版平家物語

第十七。（巻第四）那須の与一が扇を射たこと

右馬之允「先をも略してなりともお語りあれ。

喜一「心得まらした。その日ははや暮れ方になれば、勝負は決すまじい、明日の軍と定めて、源氏引き退かうとするところに、沖の方から尋常に飾った小船一艘汀に寄するを何ごとぞと見るところに、赤い袴に、柳の五衣きた女のまことに優なが、船中から出て、皆紅の扇の日いだいたをふなばたにさしはさうで立て、陸へ向うて招いた。義経後藤兵衛を召して、あれは何ごとぞと、おほせらるれば、射よと申すことでござらうず。ただし謀でもござらうず。大将さだめて進み出させられて、傾城を御覧ぜられうずる、その時手たれをもって射落さうずるとの儀でござるか、扇をばいそいで射させられうずるかと申せば、射さうな者はないか？　那須の与一は小兵なれども、手はきいてござる。証拠はあるか？　そのことでござる。かけ鳥を三よりに二よりはたやすうつかまつると申す。さらば召せとて、召されたに、与一そのころ十八九ばかりであったが、お前に出て畏まったを義経いかに与一、傾城の立てた扇のまん中射て、人に見物させいとおほせらるれば、与一これをつかまつらうずることは不定な。射損じてござらば味方の長いきずでござらうず、自余の人におほせつけられいかしと申せば、義経怒らせられて鎌倉を出て西国へ向はうずるともがらは義経が命

をそむくまじい儀ぞ。それに子細を申さう人は急いで鎌倉へ帰り上られい。その上大勢の中から一人選ばるるは、後代の冥加ぢゃと喜ばぬ侍は何の用にたたうかと、おほせられたれば、与一重ねて申さば、悪しからうずるとお前をつい立って馬にうち乗り、磯の方へ歩ませゆけば、兵どもおっさまにこれを見て、ふりかかり静まって一定この若い者はつかまつらうとおぼゆると、口々に申せば、義経も世に頼もしう思はれた。磯からうちのぞうで見れば、遠かった。遠浅なれば、馬の太腹ひたるほどにうち入るれば、いま七八段と見えた。をりふし風が吹いて船を揺りすゑ揺り上げ、扇座席も定まらいでひらめいた。沖には平家一面に船を並べて見物する。うしろを見れば、汀に味方の源兵ども轡を並べてひかへたれば、いづれも晴れでないといふことはなかった。なほ風も静まらねば、扇の座席も定まらず。与一何ともせうやうもなうて、しばしたったが、風が少し静まり、扇射よげに見えた。小兵なれども、十三束の鏑とってつがひ、しばしたもって放すに、弓は強し、浦に響くほどに、鳴りわたって、扇の要からかみ一寸ばかりおいてひっぷっと射切ったれば、扇こらへいで三つにさけ、空へ上がり、風に一もみもまれて、海へざっと散った。皆紅の扇の日いだいたが、夕日に輝いて白波の上を浮きぬ、沈みぬ揺られた。陸海上の敵味方ふなばたを叩き、箙を叩き、一度にどっとほめて、しばしは鳴りも静まらなんだ。

亀井高孝・阪田雪子翻字「平家物語」より

二十三、イソポのハブラス

盗人と、犬のこと

ある盗人福人の家に忍びいらうずると思へども、番の為に犬をあまた飼うておいたれば、吠え立てられてえ入らなんだ、それによって盗人のはかりことに、先づたび〳〵パンを持って来て犬に食はせて、その身を見知られうとした。さて犬ども漸く見知ったと思ふ時、ひそかに忍び入らうとすれば、常よりも犬どもが猶吠えまはるところで、盗人犬に言ふは、「さてもおのれは我が恩を知らぬものかな！　身がおのれに常に不びんを加へたはこの時見知られう為ぢゃ」と、犬が又盗人に答へて言ふは、「そちがたま〳〵一口のパンをくれ、多年の主人の過分の財宝を取りごとはくせごとぢゃ、急いでそこを立ち去れ」と言うた。

下心

主人に志を深うする者は少しの利によって、多くの恩を忘れぬものぢゃ。されどもふたごころの有る者は少しの利をもってもあまたの恩を忘るゝ。

獅子と、狐のこと

獅子もってのほかにあひ煩うてさん〴〵のていであったれば、よろづのけだものそれを問ひとむ

らふこと隙（ひま）も無かった。その中に狐ばかり見えなんだ。こゝにおいて獅子、狐の許へ消息して言ひやるは、「何とてそれには見えられぬぞ？ 自余の衆は多分見舞はるゝ中に余りうと／＼しうおとづれも無いは曲（くせ）も無い次第ぢゃ。生得それにと我とは深切の中なれば、隔心（きゃくしん）あらうずる儀で無い、もし又身が上を疑はるゝか？ 少しも別心は無い、たとひ害を為したうても今このていでは叶はねば、お出でを待ち存ずる」と書いたところで、狐謹んで、「仰せかたじけなう存ずる、さほどのことゝも存ぜいで、このごろは無音（ぶいん）本意を背（そむ）いてござる、只今も参りたう存ずれども、こゝに一つの不審がござる、よろづのけだもののお見舞ひに参られたとは覚しうて、御座どころへいった足跡は有れども、出た足跡は一つも見えねば、覚束（おぼつか）なう存ずる」と返事した。

下心

言葉の行跡（かうせき）にたがふ時は、人がこれを信ぜぬものぢゃ。

日本古典全書「吉利支丹文學集下」より

二十四、仁勢物語

九、をかし、おとこ有けり。其おとこ、身をゑうなき物におもひなして、「京にはあらじ。東のかたにすむべき」とてゆきけり。つれとする人、ひとりふたり行けり。道しれる人もなくて、とふてゆきけり。三河国おかざきといふ所にいたりぬ。そこをおかざきとは、ちやうりあるによりてな

む、おかざきとおもひける。其やどの家に、たちよりてはたごめしくひけり。そのたなに、かきつへた、いとおほくありけり。それを見てつれ人、「かきつへた、といふ五もじを、くのかみにすへて、たびのこゝろをよめ」といひければ、よめる。

かちみちをきのふもけふもつれだちてへめぐりまわるたびをしぞおもふ

とよめりければ、皆人わらひにけり。

ゆき〳〵て、するがのくに、うつの山にいたりて、わがのぼらんとする道は、いとくらう高きに、つた・かゑではしげり、物こゝろぼそく、ひだるき目をみることゝおもふに、すき行者あふたり。「かゝる道はいかでかいまする」といふをみれば、知人なりけり。京に其人のもとにとてことつてす。

するがなるうつの山辺のたうだんごぜにがなければかはぬなりけり

ふじの山をみれば、五月の卅日に雪ありて、めしにゝたり。

ときしらぬふじのねほどのいひもがなかのこかたびらかへてくふべき

その山を物にたとへば、ひゑめしをかさねあげたらんやうにて、なりはすり鉢のしりのやうになんありける。

なをゆき〳〵て、むさしの国としもつふさの国との中におほきなるかわあり。それを角田川といふ。その河のほとりにむれいておもひやれば、かぎりなく、ひだるくもあるかなとわびあへるに、わたし守「はやふねにのれ。日もくれぬ」といふ。さるおりしも、白きかほにおびと小袖とあかき、舟のうへにあそびていひをくふ。わたし守にとへば、「これなん都人」といふを聞て、

なめしあらばいざちとくわん都人わがおもふほどはありやなしやと

とよめりければ舟こぞりてわらひにけり。

日本古典文學大系「假名草子」より

二十五、きのふはけふの物語

ある人、てらへまいり、「ちやう老さまは」といへば、「御るすぢや」と申。「はる〲参りたるに御残りおほひ事ぢや」とて、しばらくやすらひけるに、おりふしたけの子の時ぶんぢやとて、やぶをのぞきまわれば、ちやう老さま、見事成がんのけをぬいて御座ある。此人、そろりとそばへより、御みまひにまいりたるよし申せば、ちやうらう、げふてんして、「さて〲此鳥のけをまくらに入候へば、つふうのくすりぢやと申ほどに、かやうにいたすが、何としても、手なれぬ事はならぬ物ぢや」とおほせらるゝ。だんなきゝて、「其はやすひ事で御座候。是へくだされよ」とて、くる〲とひきむしり、けをばをしよせて、「此身はこなたにいらざる物よ」とて、やがてとつてかへり、しやうぐわんした。

さる寺にて、じゆん礼とはちひらきとね物がたりするをきゝければ、じゆんれい申やう、「さて〲、いかなるゐんぐわにて、われらはかやうにあさましき事や。せめて天下を三日しりたひ。さあらば、国々のつじだふのいたじきをたか〲とつくらせ、ゐんのしたにて、其方たちとゆる〲とはなしたひ」といふ。はちひらいがきゝて、「き所はそれほどどんなゆへに、しよ国をめぐる事

ぢや。その身におうじたるねがひをしたがよひ。たゞ我らは、京の国を一日なりともしりたひ」「なぜに」「町中のいぬどもをみなうちころさせて、ゆる〳〵とはちをひらきたい」といふた。

くろたにから京へ、まい月ときに出る坊ずあり。正月十日に、かなや長春所にて大酒をして、かへりに道にて田の中へころび、けさ、ころも、小袖こと〴〵くよごし、やう〳〵下人のかたにかゝりてかへり、ゑひさめてから、「扨〳〵よしなきさけをしいられて、このごとくそんをする」とて、事のほかうらむる。扨、ほどなく二月に又さけをしいらるゝ。その時、かのとものまかり出、「先の月も御しゆがすぎて、道にてころばせられ、御いしやう共、みな御よごしなされて候。さのみ御無よう」と申せば、「其儀ならば申まひ」とて、おさめとる。さて、かへりざま、まへのところにてまたころび、ともにひきおこされて、「なんぢよくきけ。正月にはようてころぶ。けふはよはねどころぶ。これみなぜんせのさだまり事なり。きやうこうは、そばからさけのしんしやくはむよう」と申された。

日本古典文學大系「江戸笑話集」より

二十六、俳諧

猿蓑

市中は物のにほひや夏の月　凡兆

あつし〳〵と門〳〵の声　芭蕉

二番草取りも果さず穂に出て　去来

灰うちたゝくうるめ一枚　凡兆

此筋は銀も見しらず不自由さよ　芭蕉

たゞとひやうしに長き脇指　去来

草村に蛙こはがる夕まぐれ　凡兆

蕗の芽とりに行燈ゆりけす　芭蕉

道心のおこりは花のつぼむ時　去来

能登の七尾の冬は住うき　凡兆

魚の骨しはぶる迄の老を見て　芭蕉

待人入し小御門の鎰　去来

立かゝり屏風を倒す女子共　凡兆

湯殿は竹の簀子侘しき　芭蕉
茴香の実を吹落す夕嵐　去来
僧やゝさむく寺にかへるか　凡兆
さる引の猿と世を経る秋の月　芭蕉
年に一斗の地子はかる也　去来
五六本生木つけたる潴(ミツタマリ)　凡兆
足袋ふみよごす黒ぼこの道　芭蕉
追たてゝ早き御馬の刀持　去来
でつちが荷ふ水こぼしたり　凡兆
戸障子もむしろがこひの売屋敷　芭蕉
てんじやうまもりいつか色づく　去来
こそ〳〵と草鞋を作る月夜さし　凡兆
蚤をふるひに起し初秋　芭蕉
そのまゝにころび落たる升落　去来
ゆがみて蓋のあはぬ半櫃　凡兆
草庵に暫く居ては打やぶり　芭蕉
いのち嬉しき撰集のさた　去来
さま〴〵に品かはりたる恋をして　凡兆
浮世の果は皆小町なり　芭蕉

なに故ぞ粥すゝるにも涙ぐみ　去来
御留主となれば広き板敷　凡兆
手のひらに虱這はする花のかげ　芭蕉
かすみうごかぬ昼のねむたさ　去来

日本古典文學全集「連歌俳諧集」より

二十七、世間胸算用

訛言も只はきかぬ宿

万人ともに、月額剃て髪結ふて、衣装着替て出た所は、皆正月の気色ぞかし。人こそしらね、年のとりやうこそさま〳〵なれ。内証の迚も埒の明ざる人は、買がかり万事一軒へも払はぬ胸算用を極め、大晦日の朝めし過るといなや、羽織脇ざしさして、きげんのわるひ内義に、「物には堪忍といふ事がある。すこし手前取直したらば、駕籠にのせる時節もまたあるものぞ。夕べの鴨の残りを酒いりにして喰やれ。掛どもをあつめて来たらば、先そなたの宝引銭一貫のけて置て、有次第に払うて、ない所はまゝにして、掛乞の皃を見ぬやうに、こちらむきて寐ていやれ」と、口ばやにいひ捨て出行商人、何として身躰つゞくべし。一日〳〵物のたらぬこしらへ、おのれも合点ながら、俄かに分別も成がたし。こんな者の女房になる事、世の因果にて、子をもたぬうちに年をよらしける。

一銭も大事の日、鼻紙入に壱歩二ツ三ツ、豆板三十目ばかりも入て、かゝりのない茶屋に行て、「爰にはまだ得しまはぬかして、取みだしたる書出し千束のごとし。是皆ひとつにしてから、高で二貫目か三貫目。人の家にはそれ〴〵の物入、われらが所は呉服屋へばかり六貫五百目、物好過たる奥さまに迷惑いたす。さらりと隙あけて、此入目を女郎ぐるひにいたすで御座る。去ながら、さられぬ事は、三月からお中にありて、日もあるに今朝からけがつきて、けふ生るゝとて、うまれぬさきの褟さだめ。乳母をつれてくるやら、三人四人の取あげ祖母、旦那山伏が来て変生男子の行ひ。千代の腹帯、子安貝、左りの手に握るといふ海馬をさいかくするやら、不断医者は次の間に鍋を仕かけ、はやめ薬の用意。何に入事じやゝら、松茸の石づき迄取よせて、姐が来てせはをやく。さても〳〵やかましい事かな。されども、こなたは内に御座らぬものといふを幸はひに、ふら〳〵と爰へ御見廻申た。われらが身躰しらぬ人は、もしは借銭こはれて出違ふかとおもふもあれば、気味がわるひ。此嶋中に一銭も指引なしの男、ことに限銀にて、子のできるまでの宿をかし給ふか。爰のさかなかけの鰤がちいさくて、われら気にいらぬ。早ゝ買給へ」と、一かくなげ出せば、「是はうれしや、亭主に隠しまして、ほしき帯よ〳〵」と笑ひ、「此年のくれには心よきお客の御出、来年中の仕合はしれた事。さて台所はあまりしやれ過ました、ちと奥へ」と申。「馳走も常に替りてすき、合点か」といふ。樽の酒のかんするもおかし。其のちかゝは畳占おきて、「三度までいたして同じ事、御男子さまに極まりました」と、かゝが推量と客の跡かたもなきうそと、ひとつに成ける。あそび所の気さんじは、大晦日の色三絃、誰はゞからぬなげぶし、なげきながらも月日を送り、けふ一日にながひ事、心にものおもふゆへなり。常はくるゝを惜みしに、各別の事ぞかし。

女は勤とて、心を春のごとくにして、おかしうないを笑ひがほして、「ひとつ〳〵行年のかなしや。此まへは正月のくるを、はねつく事にうれしかりしに、はや十九になりける。追付脇ふたぎて、かゝといはるべし。ふり袖の名残も、ことしばかり」といふ。此客わるひ事には覚えつよく、「汝此まへ花屋に居し時は、丸袖にてつとめ、京で十九といふた事、大かた二十年にあまる。せんさくすれば、三十九のふりそで、うき世に何か名残あるべし。小作りにうまれ付たる徳」と、あたまおさへてむかしをかたれば、此女「ゆるし給へ」と手を合せ、気のつまる年ぜんさくやめて、うちとけて夢むすぶうちに、此女の母親らしきものゝ来て、ひそかによび出し、ひとつふたつ物いひしが、何の事はない、「是が皃の見おさめ、十四五匁の事に身をなげる」といふ。此女泪ぐみて、今までうへに着たるぐんない嶋の小袖を、ふろしきづゝみに手まはしばやくして、親にわたすありさま、いかにしても見かねて、又一かくとらせて戻し、心おもしろう声高に物いふを聞付、若衆のぞうり取めきたる者二人つけこみて、「旦那これに御座ります。御宿へけさから四五度もまいれど、御留守は是非なし。お目にかゝるこそ幸はひ」と、何やらつめひらきしてのち、銀有次第、羽織・わきざし・きるものひとつ預かり、「跡は正月五日までに」といひ捨て帰る。此おきやくしゆびあしく、「人にいひかけられて、合力せねばならず。とかく節季に出ありくがわるひ」と、これにも分別がほして、夜の明がたに爰を帰る。「たはけといふは、すこし脈がある人の事」と、笑ふて果しける。

日本古典文學大系「西鶴集下」より

二十八、曾根崎心中

此のよのなごり。よもなごり。しにに行く身をたとふれば。あだしがはらの道のしも。一あしづゝにきえてゆく。夢のゆめこそあはれなれ。あれかぞふればあかつきの。七つのときが六つなりてのこる一つがこんじゃうの。かねのひゞきのききをさめ。じゃくめつゐらくとひゞくなり。かねばかりかは。くさも木も空もなごりと見あぐれば。くも心なき水のおとほくとはさえてかげうつるほしのいもせのあまのがは。むめだのはしをかさゝぎのはしと契りていつまでも。われとそなたはめをとぼし。かならずそふとすがりより。二人が中にふる涙。かはのみかさもまさるべし。むかふのにかいは。なにやとも。おぼつか情さいちゅうにて。まだねぬひかげこゑたかく。ことしの心中よしあしの。ことのはぐさや。しげるらん。きくに心もくれはどりあやなやきのふけふまでも。よそにいひしがあすよりはわれもうはさのかずに入り。よにうたはれんうたはばうたへ。うたふを聞けば。どうで女ばうにゃもちゃさんすまい。いらぬものぢゃと思へども。げに思へどもなげけども身もよもおもふまゝならず。いつをけふとてけふが日まで。心ののびしよはもなく。思はぬ色にくるしみに。どうした事のえんぢゃやら。わするゝひまはないわいな。それにふりすてゆかうとは。やりゃしませぬぞ手にかけて。ころしておいてゆかんせな。はなちはやらじとなきければ。うたもおほきにあのうたを。ときこそあれこよひしも。うたふはたそや聞くはわれ。すぎにし人もわれ

〱も。ひとつおもひとすがりつき。こゑもをしまずなきゐたり。いつはさもあれ此のよはは。せめてしばしはながからで心もなつのよのならひ命をおはゆる雞のこゑあけなばうしやてんじんの。もりでしなんと手を引いて。むめだづゝみのさよがらす。あすは我が身をゑじきぞや。誠にことしはこなさまも廿五さいのやくのとし。わしも十九のやくどしとて。思ひあうたるやくだゝりえんのふかさの。しるしかや。神やほとけにかけおきしげんぜのぐゎんを今こゝで。みらいへゑかうし後のよもなほしも一つはちすぞやと。つまぐるじゅずの百八に。涙の玉の。かずそひて。つきせぬ。あはれつきる道。心も空に。かげくらく風しん〱たるそねざきの。森にぞ。たどり着きにける。かしこにかこゝにかとはらへどくさにちるつゆのわれよりさきにまづきえて。さだめなきよはいなづまか。それか。あらぬか。ア、こは。いまのはなにといふものやらん。オ、あれこそは人だまよ。こよひしするは我のみとこそ思ひしに。さきだつ人も有りしよな。たれにもせよしでの山のともなひぞや。なむあみだ仏。なむあみだ仏のこゑの中。あはれかなしや又こそたまのよをさりしは。南無あみだ仏といひければ。女はおろかに涙ぐみ。こよひは人のしぬるよかやあさましさよと涙ぐむ。をとこなみだを。はら〱と。ながし。二つつれとぶ人だまをよそのうへと思ふかや。まさしう御身と我がたまよ。なになう二人のたましひとや。はや我ゝはししたる身か。オ、常ならばむすびとめつなぎとめんとなげかまし。今はさいごをいそぐ身のたまのありかをひとつにすまん。道をまよふなたがふなと。いだきよせはだをよせ。かっぱとふして。なきゐたる。ふたりのこゝろぞ。ふびんなる。涙のいとのむすびまつ。しゅろの一木のあひおひを。れんりの契になぞらへつゆのうき身のおきどころ。サアこゝにきはめんと。うはぎのおびを徳兵衛もはつも涙のそめこそで。ぬいでかけたるしゅろのはの。その玉はゝき今ぞげに。うきよのちりを。はらふらんはつがそでよ

りかみそり出し。もしも道にておってのかゝりわれ〳〵になるとても。うき名はすてじと心がけかみそりよういいたせしが。のぞみのとほり一所でしぬることのうれしさと。いひければ。オゝしんべうたのもしゝ。さほどにこゝろおちつくからはさいごもあんずることはなし。さりながら今はのときのくげんにて。しにすがた見ぐるしといはれんもくちをしゝ。此のふたもとのれんりの木にからだをきっとゆはひつけ。いさぎようしぬまいか世にたぐひなきしにやうの。てほんとならんいかにもとあさましやあさぎぞめ。かゝれとてやはかゝへおび両はうへ引はりて。かみそりとってさら〳〵と。おびはさけてもぬしさまとわしがあひだはよもさけじと。どうどざをくみふたへみへ。ゆるがぬやうに。しっかとしめ。ようしまったか。オ、しめましたと。女はをっとのすがたを見をとこは女のていを見て。こはなさけなき身のはてぞやと。わっとなきいる。ばかりなり。ア、なげかじと徳兵衛。かほふり上げて手をあわせ。我えうせうにてまことの父母にはなれをぢといひおやかたのくらうとなりて人となり。おんもおくらず此のまゝに。なきあとまでもとやかくと。御なんぎかけん。もったいなや。つみをゆるして下されかしめいどにまします父母にはおっ付御めにかゝるべし。むかへ給へとなきければ。おはつもおなじく手をあはせ。こなさまはうらやましやめいどのおやごにあはんとあるわれらがとゝさまかゝさまはまめで此の世の人なれば。いつあふことの有るべきぞたよりは此の春聞いたれど。あうたは去年の初秋のはつが心中とりざたの。あすは在所へ聞えなばいかばかりかはなげきをかけんおやたちへも兄弟へもこれから此の世のいとまごひ。せめて心がつうじなば夢にも見えてくれよかし。なつかしのはゝさまやなごりをしのとゝさまやと。しゃくりあげ〳〵。声も。をしまずなきければをっともわっとさけびいり。りうていこがるゝこゝろいきことわりせめてあはれなれ。いつまでいうてせんもなし。はや〳〵ころして〳〵とさいごをい

そげば心えたりと。わきざしするりと、ぬきはなし。サアたゞいまぞなむあみだなむあみだと。いへどもさすが此のとし月いとしかはいとしめてねし。はだにやいばがあてられうかと。まなこもくらみ手もふるひよわる。心を引なほし。とりなほしてもなほふるひつくとはすれどきっさきは。あなたへはづれこなたへそれ。二三どひらめくつるぎのは。あっとばかりに。のどぶえに。ぐっととほるかなむあみだ。なむあみだなむあみだぶつと。くりとほしくりとほすうでさきも。よわるを見れば両手をのべ。だんまつまの四く八く。あはれと。いふもあまり有り。我とてもおくれうかいきは一どに引とらんと。かみそりとってのどに。つき立て。つかもをれよはもくだけとゑぐり。くり〳〵目もくるめき。くるしむいきもあかつきの。ちしごにつれてたえはてたり。たがつぐるとはそねざきのもりの下風おとにきこえ。とりつたへきせんくんじゅのゑかうのたね。みらい成仏。うたがひなき恋の。手ほんとなりにけり。

日本古典文學大系「近松浄瑠璃集上」より

二十九、雨月物語

吉備の国賀夜郡庭妹の郷に、井沢庄太夫といふものあり。祖父は播磨の赤松に仕へしが、去ぬる嘉吉元年の乱に、かの舘を去てこゝに来り、庄太夫にいたるまで三代を経て、春耕し、秋収めて、家豊にくらしけり。一子正太郎なるもの農業を厭ふあまりに、酒に乱れ色に酖りて、父が掟を守ら

ず。父母これを歎きて私にはかるは、「あはれ良人の女子の㒵よきを娶りてあはせなば、渠が身もおのづから脩まりなん」とて、あまねく国中をもとむるに、幸に媒氏ありていふ。「吉備津の神主香央造酒が女子は、うまれだち秀麗にて、父母にもよく仕へ、かつ歌をよみ、筝に工みなり。従来かの家は吉備の鴨別が裔にて家系も正しければ、君が家に因み給ふは果吉祥なるべし。此事の就んは老が願ふ所なり。大人の御心いかにおぼさんや」といふ。庄太夫大に怡び、「よくも説せ給ふものかな。此事我家にとりて千とせの計なりといへども、香央は此国の貴族にて、我は氏なき田夫なり。門戸敵すべからねば、おそらくは肯がひ給はじ」。媒氏の翁笑をつくりて、「大人の謙り給ふ事甚し。我かならず万歳を諷ふべし」と、徃て香央に説ば、彼方にもよろこびつゝ、妻なるものにもかたらふに、妻もいさみていふ。「我女子既に十七歳になりぬれば、朝夕によき人がな娶せんものをと、心もおちゐ侍らず。はやく日をえらみて聘礼を納給へ」と、強にすゝむれば、盟約すでになりて井沢にかへりことす。即聘礼を厚くとゝのへて送り納れ、よき日をとりて婚儀をもよほしけり。

猶幸を神に祈るとて、巫子祝部を召あつめて御湯をたてまつる。そも〳〵当社に祈誓する人は、数の秡物を供へて御湯を奉り、吉祥凶祥を占ふ。巫子祝詞をはり、湯の沸上るにおよびて、吉祥には釜の鳴音牛の吼るが如し。凶きは釜に音なし。是を吉備津の御釜秡といふ。さるに香央が家の事は、神の祈させ給はぬにや、只秋の虫の叢にすだくばかりの声もなし。こゝに疑ひをおこして、此祥を妻にかたらふ。妻更に疑はず、「御釜の音なかりしは祝部等が身の清からぬにぞあらめ。既に聘礼を納めしうへ、かの赤縄に繫ぎては、仇ある家、異なる域なりとも易べからずと聞ものを。ことに井沢は弓の本末をもしりたる人の流にて、掟ある家と聞けば、今否むとも承がはじ。こ

とに佳婿の麗なるをほの聞て、我児も日をかぞへて待わぶる物を、今のよからぬ言を聞ものならば、不慮なる事をや仕出ん。其とき悔るともかへらじ」と言を尽して諫むるは、まことに女の意ばへなるべし。香央も従来ねがふ因みなれば深く疑はず、妻のことばに従て婚儀とゝのひ、両家の親族氏族、鶴の千とせ、亀の万代をうたひことぶきけり。

香央の女子磯良かしこに徃てより、夙に起、おそく臥て、常に舅姑の傍を去ず、夫が性をはかりて、心を尽して仕へければ、井沢夫婦は孝節を感たしとて歓びに耐ねば、正太郎も其志に愛てむつまじくかたらひけり。されどおのがまゝの姧たる性はいかにせん。いつの比より鞆の津の袖といふ妓女にふかくなじみて、遂に贖ひ出し、ちかき里に別荘をしつらひ、かしこに日をかさねて家にかへらず。磯良これを怨みて、或は舅姑の忿に托て諫め、或ひは徒なる心をうらみかこてども、大虚にのみ聞なして、後は月をわたりてかへり来らず。父は磯良が切なる行止を見るに忍びず、正太郎を責て押籠ける。磯良これを悲しがりて、朝夕の奴も殊に実やかに、かつ袖が方へも私に物を餉りて、信のかぎりをつくしける。一日父が宿にあらぬ間に、正太郎磯良をかたらひていふ。「御許の信ある操を見て、今はおのれが身の罪をくゆるばかりなり。かの女をも古郷に送りてのち、父の面を和め奉らん。渠は播磨の印南野の者なるが、親もなき身の浅ましくてあるを、いとかなしく思ひて憐をもかけつるなり。我に捨られなば、はた船泊りの妓女となるべし。おなじ浅ましき奴なりとも、京は人の情もありと聞ば、渠をば京に送りやりて、栄ある人に仕へさせたく思ふなり。我かくてあれば万に貧しかりぬべし。路の代身にまとふ物も誰がはかりことしてあたへん。御許此事をよくして渠を恵み給へ」と、ねんごろにあつらへけるを、磯良いとも喜しく、「此事安くおぼし給へ」とて、私におのが衣服調度を金に貿、猶香央の母が許へも偽りて金を乞、正太郎に与へける。此金

を得て密に家を脱れ出、袖なるものを倶して、京の方へ逃のぼりける。かくまでたばかられしかば、今はひたすらにうらみ歎きて、遂に重き病に臥にけり。井沢香央の人ゝ彼を悪み此を哀みて、専医の験をもとむれども、粥さへ日ゝにすたりて、よろづにたのみなくぞ見えにけり。

日本古典文學大系「上田秋成集」より

三十、椿説弓張月

この折しも八郎為朝は当国に到着ありて、阿蘇の宮へ詣ん為、彼鶴を従者に扛担せ、文殊院のほとりを過り給ふに、人夥馳あつまり、門の柱には、しか〴〵の趣を書て貼おきたれば、是わが夢の告に、妍き妻を娶る事あらんと聞えしは、この事なるべしと暁得給ひつ。やがて門内にすゝみ入りて忠国に対ひ、「それがし彼猴を射おとして進らすべし」と宣ひけり。忠国これを聞て、まづその人を見るに、年紀は、十六七にして、筋骨逞しく、面白く鼻高く、眉は緑にして青山のごとく、唇は紅にして春花のごとく、耳厚、瞳二ッありて、身の丈七尺あまりなるべく、平人ならず見えしかば、心にふかく驚嘆し、「御身よく彼猴を射て給はらば、わが婿にせん事子細あらじ」といふ。「さらば弓勢の程をもしらせまゐらすべし」とて、為朝は従者に持せたりし、弓矢をとりて岳のほとりに歩み寄り給ふを見るに、弓は鉄の枴を押たはめつるやうなれば、忠国はさら也、人みな大に驚きて、「かゝる強弓を引んものは、いにしへにもたえて聞ず。まして後の世にはなほ

ありがたかるべし」と称て、いと頼もしくおぼえける。猴は遥に為朝を見て、脱れがたきをしりたりけん、泫然としてうち歎くがごとし。浩処に当寺の住持、この事を洩聞けん。職事僧を遣して、忠国にいはせけるは、「抑 わが山は、仁明天皇の勅願にして、弘法大師の開基たり。特に彼塔には、勅封の仏舎利を納たるに、これに対ひて弓を引んは、朝敵仏敵に斉しかるべし。且縦彼猴罪ありとも、一たび寺内に入りしものを、無下に殺さんは、法師の忍びざる所なり。彼といひ是といひ、此事有免に預るべし」と述たりける。忠国聞て眉を顰、彼猴霊場に走り入るといふとも、既に人を殺せしからは、敢て恕すべきにあらず。しかはあれど、勅封の仏舎利を納たる宝塔に対ひて矢を発さんには、後難はかりがたし。こは何とせんと愁悶るにぞ、為朝も用意忽地相違して、旧の処へ退き給へば、猴はふたゝび勢力出て、指さし恥る事はじめにも過たれば、忠国ます〳〵憤りに堪ず。為朝も心の中ふかく望をうしなひ、われ今猴を射ん事はいと易けれど、事かなはねばせんすべなし。もし彼八町礫紀平治だにあるならば、弓矢を用ひずして打落す事難きにあらざめれど、国を隔たればそれもかひなしなど、とさまかうさま思ひ屈し給ふに、彼鶴笯の中にありて、俄頃に羽たゝきし、しば〳〵飛出んと欲する気色なれば、為朝見そなはしてふたゝび暁得、この鶴が夢に告て、阿蘇の宮のほとりにて、放てよといひしはけふの事にて、彼みづからなす事あるべし。かゝれば深く疑ふべきにあらずとて、胆太くも重て忠国に対ひ、「それがし弓矢を用ずして、猴を打落進らすべし」と宣へば、忠国斜ならず悦びて、「既に宣ふごとくならば、幸これにますものあらじ。とく〳〵用意し給へ」と回答せり。為朝はこゝろに祈請しつゝ、笯の門をひらき給ふに、予てこゝにて放べく思しければ、足には旧のごとく牌を着たるが、鶴は笯を出るとやがて、虚空遥に翔揚り、ゆくへもしらずなりにけり。忠国主従はさらなり、是を見るもの冷笑ひ、「こは

嗚呼なる愚者もあるかな。鷲鵰なんどこそ、猨をも捉らめ。鶴の獣を捉といふ事は、たえて聞も及ばず。さればこそそらしらず顔して飛うせたり」などさゞめきあへり。為朝もこの光景にふたゝび疑念を生じ、そなたの空をうち眺ておはしけるに、且くして彼鶴は、西のかたより翔来り、塔の火珠をはなるゝ事一丈ばかりにして、処も去らず翔居たるを、猨はうち仰ぎて瞬もせず、ちかくよらば攫みもすべき気色なり。鶴はなほ高く翔低く翔て、やゝその間ちかくなるとき、何とかしけん猨は大に慌忙き、火珠を走り下りんとするところを、鶴はさとおとし来て、觜もて丁と衝やうなりしが、猨は忽地血に塗れながら撞と堕、鶴は高く翔あがりて、南を投て飛去りける。これを見るものみな声を揚、嗚呼と感じて鳴も已ず。忠国は喜びに堪ず。為朝とともに彼猨を見るに、猨は脊より胸さかをいたくつらぬかれて死たるが、目鼻の間に夥しく砂のかゝりてありしかば、忠国掌を拍していふやう、「はじめ彼鶴が、いづ地ともなく飛ゆきしは、この砂を銜来て、猨の眼つぶしにせんが為なり。飛禽といへども事に臨て、よく剛敵を拉ぐ。その智ははかりしるべからず。嗚呼奇なるかな」と嘆賞し、更に為朝に対て礼儀を正くし、「そも御身はいかなる人なれば、輙くわが仇を亡し給ひたる。もし仙境の客ならずは、必ず名ある武士ならん。今日の事いと不思議に候」といへば、為朝含笑て、「名告申さんも嗚呼にはあれど、久しく父為義が不興を得て豊後のかたに身を寓せし、八郎為朝といふもの也。彼鶴の事につきては、種々の物がたりあれど、一朝には説尽しがたし。われ幸にして御身が望をかなへ、いとよろこばしく候」と宣へば、忠国且驚き、且うれしみていふやう、「こは思ひもかけぬ、源家の御曹子にて在せしかな。器量骨柄平人ならずと見まゐらせしが、果してしかり。それがし不才なれども弓矢とる身の数にも入れり。もし嫌ひ給はずは、女児白縫を進らせて、ながく晋秦の好を締候べし。いかに諾ひ給はんか」といへ

ば、為朝(ためとも)も、「こは希(こひねがふ)ところ也。親兄弟(おやはらから)にも遠(とほ)ざかりて、頼(たの)むかたなき身にしあればよきに計(はか)りて給はり候へ」と宣(のたま)ふにぞ、阿曾(あそ)の家隷(いへのこ)どもよろこぶ事限(かぎ)りなく、みな万歳(ばんぜい)とぞ祝(ことぶ)きける。

日本古典文學大系「椿説弓張月上」より

三十一、玉勝間

あがたゐのうしは古(へ)学のおやなる事

からごゝろを清くはなれて、もはら古(へ)のこゝろ詞をたづぬるがくもむは、わが県居大人(ノ)よりぞはじまりける、此大人の学の、いまだおこらざりしほどの世の学問は、歌もたゞ古今集よりこなたにのみとゞまりて、万葉などは、たゞいと物どほく、心も及ばぬ物として、さらに其歌のよきあしきを思ひ、ふるきちかきをわきまへ、又その詞を、今のおのが物としてつかふ事などは、すべて思ひも及ばざりしことなるを、今はその古言(へ)をおのがものとして、万葉ぶりの歌をもよみいで、古(へ)ぶりの文などをさへ、かきうることゝなれるは、もはら此うしのをしへのいさをにぞ有ける、今の人は、たゞおのれみづから得たるごと思ふめれど、みな此大人の御蔭(ミカゲ)によらずといふことなし、又古事記書紀などの古典(イニシヘノフミ)をうかゞふにも、漢意(カラゴヽロ)にまどはされず、まづもはら古言(へ)を明らめ、古意(へ)によるべきことを、人みなしれるも、このうしの、万葉のをしへのみたまにぞありける、そもそもかゝるたふとき道を、ひらきそめられたるいそしみは、よにいみしきものなりかし、

もろこしぶみをもよむべき事

から国の書をも、いとまのひまには、ずゐぶんに見るぞよき、漢籍も見ざれば、其外国のふりのあしき事もしられず、又古書はみな漢文もて書たれば、かの国ぶりの文もしらでは、学問もことゆきがたければ也、かの国ぶりの、よろづにあしきことをよくさとりて、皇国だましひだにつよくして、うごかざれば、よるひるからぶみを見ても、心はまよふことなし、然れども、かの国ぶりとして、人の心さかしく、何事をも理をつくしたるやうに、こまかに論ひ、よさまに説なせる故に、それを見れば、かしこき人も、おのづから心うつりやすく、まどひやすきならひなれば、から書見むには、つねに此ことをわするまじきなり、

神わざのおとろへのなげかはしき事

よろづよりも、世中に願はしきは、いかでもろ〳〵の神社のおとろへを、もて直し、もろ〳〵の神わざを、おこさまほしくこそ、今の世の神社神事のさまは、おほかた中ごろのみだれ世に、いたくおとろへすたれたるまゝなるを、今の世の人は、たゞ今のさまをのみ見て、いにしへよりかゝるものとぞ思ひためる、まれ〳〵書をよむ人なども、たゞからぶみをのみむねとはよみて、其心もて、よろづをさだして、皇国のふるきふみどもをば、をさ〳〵よむ人もなければ、古の御世には、神社神事を、むねと重くし給ひしことをばしらず、又まれにはしれる人もあれども、なほ今の世のならひにまぎれては、いにしへを思ひくらべて、これを深く歎く人のなきこそ、いと悲しけれ、

日本思想大系「本居宣長」より

三十二、遊子方言

宵の程

大勢つきそい、挑灯三張にて、はしごを上ル。新ぞう客の後に付、新ぞう「はしごをば、しづかに、おあがりなんせ。客よほど酔ている。「心得ました。新ぞう「こはばからしうおざんす。人の座敷でおざんす。こッちらへ、お出なんし。客「又せまい所へ入るのか。新ぞう「なにせまい所じやおざんせん。せんどおまへの酔なんした所でおざんす。客「あのおくのか。新ぞう「あいおくのでおざんす。はやくお出なんし。と廊下を行と、方ゝの座敷より名をよび、誰さん〳〵といふ。客うれしそふな顔見ゆる。舟宿・茶屋「これでまづおめでたふ御座ります。御座敷も定りました。客「全体こよひは、おれひとりじやによつて、此座敷がよいではないか。舟宿・茶屋「さやうで御座ります。此うちに、盃・てうし・硯ぶた・吸ものや、くわしや、たばこ盆いづる。女郎やの若ゐ者「旦那一ッ召上られませ。客「さあ〳〵座がしめッて面白くないではないか。なんと此ふたでまはそふではないか。みな〳〵「よふ御座りましよう。客「とかく、おればかりが、いつも呑かぶだ。おみよやお秀を、呼にやらんか。茶屋「只今参るはづで御ざります。客「今夜は後には、大ぶ賑に成ろうぞ。さッき道で呂州に逢た。これも来よふといふた。それで今夜は藤兵衛を呼ん。こゝがおれが粋じや。呂州が来てゐるに、藤兵衛にうたわせるは、互におもしろくない。よつて呼ん。茶屋「成ほど、万事に、あのやうにお心がお付なさる。舟宿「あい左様さ。茶屋「私はちよッと、行てさんじましよ。客「ま、ま、そんなら一盃のんで行やれ。今の盃を帰しもせいで。

茶屋「また私はふせります。客「はてねたがよい。しかし、其やうな事で酒はのめる物ではない。さあ〱わしも呑ぞ。新ぞう「もしぇ、もふそれ切で、かならず呑なんすなへ。客「これはつれない事じや。新ぞう「おゐらんで、いゝなんすには、かならず上申などいゝなんしたによつて、留申さにや成んせん。客「はてこまッたものじや。といふ内に、五六人ざは〱と来て、すはりながら、口〱に、新ぞう「御亭さん、お出なんし。兄さん、どふなんした。客「これは〱うつくしいぞ。これはいかい事。客ひとりに、むこ八人じや。賑で、どふもいへぬ。面白う成た。さあ〱君たち、ちと呑給へ。あ、どれへさし上やうやら。新ぞう「わッちに差なんせ。と引うけ、うまそふにのむ所へ、やり手来る。やり手「いやのみなんすの。といふて、客にむかいて、御出あそばしましたか。すッきと御足が御遠く成なんしたの。客「いやこれは〱かゝさま、どふじや〱、一ッ呑給へ〱。茶屋をよび、ひそ〱いふ。茶屋「これ申、御しうぎが、御ざりましたぞへ。やりて「はははゝお有がたふ御座りんす。私はまあ行ッて参りましよ。新ぞう「今のお盃、あぎんしよ。此所へ、台の物、菓子、重箱のふたをとれば、あたゝかそふな物、方々より持来る。客「さあ〱これほど御肴が出た。おさへます〱。いやおみよお秀、いやあ呂州丈、さあ御出〱。なに今の盃は、こふおまはし〱。かぶろ「兄さん、其三みせん箱、あちらへ上てくんなんし。あれ御亭さん、くるひなんすな。あれよびんす。おう〱。みな〱「旦那は大ぶお酔なさつた。休ませ申たら、よかろう。

日本古典文學大系「黄表紙・洒落本集」より

三十三、東海道中膝栗毛

斯(かく)てこの宿(しゆく)はづれなる、茶みせによりて、休ゐたるに　馬士「モシおまいがたア、おまにのつて下んせんか　弥次「いかさま、もどりならのるべい　馬士「上野までもどるおまじやわい。荷(に)をつけて弐百五十くだんせ　北八「二ほうくはうじんで百五十やるべい　馬士「けふは枠(わく)をもてこんわいの。爰からうへ野まで三里の所じや。白子(しろこ)へ壱里半、かはりやつてのつていかんせ　弥次「ふたりのられにやアいやだ　馬士「そしたらおふたりとも、おまの鞍(くら)へくゝしつけていこまいか。この縄(はな)でしめりや、きづかひはないがな　北八「とんだことをいふ。それじやアたばこものまれぬ　弥次「そんならかはり〴〵のろふ。百五十でやるか　馬士「まゝよかし、やらかしましよ　ト馬のそうだんできて、ふたりのにをつけ、此所より先北八のつて出かける　弥次「おらアそろ〳〵さきへいくぞ。ソレ北八、右のほうへかしぐよふだ　馬「ヒイン〳〵　すゞのおと「しやん〳〵〳〵　此内向ふよりきたるおとこ、こんじまのせんだくしたる、ひきまはしをきて、ぜに壱かんめばかり、さしこのふるきふろしきに包かたに引かけ、ぞうりがけにて来り、此馬士をみつけ「ヒヤアのしやアうへのゝ長太じやないか。今のしがとこへいた戻(もど)りじや。ゐいとこでいきあふた　馬かた長太「ハア権平次(ごんべいじ)さまかいな。コリヤさて、わしやめんぼくがないがな　どん平「あろまい〳〵、あろはづがないわい。晦日(みそか)〳〵にいこすはづを、まんだびた銭壱文もいこさんがな。どふしさるのじや。ソレきこわい　馬士「マア〳〵こち来て下んせ　此馬士、しやつきんのことはりと見えて、かのおとこを、日あたりのよいところへともなひ、おのれも土手にゆう〳〵とこしうちかけて「そないにごうにやらかいてくだんすな。マアこゝへかけさんせ。イヤそこの

ねきには、犬のくそがある。けふおいでるとしりおつたら、そうぢしておこもの。コリヤ〳〵、権平さまへちやなとあげんか、酒かふてこいといふ所じやが、こゝは大道なかでそれもでけぬくい

北八「コリヤどふする。はやくやらぬか　馬士「はてせわしない。ちとまたんせ。いんま、だいじのおきやくがある。さてマアきいてくだんせ。去年の冬から、うちのかゝめが病気を煩ひおつて、がきどもにはせちがはれる。雑役にさへ出やせんものを、何じやろと、こうして下んせ。四五日のうちには、ひゆつとこちらからもていこがな　どん平「イヤじやうちならんわい。そないにいふても、よふいこしやしよまいがな。でんない〳〵。もふ三年ごしといふもの、かした銭じや。利に利がくつて、二十貫あまりといふもんじやもの。いこすな〳〵。そのかはり、あのおまをとていのかい。ハテまさかの時は、のしがおまをわたそと、証文にかいたじやないか。そしたらいひぶん、ありやしよまいがな。サア〳〵もし、おまのうへな旦那さま、いんまきかんすとふりじや。借銭のかはりに、請とるおまじや。どふぞ、こゝからおりさんせ。きのどくながら　北八「ハアおいらもさつきにから、じれつたくてならなんだ。ひよんな馬にのり合せたは、こつちの不仕合。しかしまだ銭はやらず、是までのつたを徳にして、ドレおりて行やしやうか　トかのごん平に口をとらせて馬からおりると、馬士かけより「モシだんな、おまへがおりては、このおまをとられる。マアのつてゐて下んせ　どん平「イヤならんわい

馬士「ハテどないにもするわいの。旦那をおろしてはきのどくな。サア〳〵めして下んせ　北八「またのるのか。しつかりたのむぞ　トきた八又馬にのれば権平やつきとなり「コリヤ〳〵長太、どふしさるのじや。旦那おりて下んせ　北八「ヱ、又おろすのか。イヤきさまたちやア、おれをいゝてうさいぼうにする。おろしたりあげたり、足も、こしもくたびれはてた　どん平「それじやて、わしがおまじや。どふぞかし、おりてくだんせ　北八「ヱ、めんどふだ　ト小じれがきてぐつととびおりる　馬士「はて扨、おりさんせずとよいが

な。コレ権平(ごん)さま、こうしてくだんせ。わしも途中(とちう)じや、しよことがない。せめて、うちへいぬまで、まつてくだんせ。そのかはり、こゝで此ぬのこをわたすに　ごん平「そしたらいんで、わけつけるか　馬士「もふよいわい。サア旦那、めさぬかい　北八「ナニ又のれか。もふかんにしてくれ。おらアこれからあるいてゆかふ。なんならせう〱は銭を出しても、のるこたアいやだ　馬士「そふいはんせずと、のつてくだんせ。もふよいがなサア〱　ト馬のくちをとりてすゝむるゆへ、きた八またしかたなく馬にのれば　ごん平「サアやくそくの布子(ぬのこ)、ぬごまいか　馬士「イヤそないにはいふたものゝ、これもうちへいぬまで、まつて下んせ　ごん平「イヤおのれ、もふりやうけんならんわい。サア〱旦那、又おりてくだんせ　北八「ヱ、この唐人(とうじん)めらア、又おりろとぬかしやアがるか。もふいやだ。サアはやくやらねへか。どふしやアがるのだ　馬士「だんな。そふはかいの。おりずとよいに　ごん平「イヤおりずとゑいとは、なんでぬかす　トまつくろになり、馬にとりつきかゝる所を、馬士つきのけて、馬のしりをおもふさまたゝきたてると、馬はいつさんにかけいだせば、きた八うへにて、まつさほになり、大ごへあげて「ヤアイ〱、たすけてくれ、コリヤどふする〱　ごん平「馬をにがしてはならん。ヲ、イ〱　トおつかける。北八はごしやうだいじに、馬のくらにとりつきても、馬はやみくもにはしるゆへ、きた八とびおりよふとして、くらのなはにあしがひつかゝり、まつさかさまにおちて、こしのほねをうち「ア、いたい〱、だれぞ来てくれアイタ、、、、　トひとりもがきてくるしむていに、馬かたいつさんにかけつけきたり「モシ旦那、おけがはないかなドリヤ〱　ト手をとりて、引おこすうち、ごん平は馬をとらへんと、かけぬける。馬かた、これを見て、そうはさせぬと、北八にかまはずかけだして行　北八「ヲ、イまちあがれ、おれをばひどいめにあはしやアがつた　トこゞとをいひながらおきあがり、はらはたてどもせんかたなく、おつかけんには、あしこしがいたみ、やう〱のことにて、ふみしめ〱、そろ〱とたどり行つゝ

借銭(しやくせん)をおふたる馬にのりあはせひんすりやどんとおとされにけり

日本古典文學全集「東海道中膝栗毛」より

三十四、春告鳥

くま「ヲヤ／＼奇麗でござゐますネヱ　梅里「その箱のふたをかへして、その上にならべるといゝヨ　トいひながら箱のふたをひッくりかへし、畳のさいしきの所を出してやる　くま「ヲヤマアどふも／＼よく出来て居るぢやァござゐませんかねへ。そしてマア、此髪の風をこしらへた所から何から、モウ／＼何とも賞様のない様でござゐますねへ。ヲヤ此蓋がおざしきでござゐますネ。どふしたらよかろふ。どふも／＼感心ぢやァございませんか。このお座敷へみんな乗つて仕舞のだものを、小細はづだ　トいひながら段取をしてならべ　くま「どふも寔にありがたいねへ。どふしてこれが考たと申て推量ますものかねへ。まことに／＼嬉しひ　ト余念もなく悦ぶ風情、自然とあどけなく見へて十五六の娘のごとし　梅里「なんぼ才物なおまへでも当なかつたネ　くま「ヲヤ才智が否でございますヨ。おまへさんこそ御才物とやらでござゐますは。人の嬉しがる様なことばッかりおつしやつて。そしてマアおせじがよくッて、下女にまで叮嚀に物をおつしやッて。それだからあの子や おはなのことをさしていふ お清までか理介でも誰でも不躾ながらお賞申て居ますは　梅里「イヱまたおまへのお口前はその通りだものを。それだから私なんぞは行届ねへから、帰つた跡ではさぞ／＼うるさい奴が何時までも居て怠屈だといはれなひうち、帰らふと思つても、ツイ長くなつて後ではどふも気の毒でならなひから、言解ながら参つてなんぞと思つて、やつぱり来たいからだねへ。さぞさげすんでお

出なさるだらふ　くま「まことにどふもおまへさんは女郎衆でも買にお出なさるか、可愛と思召情人の所へでもお出なさつたら、さぞ先よりは手とやらがおあんなさるだらふねへ　トいふ所へ出し抜に下女　きよ「マア〳〵左様お二人で賞美ッくらばかりしてお出なさらずと、お燗が出来ました。お肴の参りますまで御漬物でも一口お上んなさいまし　ト燗ぢやうしを袴へ入れ、足なしの好風な台のうへに小品丼を種々ならべ、ひやうたんの清しどんぶりへ水を入れ、かはひらしき猪口を二ッばかりならべ持出　きよ「やつぱり中の間で宜ござゐますか。奥の火鉢へ火を入れませうか　くま「ヲヤ清か。びッくりしたョ。何時の間に帰ッて来たのだへ。障子の音もしなかつたのにョ。内証ばなしをして居ないでよかつたねへ　ト男の顔を見て笑ふ愛らしさ。何とか思入ある女のかゝる言葉をいだす節は、誰とても胸のとゞろくものなるべし　梅里「どふぞ内証ばなしといふことを一生の中にして見たいもんだねへ、お清さん　きよ「ヲホヽヽヽ、おまへさん、其様なことをおつしやつて。ネエ姉さん　くま「左様サ。それぢやァ私が内証ばなしをしなひでよかつたと申たが自惚らしいと思召だらふノウ　きよ「左様サねへ。余事何もおつしやらないがよふございます。下目でお出なさるも知れませんョ　梅里「コウ〳〵おぼへてお在よ。おまへまでが其様なことをいつて。何様してもまた違つたものだねへ、お召仕までが　くま「アレまたあんな世事をおつしやるョ。夫ゃァ宜が、此所ぢやァ余り麁末らしいねへ。奥へ参りませうぢやァなひかねへ　梅里「ナニ〳〵こゝがよふござゐます。またお客でもお出なさるとわるひから　トいひながらちよいと立て居直り　梅里「サアマアおもちやは後にして、御酒におかゝんなせへナ　トおくまはわらひながら人ぎやうをかたよせ　くま「さようサねへ。放蕩きつておまへさんが内の者の様だねへ、可笑。しかしどふも大事で気になりますョ　トいひながら人形を吉野紙に包み、元のごとくに仕舞　きよ「何でございましたか。私も見たふござゐましたねへ。よく〳〵お気

に入ッたと見へますネ　くま「ア、モウ〳〵気に入の何のどころではなひョ。今出すとまた御酒をあげるのに邪魔になるから、跡でゆつくりと見せるョ。あの嬢に見せたらさぞ嬉しがるだらう。サアマアーッおあがんなさいまし　ト猪口を清しておく　梅里「マア〳〵おはじめなさい　トいひながら燗でうしをとる　くま「マア〳〵其様なことをいはねへで　ト麁末に言て心付、くま「ヲヤ御免なさいましョ。サアおまへさんからおはじめなさいましな。今家内の者の様におなんなすつたからサ　梅里「そんなら仰にしたがつて始めませう。少しの内もお宿のものになる気でと自惚のお猪口はじめといたしませう　ト猪口をとる。

日本古典文學全集「洒落本・滑稽本・人情本」より

三十五、文字之教

一　日本に仮名の文字ありながら漢字を交へ用るは甚だ不都合なれども、往古よりの仕来りにて全国日用の書に皆漢字を用るの風と為りたれば、今俄にこれを廃せんとするも亦不都合なり。今日の処にては不都合と不都合と持合にて、不都合ながら用を便ずるの有様なるゆへ、漢字を全く廃するの説は願ふ可くして俄に行はれ難きことなり。此説を行はんとするには時節を待つより外に手段なかる可し。

一　時節を待つとて唯手を空ふして待つ可きにも非ざれば、今より次第に漢字を廃するの用意専

一なる可し。其用意とは文章を書くに、むづかしき漢字をば成る丈け用ひざるやう心掛ることなり。むづかしき字をさへ用ひざれば、漢字の数は二千か三千にて沢山なる可し。此書三冊に漢字を用ひたる言葉の数、僅に千に足らざれども、一と通りの用便には差支なし。これに由て考れば、漢字を交へ用るとて左まで学者の骨折にもあらず。唯古の儒者流儀に倣て妄に、難き字を用ひざるやう心掛ること緊要なるのみ。故(こと)さらに難文を好み、其稽古のためにとて、漢籍の素読などを以て子供を窘(くるしむ)るは、無益の戯と云て可なり。

一　医者、石屋などの字は、仮名を用るよりも漢字の方、便利なれども、上る、登る、昇る、攀るなどの字を一々書き分るは甚だ面倒なり。猿が木に攀るも、人が山に登るも、日本の言葉にては、ノボルと云ふゆへ、漢字を用るよりも仮名を用る方、便利なり。都て働く言葉には成丈け仮名を用ゆ可し。

一　易き漢字を見分けて素読するはあまり難きことに非ざれども、唯字を素読するよりも、文章の義を解すことに心を用ひざる可らず。即ち此書は子供をして文章の義を解さしめんがための趣向にて作りたるものなり。其教授の法、左の如し。

一　書中、文字の大なるものを題字と名け、細なるものを文章と名く。即ち題字は文章を作るたねの言葉なり。子供へ先づ題字の素読を授け、次で其字義を教へ、細字の文章をば、子供の考にて自ら素読し自から義を解かしむるなり。或は学校などにては、教授の席にて子供の書物を取上げ筆紙を渡し置き、教師一人書物を見て黒板へ其題字のみを写し、大勢の子供へ其字義を解き聞かせ、然る後に細字の文章を読て、其読む音の通りに文章を書かしむるなり。譬へば第四教の処に、男、女、父、母等の題字を黒板に書て其義を解き聞かせ、然る後に、男、犬を打つと、細字の文を読むとき、

子供は其音を聞て黒板を見れば、男と云ふ字と打つと云ふ字はあれども、犬と云ふ字なし。記憶よき子は第二教の犬の字を覚へて其文章を書き、記憶なき子は犬の字を知らず。これに由て子供の学力を試み黒白の点を付く可し。

一　此書、紙の数を増すときは本の価を増して小学の読本に用ひ難し。故に細字の文章を少なくして紙数を省きたるは、敢て著者の骨折を愛(をし)むに非ず。本を買ふ者のために銭を愛みたるなり。斯く細字の文章は少なしと雖ども、書中既に題字の順序仕組あるゆゑ、文章は教授の即席にて作るも可なり。譬へば第二教の文章「人、犬を見る」までにて教授に不足なることあらば、其席にて文章を工夫し、「犬と猫とを見る」「牛は車を見れども車は牛を見ず」などゝ様々に考へ、腹の中に文を作てこれを口に唱へ、稽古人をして其音の通りに書き記さしむること、前の法の如くす可し。但し第二教の日には第一教より二教までの題字を用ひ、第三教の日には三教までの字を用るのみにて、決して他の字を用ゆ可らず。若し止む得ずして用るときは、これを別段の題字として、其日其席の黒板に記す可し。

一　右の法に従て次第に進むときは、漢籍の難文に窘めらるゝこともなく、所謂四書五経の素読をも止めにして、別に読書作文の手掛りを得べし。著者の深く願ふ所なり。明治六年八月、著者記す。

大島田人・河村清一郎・八角真編「資料近代文章史」より

三十六、浮　雲

お勢も今日は取分け気の晴れた面相で、宛然籠を出た小鳥の如くに、言葉は勿論歩風身体のこなしにまで何処ともなく活々とした所が有ツて、冴が見える。昇の無駄を聞ては可笑しがツて絶えず笑ふが、それもさうで、強ち昇の言事が可笑しいからではなく、黙ツてゐても自然と可笑しいからそれで笑ふやうで。

お政は菊細工には甚だ冷淡なもので、唯「綺麗だことネー。」と云ツてツラリと見亘すのみ、さして眼を注める様子もないが、その代り、お勢と同年配頃の娘に逢へば、叮嚀にその顔貌風姿を研窮する。まづ最初に容貌を視て、次に衣服を視て、帯を視て爪端を視て、行過ぎてからズーと後姿を一瞥して、また帯を視て髪を視て、其跡でチヨイとお勢を横目で視て、そして澄まして仕舞ふ。妙な癖も有れば有るもので。

昇等三人の者は最後に坂下の植木屋へ立寄ツて、次第々々に見物して、とある小舎の前に立止ツた。其処に飾付て在ツた木像の顔が文三の欠伸をした面相に酷く肖てゐるとか昇の云ツたのが可笑しいといつて、お勢が嬌面に袖を加てゝ、勾欄におツ被さツて笑ひ出したので、傍に鵠立でゐた書生体の男が、俄に此方を振向いて、愕然として眼鏡越しにお勢を凝視めた。「みツともないよ」ト母親ですら小言を言ツた位で。

漸くの事で笑ひを留めて、お勢がまだ莞爾々々と微笑のこびり付てゐる貌を擡げて傍を視ると、昇は居ない。「ヲヤ」と云ツてキヨロ〳〵と四辺を環視はして、お勢は忽ち真面目な貌をした。

其内に紳士の一行がドロ〳〵と此方を指して来る容子を見て、お政は、茫然としていたお勢の袖を匆はしく曳揺かして疾歩に外面へ立出で、路傍に鵠在で待合はせてゐると、暫らくして昇も紳士の後に随つて出て参り、木戸口の所でまた更に小腰を屈めて皆其々に分袂の挨拶、叮嚀に慇懃に喋々しく陳べ立てゝ、さて別れて独り此方へ両三歩来て、フト何か憶出したやうな面相をしてキヨロ〳〵と四辺を環視はした。

「本田さん、此処だよ。」

ト云ふお政の声を聞付けて、昇は急足に傍へ歩寄り、

「ヤ大にお待遠う。」

「今の方は。」

「アレが課長です。」

ト云つて如何した理由か莞爾々々と笑ひ、

「今日来る筈ぢや無かツたんだが……」

「アノ丸髷に結ツた方は、あれは夫人ですか。」

「然うです。」

「束髪の方は。」

「アレですか、ありや……」

ト言かけて後を振返つて見て、

「妻君の妹です……内で見たよりか余程別嬪に見える。」

「別嬪も別嬪だけれども、好いお服飾ですことネー。」

「ナニ今日は彼様なお嬢様然とした風をしてゐるけれども、家にゐる時は疎末な衣服で、侍婢がはりに使はれてゐるのです。」

「学問は出来ますか。」

ト突然お勢が尋ねたので、昇は愕然として、

「エ学問……出来るといふ噺も聞かんが……それとも出来るかしらん。此間から課長の所に来てゐるのだから、我輩もまだ深くは情実を知らないのです。」

ト聞くとお勢は忽ち眼元に冷笑の気を含ませて、振反つて、今将に坂の半腹の植木屋へ這入らうとする令嬢の後姿を目送ツて、チヨイと我帯を撫でゝ而してズーと澄まして仕舞ツた。

坂下に待たせて置た車に乗ツて三人の者はこれより上野の方へと参ツた。

車に乗ツてからお政がお勢に向ひ、

「お勢、お前も今のお娘さんのやうに、本化粧にして来りやア宜かツたのにネー。」

「厭サ、彼様な本化粧は。」

「ヲヤ何故へ。」

「だツて厭味ツたらしいもの。」

「ナニお前十代の内なら秋毫も厭味なこたア有りやしないわネ。アノ方が幾程宜か知れない、引立が好くツて。」

「フヽン其様（そん）なに宜（よ）きやア慈母（おつか）さんお做（し）なさいな。人が厭だといふものを好々（いよいよ）ツて、可笑しな慈母（おつか）さんだよ。」

「好（いゝ）と思ツたから唯好ぢや無いかと云ツたばかしだアネ、それを其様（そん）な事いふツて真個（ほんと）に此娘（このこ）は可笑しな娘だよ。」

お勢は最早弁難攻撃は不必要と認めたと見えて、何とも言はずに黙して仕舞ツた。それからと云ふものは、塞（ふさ）ぐのでもなく萎（しほ）れるのでもなく、唯何（なに）となく沈んで仕舞ツて、母親が再び談話（はなし）の墜緒（つゐしよ）を紹（つが）うと試みても相手にもならず、どうも乙な塩梅（あんばい）であつたが、シカシ上野公園に来着いた頃にはまた口をきゝ出して、また旧（もと）のお勢に立戻ツた。

現代日本文學全集1「坪内逍遙・二葉亭四迷集」より

三十七、蝴蝶

壇の浦つゞきの磯づたひ、白沙の晃（きら）めきを鏡として翠色（すゐしよく）の色上げをば生温い浦風にさせながら思ふまゝに悠然と腹這して居る黒松の根方に裸体のまゝ腰を掛けて居るのは、前回に見えた蝴蝶といふ少女です。実に西の嵐に東の日和（ひより）、花をたしなめる風雨を見ては誰が実を結ばせる末を思ひましやう。わづか離れた処の修羅の巷はここに蜃楼の影も留めず、一網の魚に露命を恃（たの）む、いはゆる質朴の静かさばかりが苫屋の春を鎖（とざ）して居ます。波にもてあそばれて居る鷗。可愛らしい銀色の足で

ちよろ〱と磯へ這上がつて来るさゞ浪。血腥いといふ言葉は爰では只魚の料理で僅に悟るといふばかり、すべて景色が、言ふもおろか、さて空気を汚すべき非理の福原の別荘も、否、別殿も、有難いこと、まだ有りません。

濡果てた衣服を半ば身に纏つて、四方には人一人も居ぬながら猶何処やら吾と吾身へ対するとでも言ふべき羞を帯びて、風の囁きにも、鳥の羽音にも耳を側てる蝴蝶の姿の奥床しさ、うつくしさ、五尺の黒髪は舐め乱した浪の手柄を見せ顔に同じく浪打つて多情にも朝桜の肌を掠め、眉は目蓋と共に重く垂れて其処に薄命の怨みを宿して居ます。水と土とをば「自然」が巧みに取合はせた一幅の活きた画の中にまた美術の神髄とも言ふべき曲線でうまく組立てられた裸体の美人が居るのですものを。あゝ高尚。真の「美」は真の「高尚」です。

見亙せば浦つゞきは潮曇りに掻暮れて、その懐かしい元の御座船の影さへ見えず、幾百かの親しい人の魂をば夕暮のモヤが秘め鎖して居るかと思はれるばかり、すべて目の触るゝその先の方は茫漠として惨ましく見える塩梅、いとゞ心痛の源です、否、「源」といふのも残念な。

「そも如何にすべき。如何に為らせ給ひしやらん、事無う御幸ましましつるよ。覚束無。さるを猶この身だに斯くて御ン跡をも失ひつ、いづくに頼りて便りを得ん。苫屋の外は無きものを、もしは敵に見認められなば、逃れ来し心尽くしも泡なれや。人目を避けて山路より御幸ますとや聞きぬるに……されば伯耆や過ぎさせ給はん。よし、さらば、如何にもして御跡を慕ひまゐらせん。久しく時を移すは甲斐なし。命めでたうてかく蘇りつ、疲れは有るとも何ならん。いでや苫屋に哀れを請ひて蜑の衣だに乞ひ受けてん。」

雄々しくも屹と思案を定めましたが、さて其処が乙女のあどけなさ、まだ裸体を人に見られる恥

かしさに、何の思慮もなく、更にやや暫くは松の根に腰を掛けて居るその処へ聞えるのは兼ねて幾度も聞馴れた鎧の袖の噛合ふ声です。

　驚いて見返つて更に一入、さて穴へも入りたい程になりました。鎧の音は一人の武者で、武者、しかも其人は兼て蝴蝶が陣中で名を知つて見覚えて居る同じ平家の旗本の二郎春風といふ人で、また而もその人は蝴蝶が常から……おゝ、つれない命……人知れずその為に恋衣を縫つて居た者です。

　駭きましたが逃げられません。逃げたくは有ますが身は縮みます。俄に顔は……はてどうでも宜いのに……潮路の紅を借りて来て……見れば、今日を晴と粧つたその武者ぶりの奥床しさ、村濃の鎧に白の鉢巻、目は涼しく、口は潤つて……

「思掛けぬ……蝴蝶ぬし、御身のみにてましますか。」

　あゝ身が慄へます、近寄らずに二郎は尋ねます。

　返辞は有りませんので二郎は重ねて、

「見たまへや、此身も落ちて来ぬるを。主上は如何に為らせたまひし。」

「御幸ますとて為りしが、」声は微かに蝴蝶の口を忍び、「恙無う在せしならん。」

「御幸。いづくへ。」

「人無き里、伯耆わたりや過ぎ給はん。」

　二郎は勇立ちました。

「さらば、蝴蝶ぬし、やよ心な為たまひそ。如何に御跡を尋ねまゐらすべきに、打連れて、君もろともに。」

日本現代文學全集「山田美妙・廣津柳浪・川上眉山・小栗風葉集」より

三十八、舞姫

或る日の夕暮なりしが、余は獣苑を漫歩して、ウンテル、デン、リンデンを過ぎ、我がモンビシユウ街の僑居に帰らんと、クロステル巷の古寺の前に来ぬ。余は彼の燈火の海を渡り来て、この狭く薄暗き巷に入り、楼上の木欄(おばしま)に干したる敷布、襦袢(はだぎ)などまだ取入れぬ人家、頬髭長き猶太(ユダヤ)教徒の翁が戸前に佇みたる居酒屋、一つの梯(きざはし)は直ちに楼(たかどの)に達し、他の梯は窖(あなぐら)住まひの鍛冶が家に通じたる貸家などに向ひて、凹字の形に引籠みて立てられたる、此三百年前の遺跡を望む毎に、心の恍惚となりて暫し佇みしこと幾度なるを知らず。

今この処を過ぎんとするとき、鎖したる寺門の扉に倚りて、声を呑みつゝ泣くひとりの少女あるを見たり。年は十六七なるべし。被りし巾を洩れたる髪の色は、薄きこがね色にて、着たる衣は垢つき汚れたりとも見えず。我足音に驚かされてかへりみたる面、余に詩人の筆なければこれを写すべくもあらず。この青く清らにて物問ひたげに愁を含める目(まみ)の、半ば露を宿せる長き睫毛に掩はれたるは、何故に一顧したるのみにて、用心深き我心の底までは徹したるか。

彼は料(はか)らぬ深き歎きに遭ひて、前後を顧みる遑なく、こゝに立ちて泣くにや。わが臆病なる心は憐憫の情に打ち勝たれて、余は覚えず側に倚り、「何故に泣き玉ふか。ところに繋累なき外人(よそびと)は、却りて力を借し易きこともあらん。」といひ掛けたるが、我ながらわが大胆なるに呆れたり。

彼は驚きてわが黄なる面を打守りしが、我が真率なる心や色に形(あら)はれたりけん。「君は善き人なりと見ゆ。彼の如く酷くはあらじ。又た我母の如く。」暫し涸れたる涙の泉は又溢れて愛らしき頬を流れ落つ。

「我を救ひ玉へ、君。わが恥なき人とならんを。母はわが彼の言葉に従はねばとて、我を打ちき。父は死にたり。明日は葬らでは愜(かな)はぬに、家に一銭の貯だになし。」

跡は欷歔(ききょ)の声のみ。我眼はこのうつむきたる少女の顫ふ項(うなじ)にのみ注がれたり。

「君が家に送り行かんに、先づ心を鎮め玉へ。声をな人に聞かせ玉ひそ。こゝは往来なるに。」彼は物語するうちに、覚えず我肩に倚りしが、この時ふと頭を擡げ、又始てわれを見たるが如く、恥ぢて我側を飛びのきつ。

人の見るが厭はしさに、早足に行く少女の跡に付きて、寺の筋向ひなる大戸を入れば、欠け損じたる石の梯(きざはし)あり。これを上ぼりて、四階目に腰を折りて潜るべき程の戸あり。少女は鏽(さ)びたる針金の先きを捩ぢ曲げたるに、手を掛けて強く引きしに、中には咳枯(しはが)れたる老媼(おうな)の声して、「誰ぞ」と問ふ。エリス帰りぬと答ふる間もなく、戸をあらゝかに引開けしは、半ば白みたる髪、悪しき相にはあらねど、貧苦の痕を額に印せし面の老媼(おうな)にて、古き獣綿の衣を着、汚れたる上靴を穿きたり。エリスの余に会釈して入るを、かれは待ち兼ねし如く、戸を劇しくたて切りつ。

余は暫し茫然として立ちたりしが、ふと油燈(ランプ)の光に透して戸を見れば、エルンスト、ワイゲルトと漆もて書き、下に仕立物師と注したり。これすぎぬといふ少女が父の名なるべし。内には言ひ争ふごとき声聞えしが、又静になりて戸は再び明きぬ。さきの老媼は慇懃におのが無礼の振舞せしを詫びて余を迎へ入れつ。戸の内は厨にて、右手(めて)の低き窗に真白に洗ひたる麻布を懸けたり。左手(ゆんで)

には粗末に積上げたる煉瓦の竈あり。正面の一室の戸は半ば開きたるが、内には白布を掩へる臥床あり。伏したるはなき人なるべし。竈の側なる戸を開きて余を導きつ。この処は所謂「マンサルド」の街に面したる一間なれば、天井もなし。隅の屋根裏より窓に向ひて斜に下れる梁を、紙にて張りたる下の、立たば頭の支ふべき処に臥床あり。中央なる机には美しき氈(かも)を掛けて、上には書物一二巻と写真帖とを列べ、陶瓶にはこゝに似合はしからぬ価高き花束を生けたり。そが傍に少女は羞(はぢ)を帯びて立てり。

彼は優れて美なり。乳の如き色の顔は燈火に映じて微紅を潮したり。手足の繊く裊(たをやか)なるは、貧家の女に似ず。老媼の室(へや)を出でし跡にて、少女は少し訛りたる言葉にて云ふ。「許し玉へ。君をこゝまで導きし心なさを。君は善き人なるべし。我をばよも憎み玉はじ。明日に迫るは父の葬(はふり)、たのみに思ひしシヤウムベルヒ、君は彼を知らでやおはさん。彼は「ヰクトリア」座の座頭なり。彼が抱へとなりしより、早や二年なれば、事なく我等を助けんと思ひしに、人の憂に付けこみて、身勝手なるいひ掛けせんとは。我を救ひ玉へ、君。金をば薄き給金を拆きて還し参らせん。縦令(よしや)我身は食はずとも。それもならずば母の言葉に。」彼は涙ぐみて身をふるはせたり。その見上げたる目には、人に否とはいはせぬ媚態あり。この目の働きは知りてするにや、又自らは知らぬにや。

我が隠しには二三「マルク」の銀貨あれど、それにて足るべくもあらねば、余は時計をはづして机の上に置きぬ。「これにて一時の急を凌ぎ玉へ。質屋の使のモンビシユウ街三番地にて太田と尋ね来ん折には価を取らすべきに。」

少女は驚き感ぜしさま見えて、余が辞別(わかれ)のために出したる手を唇にあてたるが、はら〳〵と落つる熱き涙を我手の背(そびら)に濺(そそ)ぎつ。

日本現代文學全集「森鷗外集」より

三十九、吾輩は猫である

今朝見た通りの餅が、今朝見た通りの色で椀の底に膠着して居る。白状するが餅といふものは今迄一返も口に入れた事がない。見るとうまさうにもあるし、又少しは気味がわるくもある。前足で上にかゝつて居る菜つ葉を掻き寄せる。爪を見ると餅の上皮が引き掛つてねば／＼する。嗅いで見ると釜の底の飯を御櫃へ移す時の様な香がする。食はうかな、やめ様かな、とあたりを見廻す。幸か不幸か誰も居ない。御三は暮も春も同じ様な顔をして羽根をついて居る。小供は奥座敷で「何と仰しやる兎さん」を歌つて居る。食ふとすれば今だ。もし此機をはづすと来年迄は餅といふものゝ味を知らずに暮して仕舞はねばならぬ。吾輩は此刹那に猫ながら一の真理を感得した。「得難き機会は凡ての動物をして、好まざる事をも敢てせしむ」吾輩は実を云ふとそんなに雑煮を食ひ度はないのである。否椀底の様子を熟視すればする程気味が悪くなつて、食ふのが厭になつたのである。此時もし御三でも勝手口を開けたなら、奥の小供の足音がこちらへ近付くのを聞き得たなら、吾輩は惜気もなく椀を見棄てたらう、しかも雑煮の事は来年迄念頭に浮ばなかつたらう。所が誰も来ない、いくら躊躇して居ても誰も来ない。早く食はぬか／＼と催促される様な心持がする。吾輩は椀の中を覗き込み乍ら、早く誰か来てくれゝばいゝと念じた。矢張り誰も来てくれない。吾輩はとう／＼雑煮を食はなければならぬ。最後にからだ全体の重量を椀の底へ落す様にして、あぐりと餅の

角を一寸許り食ひ込んだ。此位力を込めて食ひ付いたのだから、大抵なものなら嚙み切れる訳だが、驚いた！ もうよからうと思つて歯を引かうとすると引けない。もう一返嚙み直さうとすると動きがとれない。餅は魔物だなと疳づいた時は既に遅かつた。沼へでも落ちた人が足を抜かうと焦慮る度にぶく／＼深く沈む様に、嚙めば嚙む程口が重くなる、歯が動かなくなる。歯答へはあるが、歯答へがある丈でどうしても始末をつける事が出来ない。美学者迷亭先生が甞て吾輩の主人を評して君は割り切れない男だといつた事があるが、成程うまい事をいつたものだ。此餅も主人と同じ様にどうしても割り切れない。嚙んでも嚙んでも、三で十を割る如く尽未来際方のつく期はあるまいと思はれた。此煩悶の際吾輩は覚えず第二の真理に逢着した。「凡ての動物は直覚的に事物の適不適を予知す」真理は既に二つ迄発明したが、餅がくつ付いて居るので毫も愉快を感じない。歯が餅の肉に吸収されて、抜ける様に痛い。早く食ひ切つて逃げないと御三が来る。小供の唱歌もやんだ様だ、屹度台所へ馳け出して来るに相違ない。煩悶の極尻尾をぐる／＼振つて見たが何等の功能もない、耳を立てたり寝かしたりしたが駄目である。考へて見ると耳と尻尾は餅と何等の関係もない。要するに振り損の、立て損の、寝かし損であると気が付いたからやめにした。漸くの事是は前足の助けを借りて餅を払ひ落すに限ると考へ付いた。先づ右の方をあげて口の周囲を撫で廻す。撫でた位で割り切れる訳のものではない。今度は左りの方を伸して口を中心として急劇に円を劃して見る。そんな呪ひでは魔は落ちない。辛防が肝心だと思つて左右交る／＼に動かしたが矢張り依然として歯は餅の中にぶら下つて居る。えゝ面倒だと両足を一度に使ふ。すると不思議な事に此時丈は後足二本で立つ事が出来た。何だか猫でない様を感じがする。猫であらうが、あるまいが斯うなつた日にやあ構ふものか、何でも餅の魔が落ちる迄やるべしといふ意気込みで無茶苦茶に顔中引つ

掻き廻す。前足の運動が猛烈なので稍ともすると中心を失つて倒れかゝる。倒れかゝる度に後足で調子をとらなくてはならぬから、一つ所に居る訳にも行かんので、台所中あちら、こちらと飛んで廻る。我ながらよくこんなに器用に起つて居られたものだと思ふ。第三の真理が驀地に現前する。「危きに臨めば平常なし能はざる所のものを為し能ふ。之を天祐といふ」幸に天祐を享けたる吾輩が一生懸命餅の魔と戦つて居ると、何だか足音がして奥より人が来る様な気合である。こゝで人に来られては大変だと思つて、愈躍起となつて台所をかけ廻る。足音は段々近付いてくる。ああ残念だが天祐が少し足りない。とう／＼小供に見付けられた。「あら猫が御雑煮を食べて踊を踊つて居る」と大きな声をする。此声を第一に聞きつけたのが御三である。羽根も羽子板も打ち遣つて勝手から「あらまあ」と飛込んで来る。細君は縮緬の紋付で「いやな猫ねえ」と仰せられる。主人さへ書斎から出て来て「此馬鹿野郎」といつた。面白い／＼と云ふのは小供許りである。さうして皆んな申し合せた様にげら／＼笑つて居る。腹は立つ、苦しくはある、踊はやめる訳にゆかぬ、弱つた。漸く笑ひがやみさうになつたら、五つになる女の子が「御かあ様、猫も随分ね」といつたので狂瀾を既倒に何とかするといふ勢で又大変笑はれた。人間の同情に乏しい実行も大分見聞したが、此時程恨めしく感じた事はなかつた。遂に天祐もどつかへ消え失せて、在来の通り四つ這になつて、眼を白黒するの醜態を演ずる迄に閉口した。さすが見殺しにするのも気の毒と見えて「まあ餅をとつて遣れ」と主人が御三に命ずる。御三はもつと踊らせ様ぢやありませんかといふ眼付で細君を見る。細君は踊は見たいが、殺して迄見る気はないのでだまつて居る。「取つてやらんと死んで仕舞ふ。早くとつて遣れ」と主人は再び下女を顧みる。御三は御馳走を半分食べかけて夢から起された時の様に、気のない顔をして餅をつかんでぐいと引く。寒月君ぢやないが前歯が皆

んな折れるかと思つた。どうも痛いの痛くないのつて、餅の中へ堅く食ひ込んで居る歯を情け容赦(ようしゃ)もなく引張るのだから堪らない。吾輩が「凡ての安楽は困苦を通過せざるべからず」と云ふ第四の真理を経験して、けろ〳〵とあたりを見廻した時には、家人は既に奥座敷へ這入つて仕舞つて居つた。

日本現代文學全集「夏目漱石集(一)」より

四十、お目出たき人

その内に電車が来た。自分は友と挨拶して電車にのつて真中より少し後ろに腰をかけた。のつて暫らくしてから出た。鶴は停車場で電車を待つてゐるかも知れないと思つた。しかし今十二時頃だから飯を食つてゐるだらうと思ひ返した、しかし何時ものやうに大久保に着くことを楽しみにしてゐた。電車が柏木(かしはぎ)に着いて一寸(ちよつと)止つて柏木を出た。自分の胸はせばまるやうに覚えた。之は珍らしいことではない。さうしてから云ふ感じを何十度味つたか知れないが、鶴に逢つたことはたゞ一度だつた。それは去年の四月四日である。

電車が大久保につく時、自分はこは〳〵プラットホームを見た。六七人まつてゐる人があつた。その内に若い女が一人ゐた。鶴ぢやないかと思つてゐる内に電車は益々近づいて止つた。

鶴だつた！鶴はこの瞬間に自分に気がついたらしかつた。後ろから乗らうとした足がこの時ピタ

ッと止つた。鶴は引きかへして前から乗つた。自分と見合つた時、目と目があつた。鶴は赤い顔をして目をそむけた。さうして自分の腰かけてゐる右側に腰かけた。鶴と自分との間には三人の人がゐた。

自分は鶴の大人になつたのに驚いた。鶴は相変らず粗末な着物を着て薄く白粉（おしろい）をぬつてゐた。自分は鶴程美しい女を見たことはないと思つた。

優しい、美しい、さうして表情のある顔、生々した目、紅の口唇、顔色もいゝ。自分は鶴の顔をもつとはつきり見たいと思つた。しかし間にゐる人が邪魔になる。赤い髪の毛が一寸見えるだけだ。（鶴の髪の毛は赤い）。自分のわきには労働者がゐた。その隣りが軍人で、その隣りが四十許りの女で、その向うに鶴がゐるのだ。

自分は向ひ側の空いてゐる席に鶴の腰かけなかつたのを残念に思つた。しかしあわてた様子、自分と顔をあはせるのを気まりわるく思つて同じ側に腰をかけたことを嬉しく思つた。

新宿で可なり人がのつた。代々木では殆（ほと）んど満員になる程人がのつた。自分は老人か子供を負（お）ぶつた人が来てくれるといゝなと思つた。さうすれば自分は何げなく立つことが出来る。さうして鶴を見ることが出来る。しかし自分の前には男の人のみ立つてゐる。

千駄ケ谷で少しおりた。信濃町（しなのまち）では五六人おりて、三四人のつた。四谷につく少し前に自分は立つた。鶴の方を見た。鶴と自分の目は会つた。鶴はすぐ目を転じた。自分は思ひ切つて鶴の前を通つてとまることにした。電車はとまりかけたが鶴はたたない。さうして自分に顔を背けてゐる。電車はほんとに止つた。自分は鶴の前を通らうとした。この時不意に鶴は立つた。自分は嬉しかつた。自分の手は鶴の背中に触れた。自分は鶴について電車を降りようとした。この時入口のそばにゐた

子供をつれた人が立つた。自分は厚顔（あつかま）しくその男をかきのけて鶴のすぐあとに従ふ勇気がなかつた。自分は鶴と自分の間に二人を入れた。

自分は電車をおりると二人を逐ひこした。さうして改札口を鶴について出ようとした。しかし鶴は改札口に達した時一寸後ろを見た。自分を見た。さうして身体を少し右に寄せて自分に先にいらつしやいと云はぬ許りの態度をとつた。自分は夫の権威を以てさきに出た。しかし自分の心はあがつてゐた。切符を改札掛に渡さうとして落してしまつた。自分は落ちた切符をたゞ眺めて改札掛の拾ふのを見て、なるたけ落ついて停車場を出た。出て右に折れて段々を左側のはしを通つて登つた。さうして自分はふり向いた。鶴と又顔をあはせた。一階段を登りをはつてふりかへると鶴は自分の通つたあとを登つてくる。矢張り左側のはじを通つて。

自分は段を上りきる前に又ふり向いた。鶴は静かに自分の歩いた処を歩いてくる。自分は登りきつて右に折れて麹町（こうじまち）の方へ行つた。ふり向くと鶴は段々を上りきつて未だ自分のあとをついてくる。自分はもう夢中だ。嬉しい。

「お鶴さん」と声をかけたい程自分は親しさを感じた。さうしてさう声をかけても鶴はおどろかないで、

「なに御用？」と笑ふやうな気がした。自分は電車道をよこぎつて麹町通の左側を通つた。鶴は電車通をよこぎらずに右側を歩いてくる。

自分は何度ふり向いたか知れない。その都度、鶴と顔をあはせた。あはせるとあはてて自分は顔を元に戻した。鶴も顔をそむけたやうに思ふ。

自分は鶴が自分を愛してゐてくれたと思はないではゐられなかつた。自分の心は嬉しさにをどつ

た。

真心は真心に通ずる。自分が鶴を恋してゐるやうに、矢張り鶴も恋してゐてくれたのだ。自分の足はをどつた。自分の足はつい早くなつた。六丁目あたりに来てふり向いた時、最早（もう）鶴の姿は見えなかつた。自分は鶴は何処かの商店（みせ）に入つてゐるのではないかと思つたが見えなかつた。しかし自分は嬉しくなつてたまらなかつた。自分は自家（うち）に急いだ。

鶴は自分を恋してゐるのだ。鶴は自分の妻になるのだ。二人は夫婦になる運命を荷つて生れて来たのだ。

なにしろ今日は嬉しい日だ。記念とすべき日だ。鶴も嬉しく思つてくれるだらう。自分は自家に帰つてこの喜をもらさないではゐられなかつた。母に逢つて、今日鶴に逢つてよ、鶴はそれは美しくなつてよ、僕は万竜（まんりう）より鶴の方が何十倍美しいか知れないと思ひましたよ、と云ひたかつた。母は万竜を或日見て、美しい美しいと感心してゐたことがあつた。さうして鶴のことはさう美しいとは云はない。母は三年前自分は鶴の自分の室の窓の前を通る所を見せたことがある。

何しろ自分はおちついてゐられない。しかし母に打ちあけて云ふのは気まりがわるかつた。昼飯食つてからもじつとしてはゐられないので神田に行つた。さうして一人鶴のことを思つて微笑（ほほえ）んだ。

大島田人・河村清一郎・八角真編「資料近代文章史」より

APPENDIX

List of Heian-period *katakana*. The characters in brackets are *man'yōgana*, which were abbreviated into various forms to represent the same syllable. For instance, the character 阿 was written or abbreviated in 17 different ways to represent the syllable *a*. Also, for most syllables, more than one *man'yōgana* was used as a source for one syllable; e.g., for the syllable *a*, the two characters 阿 and 安 were used, plus one other character that has not been determined. From Nakata Norio, *Kotenbon no kokugogakuteki kenkyū sōron hen*, supplement *Ryakutai kana sōgō jitai hyō*, rev. ed. (Tokyo: Benseisha, 1979).

List of Heian-period *hiragana*. The printed characters are *man'yōgana* from which the cursive *hiragana* script was derived. Several different *man'yōgana* were used as the basis for different forms of calligraphic *hiragana* for the same syllable; e.g., *hiragana* based on the characters 安, 阿, and 悪 were used to write the syllable *a*. From Komatsu Shigemi, *Kana: Sono seiritsu to hensen* (Tokyo: Iwanami Shoten, 1968).

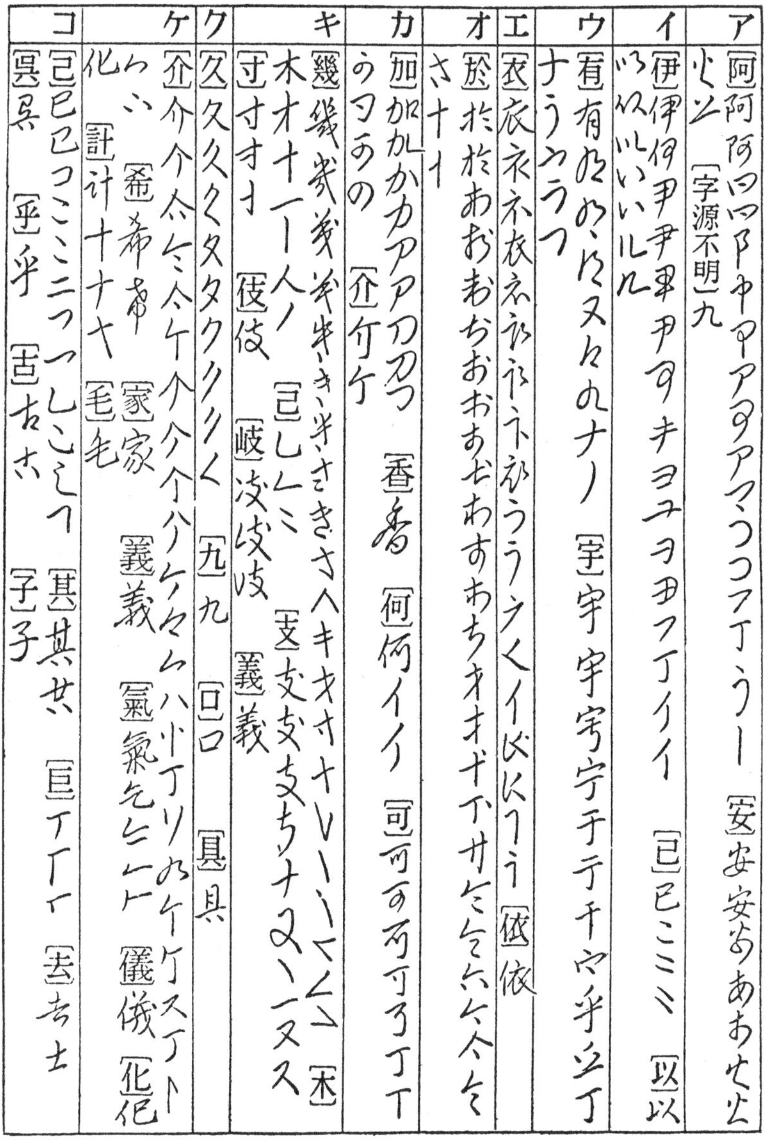

List of Heian-period *katakana*.

サ	[佐] [坐] [左] [沙] [在] [差] [散]
シ	[之] [自] [志] [四] [士]
ス	[須] [寸]
	[受] [爲]
セ	[世] [西]
ソ	[曽] [十]
タ	[多] [太]
	[他] [田] [陁] [字源不明]
チ	[知] [智] [地]
	[千] [字源不明]
ツ	[州]
	[字源不明] [都]
テ	[弖] [天]
	[手]
ト	[止] [刀] [土] [士]
	[字源不明]
ナ	[奈]

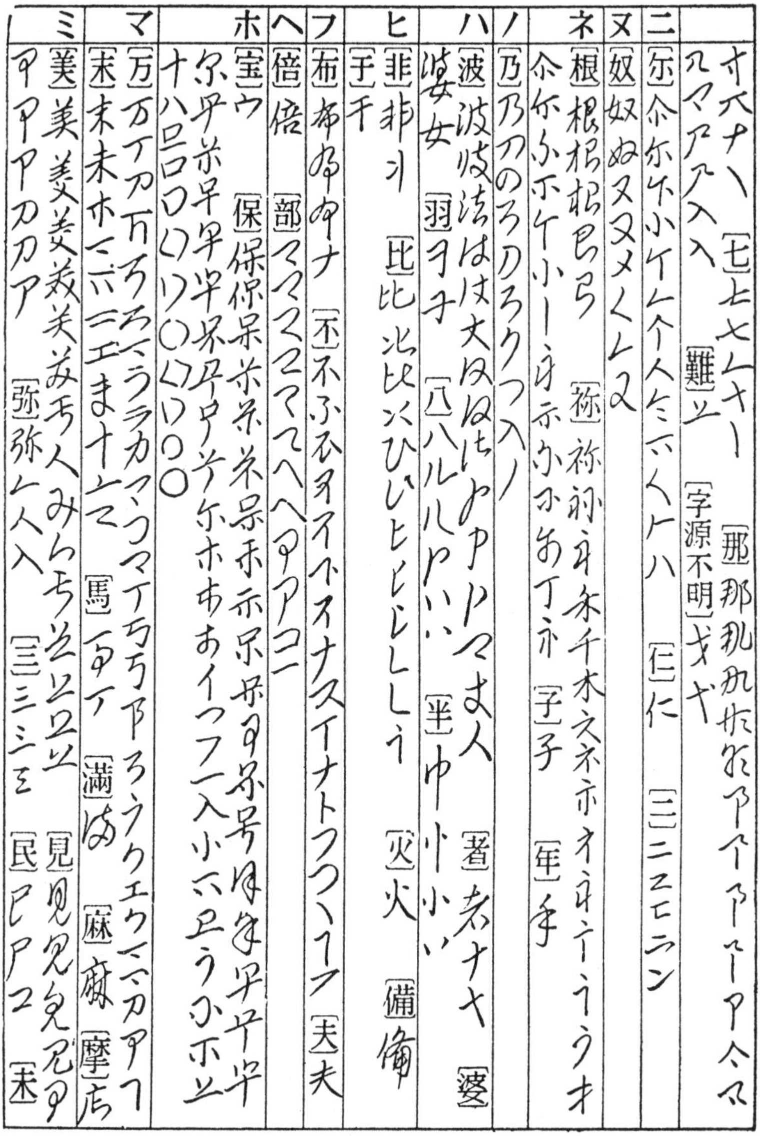

[七] [難] [字源不明] [那]
ニ [尓] [仁] [三]
ヌ [奴]
ネ [根] [祢] [子] [年]
ノ [乃]
ハ [波] [羽] [八] [半] [者] [婆]
ヒ [非] [比] [火] [備]
フ [干] [布] [不] [夫]
ヘ [倍] [部]
ホ [宝] [保]
マ [万] [末] [馬] [満] [麻] [摩]
ミ [美] [弥] [三] [見] [民] [未]

	末丁マ
ム	[牟]牟牟牟牟厶厶厶个厶ムレら [无]无无无无无九え [六]六 [武]む
メ	[米]米ソ丶十ヰソメ [目]目ニ丨 [女]女めサソメ又ㄨメヌくㄥ ユ [免]免 [命]仒人
モ	[毛]毛毛毛毛モモもモモもモモモしモしモモもも 丁ニモモ
ヤ	[也]世也ヤ也ヤセヤアセアヒ世くカカ丨＼ [八]八
ユ	[由]由由由由山ユ二二エムレゆナヨ
エ	[延]延巡迩之乀 [江]江江にエエエ [兄]兄兄文
ヨ	[夜]夜 [與]与与与与与与与与ヨ与与ヨヨヨヨヨヨヨヨヨタ トイ二ヨ上
ラ	[良]良良良良らららららうアヨヨヨヨコアうラアラ ううララムレ十らら丨丨 [等]寸十十 [字源不明]又メ ヘソヘ
リ	[利]利利わわタリ丨 [里]里
ル	[流]流流流流流ホルルいいいツルレ、、ハ十ルルルルル九レ [留]留留留留留留留留留留ロロムロロ ()()()ロ〇
レ	[禮]礼礼礼礼不列セpムしくち [例]例列ろろ
ロ	[呂]呂呂呂呂呂呂ろろろろろろろススろろろタろムロロロロロ

	〇〇り 〔六〕六 〔魯〕曰
ワ	〔和〕和禾手わーム〇口ワワ〇〇ヲ〇〇〇ワ〇〇〇〇ワワワワ 〔王〕王ら己王巳
ヰ	〔爲〕ゐゐゐゐ 〔井〕井井キキ
ヱ	〔惠、慧、恵〕恵恵恵恵恵志恵恵卫ま丑卫丑十下丑子卫 巳寸下心ん刃卫ち卫卫巾亡ちち小ち
ヲ	〔雄〕雄 〔乎〕乎乎乎乎乎乎乎ソ、ソ、六ぶ片しシキツソ゛ソ シシシヲヲヲ
ン	〔尓〕ムレンニンし 〔三〕シ 〔撥音の象徴〕ンレレ>くフVマC2一 し

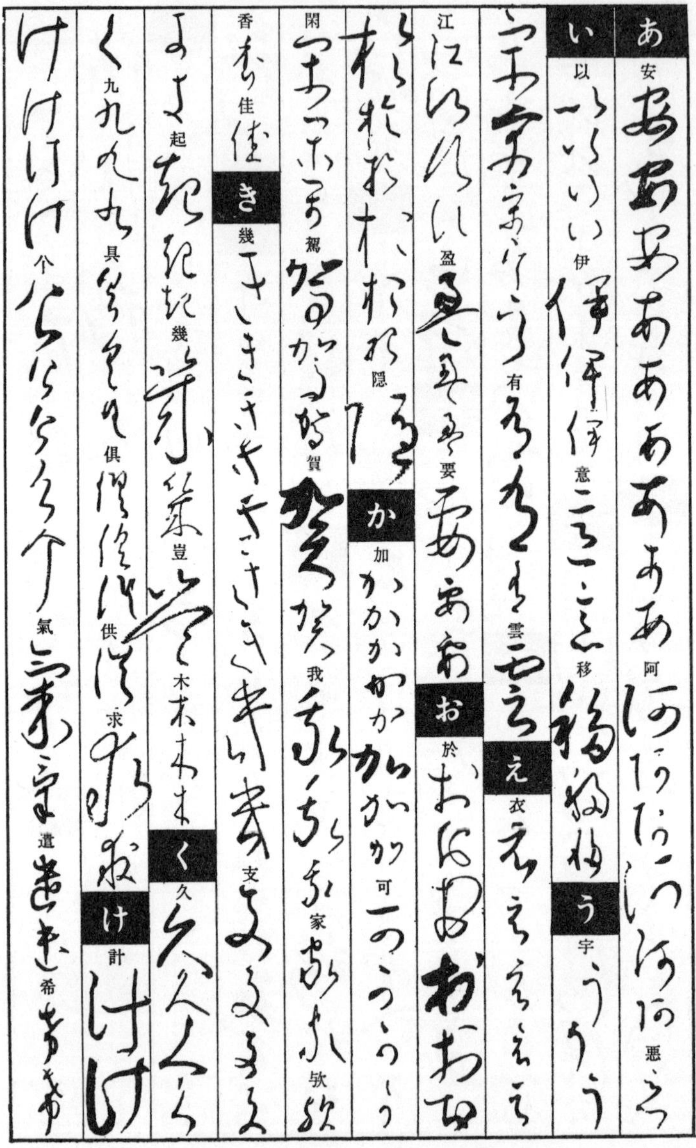

List of Heian-period *hiragana*.

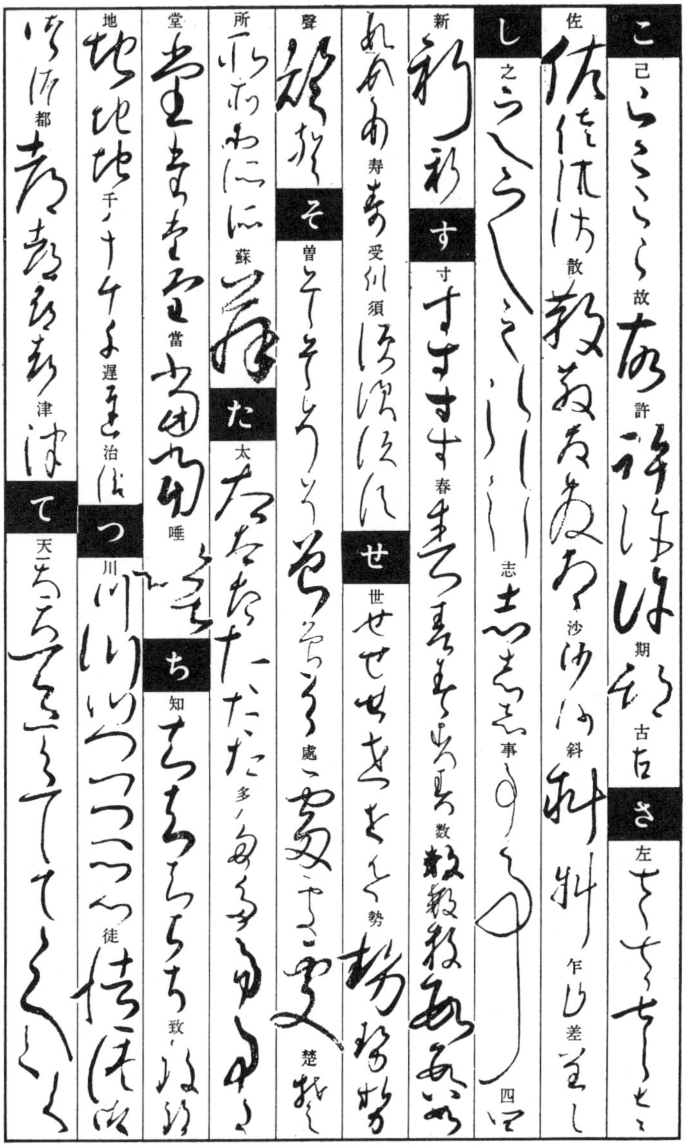
こ
己
故
許
期
古
さ
左
乍
差
佐
散
沙
斜
し
之
志
事
四
新
す
寸
春
数
寿
受
須
せ
世
勢
聲
そ
曽
處
楚
所
蘇
た
太
多
堂
當
唾
ち
知
致
地
千
遅
治
つ
川
徒
都
津
て
天

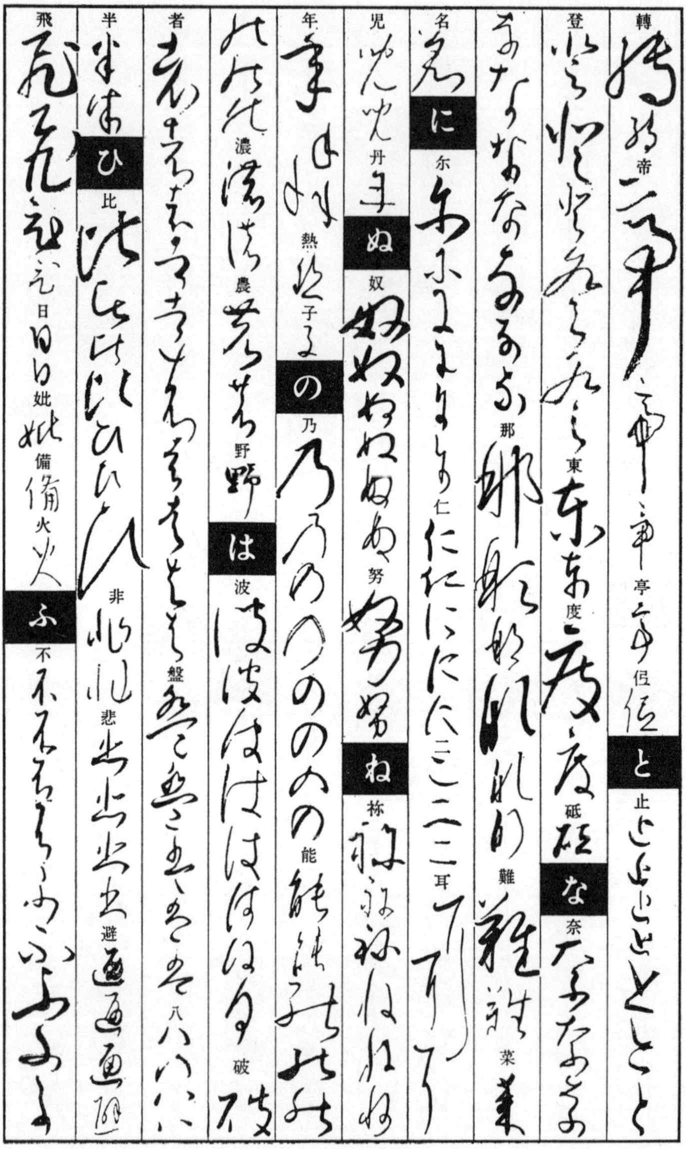
轉 帝 亭 佀 と 止
登 東 度 砥 な 奈
那 難 菜
名 に 尓 仁 耳
児 丹 ぬ 奴 努 ね 祢
年 熱 子 の 乃 能
濃 農 野 は 波 破
者 盤 八
半 ひ 比 非 悲 避
飛 日 妣 備 火 ふ 不

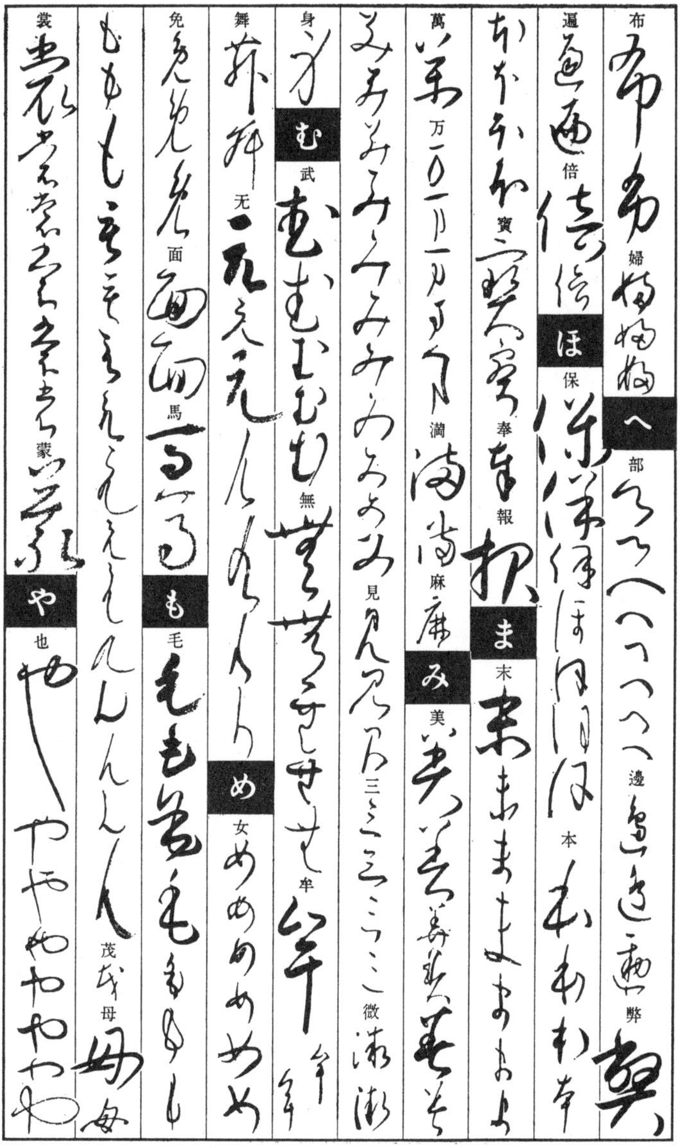
布
婦
へ
部
邊
弊
遍
倍
ほ
保
本
寶
奉
報
ま
末
萬
万
滿
麻
み
美
見
三
微
身
む
武
無
牟
舞
无
め
女
免
面
馬
も
毛
茂
母
裳
蒙
や
也

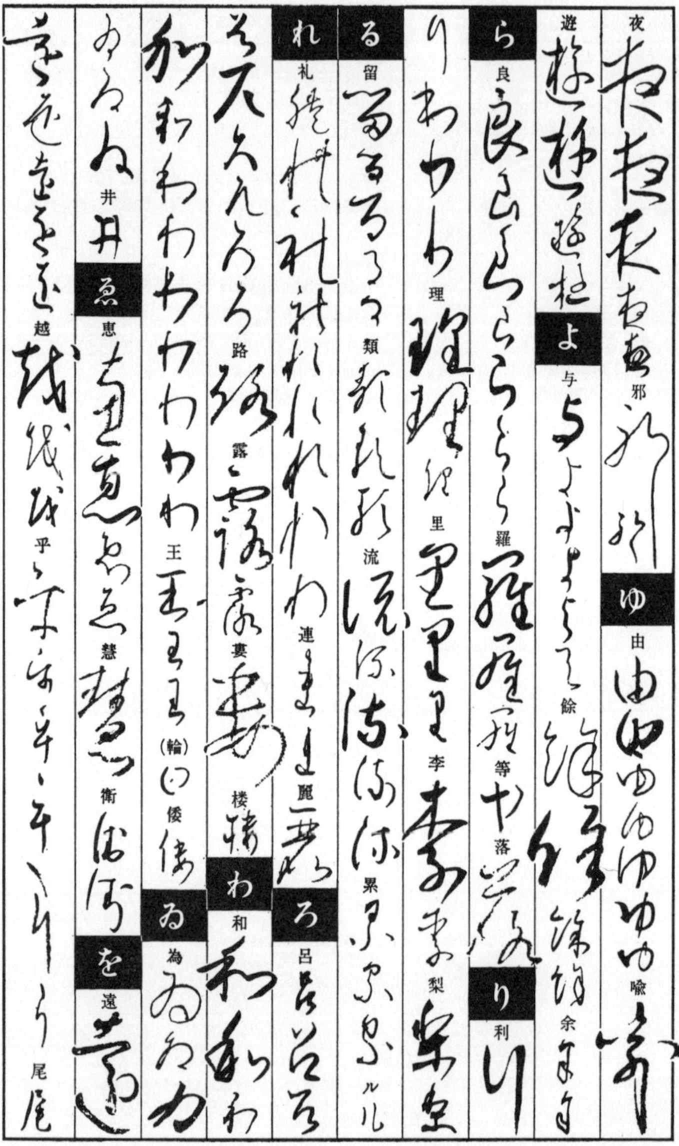

夜
邪
ゆ
由
喩
遊
よ
与
餘
余
ら
良
羅
等
落
り
利
理
里
李
梨
る
留
類
流
累
ルル
れ
礼
連
麗
ろ
呂
路
露
妻
楼
わ
和
王
(輪)
倭
ゐ
為
井
ゑ
恵
慧
衛
を
遠
越
乎
尾